BF
637
.I48
B37
1994

Barash, David P.

Beloved enemies.

$25.95

DATE			

BAKER & TAYLOR

BELOVED ENEMIES

Also by David P. Barash

Sociobiology and Behavior
The Whisperings Within
Aging: An Exploration
Stop Nuclear War! A Handbook (with Judith Eve Lipton)
The Caveman and the Bomb (with Judith Eve Lipton)
The Hare and the Tortoise
The Arms Race and Nuclear War
Marmots: Social Behavior and Ecology
The Great Outdoors
Introduction to Peace Studies
The L Word

BELOVED ENEMIES

OUR NEED FOR OPPONENTS

DAVID P. BARASH

 Prometheus Books

59 John Glenn Drive
Amherst, New York 14228-2197

Grateful acknowledgment is made to the following publishers for permission to reprint material:

Tribune Media Services for the poem by Charles Osgood, © 1991

Princeton University Press for "Waiting for the Barbarians" from C. P. Cavafy, *Collected Poems*, © 1975 by Princeton University Press

Random House, Inc., for "What I Expected, Was" from Stephen Spender, *Collected Poems 1928–1985*, © 1934, 1962 by Stephen Spender.

Published 1994 by Prometheus Books

98 97 96 95 94   5 4 3 2 1

Library of Congress Cataloging-in-Publication Data

Barash, David P.
    Beloved enemies : our need for opponents / David P. Barash.
       p.   cm.
    Includes bibliographical references.
    ISBN 0-87975-908-9 (alk. paper)
    1. Interpersonal conflict. 2. Social conflict—Psychological aspects.
I. Title. II. Title: Enemies.
BF637.I48837   1994
302—dc20

                                    94-3468
                                      CIP

Printed in the United States of America on acid-free paper.

Contents

If there were only two men in the world, how would they get on?
They would help one another, harm one another, flatter one another,
slander one another, fight one another, make it up;
they could neither live together nor do without one another.

—Voltaire, *Philosophical Dictionary*

1

The End of Enemies?

There is nothing so disorienting as the loss of a good friend, except, perhaps, the loss of a good enemy. Yet, from the personal details of our private lives to the global contortions of nation-states, we are regularly confronted with just such losses.

Try to imagine: Captain Ahab without Moby Dick, the Hatfields without the McCoys, the Montagues without the Capulets, Belfast Catholics without Protestants, Israelis without Arabs, the United States without the Soviet Union or vice versa. Each has long been defined by the other. And in the process, enmity has subtly been transformed into dependence. If Moby Dick had died of old age, or in the sweet embrace of a giant squid, or by someone else's harpoon, Ahab would probably have mourned rather than celebrated. But Ahab was a fictional character, while the rest of us—and our enemies—are very real. Equally real is the fact that sometimes these enemies go away, leaving us frustrated, empty, and strangely alone.

In 1989 Francis Fukuyama wrote a much-noticed article titled "The End of History,"[1] in which he celebrated the crumbling of communism in Eastern Europe, asserting that with the conclusion of the Cold War and its titanic struggle between communism and capitalist democracy, history itself had somehow come to an end.

9

Many critics felt that the author had overstated his case. What is important for us, however, is the implication that enemies make history, not in the simple sense of producing important and noteworthy events, but in the deeper, literal sense of *creating* history itself. Without enmity, life—or at least, its political aspect—is deprived of meaning and literally seems to stop.

The phenomenon is as old as human history, perhaps older. Ancient Rome and Carthage were mortal enemies. Yet it is reported that at the end of the Third Punic War, after Carthage had finally been destroyed and pillaged, her people all killed or enslaved, her walls torn down and her land sown with salt, a kind of sadness came over the citizens of Rome, an awareness that with its primary and defining struggle behind it, Rome itself would never be the same. (Of course, as we now see clearly through the benefit of hindsight, Rome's history did not end at that time.)

Skipping ahead two thousand years, most modern-day Americans eagerly assert that they feel no sadness whatever at being deprived of the Cold War, and Israelis, for their part, are virtually unanimous that they would not be in any way troubled if God, the United Nations, or the much-encumbered "peace process" should someday deprive them of their Arab opponents and thus the intermittent hot wars that have plagued the Middle East. (Most Arabs, to no one's great surprise, have a similar view of Israel.) Armenians and Azeris (Azerbaijanis) feel similarly, as do Serbs, Croats, and Bosnian Muslims, the Hutus and Tutsis of Rwanda, and literally millions of other human beings, locked in mutual antagonism. Not coincidentally, more than a few divorced couples subscribe to similar sentiments, as do many married couples as well, their union not uncommonly held together by shared enmity toward third parties and, sometimes, even toward each other. We are, all of us, prepared to get along just fine, thank you, without our long-standing enemies. After all, isn't that what enemies *are*: those who we yearn to be rid of?

The truth, however, may well be otherwise. And a deeper understanding of our reliance upon enemies seems likely to help illuminate the condition of the species *Homo sapiens* as the twentieth century draws to a close. Thus, from our personal lives to our relationships with nature, religion, and society, from "intrapsychic conflict" to international geopolitics, the presence (and absence) of enemies permeates our lives, and the lives of just about everything else as well.

Only rarely are these enemies of the easy-to-recognize, mustache-twirling variety. In some cases, of course, specific villains can readily be identified, but most of the time our enemies are subtle and diffuse, prone to transformation, sometimes even difficult to name. But they exist nonetheless, and more often than we care to admit, we feel their absence as strongly as their presence.

The greatest tragedy in life, noted George Bernard Shaw, is to be denied the thing one most wants. The second greatest tragedy? To get it. Getting rid of our enemies—something that is universally wanted—may in fact present us with more trouble than meets the eye, not so much because of the difficulty of achieving this goal, but because of the difficulty of living with success.

In this book, we shall explore the "enemy system," that complex of needs and circumstances, filtered through our personal experiences, which results in a peculiar relationship with others, a relationship in which those others often become enlarged and transformed, going from "others" to "Others," who are then identified and often demonized, in turn, as our enemies. Many of us would argue that we don't have personal enemies, at least not in any profound sense. I shall argue just the opposite: We do have enemies, and they are deeply ensconced within our private psyches as well as our public lives. So deeply embedded are they that we frequently deny their existence, even as they influence us in subtle but important ways. From our attitudes toward nature, our own bodies, our friends and lovers, to the larger patterns of society, an understanding of the human condition requires that we understand our penchant for enemies, as well as our remarkable ingenuity in creating them, including the challenge posed by those enemies: not only when they confront us, but also when and if they go away.

As we explore our universal "enemy system," I hope to reveal its causes and its multifaceted complexity, with the goal of illuminating some of the deeper, danker recesses of the human spirit. In doing so, we shall turn over some rocks and rotten logs, looking at those slippery and unseemly aspects of our psyche that crawl about underneath. I hope, also, to show how our need for enemies may be a "natural" inclination comparable to our need for food, sex, sleep, shelter, and companionship. This is not to say, however, that this book conveys a message of hopelessness, despair, or rigid determinism. Our exploration is powered by a search for the wisdom born of greater understanding, and it concludes with hope for overcoming— not overcoming our enemies, but rather a deeper and more urgent hope: the hope of overcoming our insistence on having enemies in the first place.

Sisyphus Reconsidered

Consider Sisyphus, wily miscreant of classical Greek mythology. Sisyphus played so many clever tricks on Zeus, Hades, and other deities that the gods eventually forced him to spend eternity pushing a heavy rock up a steep hill, only to have the rock roll back down again just as it reached the top. The work of Sisyphus, then, is never done. We might also say that the rock—or the slope, or gravity, or the curse upon him—is Sisyphus's enemy and that he was doomed to eternal misery, ever struggling with his opponent(s), and ever losing. But the French existential philosopher Albert Camus gives us an interesting twist on this story, arguing first that Sisyphus represents the perpetual human condition, struggling against a cold and uncaring universe, one that ultimately will be victorious if only because ultimately each of us will die. Furthermore, Camus maintains that Sisyphus is in fact happy rather than miserable, since Sisyphus knows his enemy, is resigned to his fate, and struggles nobly against it. This, for Camus, is what it means to be human: to define one's self in the ongoing struggle that is human existence.

Let us assume for a moment that Camus is correct, and add the further assumption that one day, Sisyphus just happens to lodge his rock firmly in a convenient cranny at the very top of his infernal, eternal hell of a hill. What then? We may presume that for a time Sisyphus would be happy, satisfied, complete. Then what? Deprived of his raison d'être, would Sisyphus grow edgy, bored, restless? Would he wonder who he is and what is his purpose? Would he start looking for other rocks to roll? Would he perhaps start throwing stones?

In the conventional myth of Sisyphus, it is assumed that Sisyphus tries his hardest not only to push the stone up the hill, but also to make it stay there once he reaches the top. But maybe it isn't that way at all. Maybe Sisyphus actually lets the rock crash back down, or gives it a slight push so it rolls over on the other side. Or maybe he doesn't really try to embed it firmly and triumphantly on the summit and lets natural instabilities do the trick. In short, maybe Sisyphus is an active participant in his life's work.

One suggestion of this book is that Camus was right. Another is that Sisyphus is even more canny than his reputation suggests. Not that he is necessarily aware of his maneuvering; Sisyphus, like most Americans, Israelis, Serbs, and millions of others involved with their identified enemies, would probably claim that he wants to do away with those enemies, or at least, to overcome them (or perhaps to transform them into friends). But we would do well to attend to what people *do*, at least as much as what they say. Moreover, so long as people—acting not only as political collectivities but also in their private lives—actually *rely* on enemies to meet real but often unspoken needs, they may stubbornly resist getting what they claim they want so badly. They may actually sabotage the end of enmity, so as to avoid relinquishing those beloved enemies in the first place. Or, if forced to do so, they may find themselves acquiring new ones with unexpected alacrity.

Tycho Brahe, Odd Metaphor for Our Times

Next, we turn to the strange case of Tycho Brahe (1546–1601), which, on inspection, turns out to be not so strange after all. Brahe is not exactly a household name, but he ought to be. An influential Danish star-charter of the late sixteenth century, Tycho Brahe served as mentor to the great German astronomer and mathematician Johannes Kepler (1571–1630). In his own right, Brahe achieved remarkable accuracy in measuring the positions of planets as well as stars. But Brahe's greatest contribution (at least for our purposes) was one that he would doubtless prefer to leave forgotten, because Brahe's Blunder is one of those errors whose very wrongness can teach us quite a lot about ourselves.

Deep in his heart, Brahe rejected the newly proclaimed Copernican model of the universe, the heretical system that threatened to wrench the Earth from its privileged position at the center of all creation and relegate it to just one of many planets that circle the Sun. But Brahe was also a careful scientist whose observations were undeniable, even as they made him uncomfortable: The five known planets of Brahe's day (Mercury, Venus, Mars, Jupiter, and Saturn) circled the Sun. This much was settled. Copernicus, alas, was right, and nothing could be done about it. But Tycho Brahe, troubled of spirit yet inventive of mind, came up with a solution, a kind of strategic intellectual retreat and regrouping. It was ingenious, allowing him to accept what was irrefutably true, while still clinging stubbornly to what he cherished even more: what he wanted to be true. And so, Brahe proposed that whereas the five planets indeed circled the Sun, that same Sun and its planetary retinue obediently revolved around an immobile Earth!

For our purposes, the crucial point is that Brahean solutions are not limited to astronomy. They reveal a widespread human tendency: Give ground—grudgingly, if you must—but only at the periphery. At the same time, strive by all means to preserve what is central, whatever is fundamentally important to your world-view.

When it comes to dealing with the loss of enemies, Tycho Brahe has nothing on us. Much in the human spirit revolves around having a reservoir of enemies, no less than the planets revolve around the Sun. And when a modern-day Copernican revolution shakes the stability of our enemy system, we respond like Tycho Brahe, defending the solar system of our childhood faith. Deprived of the Soviet Union as our enemy, we have eagerly begun to latch onto substitutes— drug lords, international terrorists, "instability" in the newly democratizing countries of Eastern Europe, ambition-crazed Middle-Eastern tyrants, Somali warlords, and so forth[2]—anything or anyone to allow us to maintain our grip on who we are *against,* and in the process, reassure ourselves about who we really *are.* As we shall explore in the chapters to come, this tendency is not limited to international affairs; it is reflected in the very patterning of modern society, in our interactions with colleagues and neighbors, and often in our most intimate relationships as well. It can even be found in our frequently unspoken assumptions about God, nature, our private lives and deaths, and our personal place in the universe.

Our fondness for Brahean solutions is most obvious, however, in the international arena, if only because these cases have been prominently displayed in the news, and they allow most of us—like astronomers—to witness events from afar, as though we were disinterested observers, which, of course, we are not.

Since 1952, the mission of the National Security Agency (NSA) has been to inform the United States government of any forthcoming Soviet military operation against Europe. Then, in 1989, something terrible happened to the good folks at the National Security Agency: The Warsaw Pact began to disintegrate, the USSR released its grip on its former satellites, and even the grimmest, most dyed-in-the-wool pessimists began finding it impossible to concoct a plausible scenario in which the Red Army marched West.

To its credit, the National Security Agency recognized the basic structure of the new Copernican solar system so rudely thrust upon it. But at the same time, it has responded in true Brahean fashion. And so, in 1990 the NSA began debating plans to redirect its global eavesdropping activities to other purposes, notably spying on world-wide financial transactions and trading practices. This transition is not just a simple matter of human psychology and the need for enemies, but also something even simpler: economics and the understandable machinations of worried military personnel and civil servants trying to keep their jobs. At least as important, however, is the effort of well-meaning, intelligent, thoughtful people to keep their mental equilibrium no less than their paychecks, to retain their pre-Copernican world-view. This world-view requires, in turn, that there be enemies that must be defended against and spied upon, whether a Soviet armored division, a Japanese steel manufacturer, or a German chemical conglomerate.

The failed anti-Gorbachev coup in Russia took place in August 1991, just after the Pentagon had delivered its annual report titled *Soviet Military Power*. This doughty publication, initiated during the Reagan administration in 1981, had become infamous for its wide-eyed, bloated overestimates of Soviet military strength, which in turn were used regularly to justify increases in the U.S. military budget. Future editions have at last been cancelled; likewise for the Hoover Institution's Yearbook on International Communism, which ceased twenty-five florid years of publication after its 1990 edition. Significantly, amid all these cancellations, the Central Intelligence Agency (CIA) at least was hard at work, coming up a year later with a report that featured the latest in enemy-spotting: *Japan 2000* unveiled a new global struggle between the "Western paradigm" and the "Japan paradigm." According to the "spooks" at the CIA, Japan is readying "an economic sneak attack, from which the U.S. may not recover." Maybe so, but one thing seems indisputable: government agencies, seeking to recover from the loss of one enemy, are quite adroit at doing so by fingering another.[3]

That great American comic-strip philosopher Pogo once said "We have met the enemy and he is us." For many, it is a hard notion to swallow. Far easier is the original, "We have met the enemy and he is ours," or Julius Caesar's "I came, I saw, I conquered." What makes Pogo's assertion so startling and difficult to swallow is that it is counterintuitive: Enemies, we all know, exist somewhere out there, not inside ourselves. And moreover, their role is to be overcome, defeated, conquered. But the end of the Cold War brought something new, something even Pogo—or Sisyphus—might find difficult to handle: We have met the enemy and he has gone away.

What then becomes of us?

At least we had been warned. Soviet policy adviser Georgy Arbatov threatened in 1987 that his government would "do something terrible" to us. It would deprive us of our enemy. The idea is not entirely unfamiliar to Western thought. Christ, for example, enjoins us to forgive our enemies. But even he does not ask that we abandon them altogether. Can we forgive those who commit the ultimate offense and become our friends?

One possibility—the most obvious and probably also the most likely—is that, more Brahe-like than Christ-like, we will latch onto a new batch of enemies and keep right on going, with the minimum possible correction in our course. For example, just as armchair cold warriors reluctantly began to admit the end of the Cold War, in their next breath they started trying to resuscitate it, pointing with alarm at the prospects of resurgent Russian nationalism. They warned that, deprived of its restless ethnic republics, Russia—angry, resentful, semi-mystical, and reactionary, the Russia of Gogol and of Solzhenitsyn at his most regressive—might be even worse than its Soviet predecessor.[4] Alternatively, they worry over the uncertain fate of market reforms in Russia, and about the possibility that Boris Yeltsin will be replaced with an old communist wolf in post-Cold War sheep's clothing. And, of course, they point out that post-Soviet Russia—no matter who leads it, and no matter what its ideology—will continue to have more than a few nuclear weapons.[5]

Just as generals typically prepare to refight the last war, our Cold War "generals" have been busily agitating to revive a cold war, any cold war, to replace the one they have lost. Among these experts in enmity, one of the most notable is Harvard political scientist Samuel P. Huntington, who for several decades labored long, hard, and influentially in the vineyards of anticommunist ideology. With the Cold War defunct, Professor Huntington reissued the same old wine in a new bottle, proclaiming his latest revelation in a 1993 issue of the prestigious establishment journal *Foreign Affairs*. His article, titled "The Clash of Civilizations?" was immediately hailed as pathbreaking and prescient. Its basic theme was that

> The fundamental source of conflict in this new world will not be primarily ideological or primarily economic. The great divisions among humankind and the dominating source of conflict will be cultural. Nation states will remain the most powerful actors in world affairs, but the principal conflicts of global politics will occur between nations and groups of different civilizations. The clash of civilizations will dominate global politics. The fault lines between civilizations will be the battle lines of the future.[6]

According to Huntington, these civilizations are Islamic, Confucian, Japanese, Hindu, Slavic-Orthodox, Latin American, "possibly African," and, definitely, Western. Later, he avers that in large part, it will be the West versus the Rest, which, in turn "will require the West to maintain the economic and military power necessary to protect its interests in relation to these civilizations." In fairness to the good professor, Dr. Huntington presents his idea as a possible paradigm, a prediction and a warning, not a statement of absolute truth. But it is likely to become self-fulfilling if taken seriously in the councils of government, where many who prospered on the Cold War are eager to do just that.

Unlike paradigms in natural science, which help to illuminate and refine our grasp of external reality, those in the realm of policy have a habit of *creating* reality. When the Copernican universe replaced the Ptolomeic, geocentric model with its more accurate, heliocentric alternative, there was no actual change in the orientation of the planets. But a Huntingtonian universe has the potential of deforming our economy and our politics, and of pandering to the worst in ethnic stereotyping and racial fears.

We have met the enemy, but can't seem to say good-bye. Our enemies, it seems, are stubbornly persistent, especially if we have anything to say about it. They stick to us like tar-babies of our souls. To Arabs and Israelis in the Middle East; Catholics and Protestants in Northern Ireland; Hindus and Moslems in India; Cambodians and Vietnamese in southeast Asia; Croats, Serbs, and Muslims in what used to be Yugoslavia; Hungarians and Romanians; Turks and Bulgarians; Armenians and Azerbaijanis; and to hundreds of millions of others throughout the world, including many Americans and Russians, much of this will seem irrelevant. Just let us overcome our enemies, they claim, and that will be the end of it. On the other hand, maybe it will not be the end after all. Tycho Brahe, erring astronomer but accurate metaphor for the human soul, would understand.

War, Peace, and In Between

Often, we find our enemies more interesting than our friends. We are far more likely to occupy ourselves with a recitation of the former's perfidy than with the latter's merits. We are notably more taken with war (the state-sponsored manifestation of political and military enmity) than with peace (the fruits of friendship and the end of enmity). It is revealing to consider, for example, the way we designate periods of history. Wars are carefully studied, identified, and given specific names, such as the War of 1812, the Spanish-American War, World War I, World War II, the Korean and Vietnam wars, and so forth. By contrast, the time between wars is simply known as "peace," and, significantly, unlike "wars," the word is never used in the plural. We do not identify "peaces," even though the peace that obtained in Europe after 1945 has certainly been quite different from that between World Wars I and II, which differed greatly from that between 1871 (the end of the Franco-Prussian War) and the assassination of Archduke Ferdinand in 1914.

We use language to focus our minds, and, in turn, our use of language reveals much about our minds and what we consider important and interesting. It is said, for example, that the Eskimo have more than eleven different words for "snow," distinguishing carefully between powder snow, sugar snow, crusty snow, heavy and wet snow, and so forth. They treat snow like we treat wars, carefully naming each variant. The Bedouins, not surprisingly, don't speak very much about snow but they have more than one hundred different words for "camel," depending on whether the animal in question is male or female, old or young, healthy or ill, nasty or agreeable, smooth or bumpy to ride, and so forth. To the English-speaking world, by contrast, there are simply "camels," just as there is simply "peace." And just as the Bedouins pay special attention to camels, and the Eskimo pay special attention to snow, we give particular heed to wars and to our enemies.[7]

If our souls have in fact been tarred (and scarred) by enemies and our reactions to them, and if we pay special attention when it comes to wars and the potential for widespread destruction, this has nowhere been more evident than in the case of nuclear weapons. The nuclear arms race also provided a textbook example of self-fulfilling prophecies, of responses to enemies creating yet more enmity. When it comes to the sticky, stubborn persistence of enemies in international relations, nuclear weapons and the whole rotten structure of deterrence belongs in a class by itself. Admittedly, some countries have real enemies and a legitimate need to be protected from these enemies. But when this "protection" involved pointing tens of thousands of nuclear weapons at someone else, no one should be surprised that someone else began to feel more than a little edgy, and even started pointing back.

"Our government kept us in a perpetual state of fear," said General Douglas MacArthur, no shrinking violet when it came to enemies; it "kept us in a continual stampede of patriotic fervor—with a cry of a grave national emergency. Always there has been some terrible evil at home or some monstrous foreign power that was going to gobble us up."[8] And of course, there is every reason to think that Americans were not alone in being subjected to this "perpetual state of fear."

Just after World War II, we pointed nuclear weapons at Stalin and his country. The Soviets pointed the Red Army at Western Europe. We got hydrogen bombs; so did they. Next came the missiles: first one warhead to each, then many. Both sides put them on submarines, on cruise missiles, and devised schemes for shooting theirs into space and for shooting down their opponents'. We each gestured with alarm at the other's arsenal as proof of how bad and aggressive *they* were, and to our own as proof of how we had been pushed into matching their nastiness with our prudence, although in *our* case (whichever side is talking) with deep regret and only the purest of defensive intentions.

Each side knew that it was peace-loving; thus, each found it inconceivable that the other could honestly feel threatened by its policies. "They must know that we mean them no harm," the experts reasoned, "so their behavior must be because they mean to cause *us* harm." The intelligence agencies of each side muttered darkly that the other had developed weapons grossly in excess of any reasonable defensive requirements. And they were right. Each also was certain that the other was following a carefully designed plan for world domination. The only way out, therefore, was to beat the other at his own game.

Notwithstanding the suffering and risk, however, at some primal level deterrence may have felt good, especially insofar as it validated a clear-cut stance toward our enemies. Thus, despite the abundantly elaborate and rarified analysis—much of it highly mathematical and imposing in its complexity—that has surrounded deterrence theory, the simple truth is that nuclear deterrence relied essentially on threat and the engendering of fear in one's enemies ("terror" and "deterrence" come from the same root, the Latin "terrere" meaning "to frighten"). Deterrence speaks a simple language, using emotional patterns that are so primitive that they even predate speech itself. Consider, for example, an ordinary spider: In order to find a common ancestor between a household arachnid and a human being, we must go back more than five hundred million years; it is as though spiders and ourselves inhabit different planets. And yet, poke at a tiny spider with a stick, or with your finger, and the angry little creature may well rear back on its legs while waving its forequarters menacingly. It is threatening you, not surprisingly. What is remarkable, however, is that you—so distantly connected—are likely to understand, because the spider is speaking in a common tongue about a widespread way of dealing with the ancient problem of enmity: When provoked or threatened, threaten back.

The nuclear dilemma at least appears, finally, to be on the road to resolution, and it is interesting that this did not occur following negotiations over these supreme weapons of enmity or as a result of the arcana of arms control and international treaties. Rather, deterrence itself is being overcome by a far deeper process of transformation: the fundamental changeover in the relationship between two former superpower rivals. We didn't so much overcome the former USSR as we both overcame our mutual enmity, largely because they have changed their system so drastically. No longer enemies, the two former rivals no longer need the lethal trappings of that animosity. Indeed, they desperately need to get rid of those trappings, to let go the tail of their shared nuclear tiger.

It has been argued that nuclear weapons kept the peace during the long Cold War. It can also be argued, however, that the distrust and fear that they engendered kept the Cold War going. The traditional wisdom, that a potential World War III between the U.S. and the Soviet Union was prevented because of nuclear deterrence, can be turned around to suggest that we avoided nuclear war not because of nuclear deterrence, but *in spite of* it. Consider, for example, the closest that we ever came to all-out nuclear holocaust: the Cuban Missile Crisis of 1962. That dispute was not about ideology or economics or even politics, but about nuclear weapons themselves. And significantly, much of the problem that remains between the former Cold War enemies still centers around these incredibly destructive trappings of superpower enmity.

But despite the negative consequences—and even though the very idea may make us uneasy—there appears to be something in the human psyche that yearns for its enemies.

Some Unexpected Peace Dividends

It doesn't take a great amount of imagination to identify war—or preparations for war—as a major threat to the quality of life on earth and, indeed, to life itself. Clearly, there are some downsides to our penchant for enemies. It does require some mental stretching to consider that to some extent our itch for opponents may also be therapeutic, a kind of self-medication.

For the collector of oxymorons, certain phrases have long been classics, among them "jumbo shrimp," "freezer burn," and "military intelligence." Another one—less commonly appreciated—is "civil war." It is often considered more "civil" to make war upon another country than to kill one's fellows, perhaps because there is a part of us that finds it easier, and perhaps even pleasant, to consider foreigners somewhat less than human or, at least, less human than ourselves. Among the Jivaro people of the upper Amazon, for example, the word *Jivaro* literally means "human being," so that members of other tribes are, by definition, not human, which enables Jivaro warriors to kill (and in the past, to eat) their neighbors during the day, then sleep soundly at night, unafflicted by pangs of conscience. With the coming of Western civilization to the Amazon, however, the Jivaro have been prohibited from practicing their lethal traditions. Not surprisingly, their own civilization has suffered.

Just as there are many ways to kill a person, there are many ways to kill a people. For one thing, they can simply be murdered, one by one. For another, the survivors can be put in situations that make them unable to carry on their cultures and traditions. Deprived of a way of life that, often as not, was predicated on certain (frequently unpleasant) ways of dealing with their enemies, such people have found themselves forced to conduct a kind of uncivil war against themselves. This process of "pacification" is especially insidious because it allows the perpetrators to sit back and claim, self-righteously, that the victims have no one to blame but themselves: A case, we like to think, of self-inflicted wounds.

It is no secret, for example, that beyond the massacres at Wounded Knee and other places, beyond the deceit and broken treaties, the original inhabitants of North America were especially devastated when they were herded onto reservations. By careful study, a virtual army of anthropologists has confirmed that what the U.S. cavalry didn't do to Native Americans, forced uprooting and confinement did. But in fact it doesn't take a highly trained expert to conclude that if people have lived for hundreds of generations as, for example, nomadic hunters following the buffalo, and then the buffalo are slaughtered and the people forced to live sedentary lives in arid, unproductive wastelands, something is likely to be lost. Rituals involving buffalo skins and buffalo hunts become irrelevant and disappear. Young men no longer graduate to the traditional role of hunter when they grow up; rather, they are forced to raise crops, hold bingo games, or rely on government hand-outs, with all the erosion of self-esteem that usually comes along with such dependency. Alcoholism goes up; life expectancy goes down.

Especially relevant for our purposes is the way that socially de-structive behavior—suicides, homicides, violent crimes—came in the wake of "pacification," even in those rare cases when the regime imposed by the self-appointed Great White Father in Washington, D.C., and his not-so-great sons and daughters appears to have been fundamentally benevolent.

Before Europeans arrived on the scene, aggression among many of the Plains Indians, for example, was often vented on neighboring "enemy" tribes. One result of being "pacified" by the white invaders was that such activity was prohibited. So far, so good. But without the buffalo and without an enemy to stalk and scalp, the warriors of the American plains turned much of their energy inward. Deprived of their traditional enemies, denied the opportunity of being *other*-destructive, they became *self*-destructive.

Abraham Kardiner examined the Comanches, who forged an ideal of courage and aggressive achievement, the so-called warrior virtues. He noted that when the Comanches were prevented from killing others, they began killing other Comanches, and also committing suicide in record numbers.[9] During precontact days, Comanche warfare "externalized aggression and reduced within-group animosity." Once their warfare was prohibited, the Comanches internalized their aggression and increased their within-group animosity. They redirected their enmity, so that instead of hurting others they began hurting each other.

Unlike the Comanches, the Teton Dakotas—another tribe of High Plains warriors and hunters—were more inclined to murder one another than to attack neighboring tribes. Mostly, the Teton Dakotas committed homicide in disputes over wealth and over women. But this was before 1850, at which time contact with white settlers became frequent and threatening to the native way of life. From about 1850 until 1880, the Tetons formed a more-or-less united front of shared hostility toward the white invaders; not surprisingly, within-group homicide decreased during that time. Then, defeated, the Tetons returned to their precontact ways: notably, murder.

It has been said that in one of his early summits with Mikhail Gorbachev, Ronald Reagan commented that maybe we needed an invasion from outer space in order for the United States and the USSR to become friends. Finally, we are becoming friends, without an invasion, but not, perhaps, without costs. In Mark Alan Stamaty's comic strip, "Washingtoon," Congressman Bob Forehead—Capitol Hill Comanche suddenly deprived of his hated Sioux—was having a terrible time. He went to see a "perestroichiatrist" who explained to the congressman's alarmed wife: "The fading of the Cold War has left a terrible void inside him. He'll need a lot of care until he finds a new enemy."

This terrible void has been even more acute among the military.

Facing a kind of forced pacification with the end of the Cold War— and fearing an end of history as they have known it—our own warriors have been getting restless, seeking other targets for their tomahawks (a name, ironically enough, now bestowed upon the Navy's cruise missiles), and looking for new reasons to beat their war drums. But things have changed, you might argue. Instead of chiefs, we have Joint Chiefs of Staff. In an age of nuclear weapons, we had all better be meek or there will be no earth for anyone to inherit. But on the other hand there looms the Dakota Teton murdering his fellow tribe member, or the equally "pacified" Comanche warrior drinking his liver into mummified shreds.

From Chiefs to the Joint Chiefs

The danger seems remote that we shall suffer the fate of the Plains Indians, acutely self-destructive when deprived of their opponents, not when international enemies provide such a heady mix of stimulation and provocation. By mid-summer 1990, for example, the United States was feeling pretty low. It had "won" the Cold War, but its triumph lacked any dramatic or thrilling victories. The former dictators of the proletariat wanted nothing more than their own American Express cards. Bits of the Berlin Wall could be purchased for $9.95 apiece at Bloomingdale's. The USSR and its minions had succumbed, not with a bang, but a whimper. Moreover, the messy problems of what would happen next in Eastern Europe and the remains of the Soviet Union itself were generating at least as much worry as celebration.

Meanwhile, the good old USA was being beaten by Western Europe and Japan on the economic and educational fronts, and the perception (accurate, it turned out) was widespread that a recession was in the offing and that the bills were coming due for a decade of profligacy and self-indulgence during the 1980s.[10] The Reagan binge was catching up with us: We had been self-indulgent, greedy, care-less—in a word, *bad*—and we were about to get our comeuppance. George Bush revealed that he had merely been lip-syncing his "no new taxes" pledge. We were in debt up to our eyebrows, including hundreds of billions to the sleazy operators of our neighborhood Savings and Loans. Our children weren't learning, the environment was in desperate shape and getting worse, the homeless were every-where, along with drugs and urban violence. Even our infrastruc-ture was rotting, while what remained intact, it seemed, was being bought up by the Japanese.

Then, *voilà*, the Iraqi invasion of Kuwait! Saddam Hussein lurched into the American consciousness: Middle-Eastern bully, terrorizer of toddlers, plunderer of petroleum, holder of hostages, gangster of the Gulf, and butcher of Baghdad. We had an enemy again, and it was neither our incompetent leaders nor our own inaction, thoughtlessness, mendacity, greed, rapaciousness, or indifference. No, it was Saddam Hussein (who, indeed, really was something of a bad guy). It was the evil Iraqis and their unspeakable crimes against innocent little Kuwait that we mobilized to punish and undo. And punish them we did, surgically striking them with our cruise missiles, carpet-bombing them with our B-52s, and knocking out their sleazy SCUD missiles with our powerful Patriots. Suddenly—at least for a time—we felt good about ourselves again. We weren't so bad, couldn't be so bad, after all, if we could do such a good job against such nefarious characters. And furthermore, as then-President Bush pointed out joyfully, we had finally licked the Vietnam Syndrome: We had proved to the world and to ourselves that we could win wars and defeat evil, and that, in Mr. Bush's memorable words, "What we say, goes." We were good at organizing and conducting a massive military effort, and—most important—good in a moral sense: the White Knights of the world socking it to the evil enemy. We weren't bad after all; they were.

Iraq served us very well indeed (until the Kurds and Shi'ites rained on our parade by suffering and dying so conspicuously, and Saddam himself dampened things somewhat, by, on the one hand, refusing to exit gracefully, and, on the other, by not being quite provocative enough to justify yet another *jihad* against him.)

It seems unlikely that our military will now turn its frustrated energies upon itself, or on the rest of us, at least so long as our leaders keep throwing them an occasional Grenada, Panama, or Iraq. Certainly, there was a revealing slip of the tongue when then-Secretary of Defense Richard Cheney, defending the B-2 bomber against attempted budget cutbacks, announced during a press conference in the autumn of 1991 that one of that billion-dollar airplane's merits was its ability to "haul a large payroll—er, payload." On the other hand, maybe there are cheaper and better ways of getting away from the Jivaro mindset and still avoiding the fate of the Comanches and the Teton Dakotas, while also stopping short of another round of waste, competition, and war. Maybe we should internationalize the National Football League, or hold a much-ballyhooed and highly competitive transcontinental spelling bee, or bring back the buffalo, and quickly.[11]

Columnist Charles Osgood captured an aspect of the problem—and possibly even part of the solution—in the following comical, yet oddly poignant account of the end of the Cold War and the dissolution of the Soviet Union:

"The Soviet Union is no more" is what the headlines read.
An obituary stating the USSR is dead.
Three republics say the country based in Moscow is now gone.
And Minsk will be the capital, they tell us, from now on.

Mine enemy grew older, I watched him fading fast.
He lost the strength that threatened in the not so distant past.

Mine enemy grew older, he did not want to die.
But time, it seems, caught up with him and finally passed him by.

When mine enemy was younger, he was filled with enmity.
He would pound his shoe and brag about how he would bury me.
Around the world he flew his flag, the hammer and the sickle.
He claimed to own the future then, but history is fickle.

I used to see mine enemy as evil, and he was.
There was an "evil empire." Evil is as evil does.
And he had been cruel and ruthless, as so many are aware.
Many nations took a mauling from that big ferocious bear.

We used to be invincible, or so we used to think.
We used to stare each other down to see which one would blink.
And when we raised our voices it seemed all the world would cower.
And the word they used to use for both of us was "superpower."

Mine enemy was also smart, and no one could deny
That he first put a satellite, the Sputnik, in the sky.
It prodded me, and challenged me so much that very soon
I was orbiting the Earth myself, and walking on the moon.

I was not about to sit back with my own dreams on the shelf.
Mine enemy was younger then, but I was young myself.
The two of us were daring, even reckless then, I think.
And we roared and rattled mighty swords as we approached
    the brink.

Mine enemy grew older though and less inclined to fight.
His hand became less steady as his hair turned thin and white.
The changing world was something that he could not understand.
It got so bad he even asked if I would lend a hand.

And now another page has turned, and now its being said,
It's all over for mine enemy. They say that he is dead.
I used to think I'd celebrate the day that he would die,
But mine enemy grew older, and so, I guess, did I.[12]

Fortunately, as Mr. Osgood recognizes, things change, including our choice of enemies, even if our need for them lingers on.

The Changing of Enemy Images

Someday, perhaps, we really shall overcome not just our enemies but also our penchant for creating, multiplying, and maintaining them, and even our perception of what it takes to be our enemy. It will not be easy, however. This sort of overcoming will require going against a tradition that existed long before the Cold War and the invention of nuclear weapons. Describing an all-too-familiar tendency on the part of ancient Rome, Joseph Schumpeter observed:

> There was no corner of the known world where some interest was not alleged to be in danger or under actual attack. If the interests were not Roman, they were those of Rome's allies; and if Rome had no allies, then allies would be invented. When it was utterly impossible to contrive such an interest—why, then it was the national honor that had been insulted. The fight was always invested with an aura of legality. Rome was always being attacked by evil-minded neighbors, always fighting for a breathing space. The whole world was pervaded by a host of enemies, and it was manifestly Rome's duty to guard against their indubitably aggressive designs. They were enemies only waiting to fall on the Roman people.[13]

Fortunately, however, we do have some examples of successful letting go of enemies: the American attitude toward Italy after World

War II, for example. Italy was forgiven and befriended almost immediately. This transition was relatively easy for most Americans because Italians were responsible for relatively few atrocities, and besides, there had been active, antifascist partisans within that country, which ultimately overthrew Mussolini and caused Italy to become a nominal ally before the war actually ended. (It also helped, perhaps, that Italy was never a very scary or effective opponent in the first place.)

The enemy images of Germany and Japan, by contrast, took quite a bit longer to be comparably refurbished, and many of us still have a hard time seeing Germans or Japanese as bona fide allies. But there is no question that in the case of Germany and Japan, the U.S. government was eager for public opinion to make that great leap from enemy to friend, and for our purposes it is especially interesting that this eagerness was due almost entirely to the emergence of another threat seen as more dangerous and more immediate than the defeated Axis powers: the Soviet Union.

The Arabs have a revealing saying: "The enemy of my enemy is my friend." It predated the Gulf War by about a thousand years, but it also helps explain the spectacle of the United States cozying up to the government of Syria in shared antagonism toward Iraq. And it also explains why, as this was taking place, Iran—which had just completed a vicious war with Iraq—actually warmed up to Saddam Hussein, since Iraq had become the enemy of Iran's other, more longstanding enemy, the United States. Similarly, in the late 1970s the United States had studiously looked the other way during the murderous rampages of the Khmer Rouge in Cambodia, because the Vietnamese, who had recently defeated us, were also enemies of those same Khmer Rouge, and we, still smarting over the Vietnam War, couldn't quite shake the notion that the enemy of our enemy— no matter how brutal and genocidal—must somehow be, if not virtuous, at least not altogether bad.

There had been a time when America and the USSR were allies, if not friends. Not coincidentally, this was when they, too, shared an enemy (Nazi Germany). Then came the end of World War II and with it the end of their "great alliance." As Winston Churchill observed, "The destruction of German military power brought with it a fundamental change in the relations between Communist Russia and the Western democracies. They had lost their common enemy, which was almost their sole bond of union."

In the United States, at least, our enemy images have begun to switch yet again. For example, as recently as the mid-1980s Americans flocked to cinematic representations of the evil empire such as *Missing in Action, Red Dawn,* and *Rambo III.* In the latter, Soviet soldiers in Afghanistan were depicted as depraved brutes who burned babies alive, tortured prisoners, and bayonetted pregnant women. More recently, however, we have been given the likes of *Fire Birds,* in which South American drug lords take over from the Soviets and their Vietnamese henchmen (e.g., *Rambo I* and *II*), as public enemy number one. In *Red Heat,* Soviet and American police officers (Arnold Schwarzenegger and James Belushi) even teamed up to defeat the evil drug dealers. And in *Iron Eagle II,* U.S. and Soviet pilots combined forces to blow up a nasty Arab missile complex. In these latter two films, initial distrust gives way to heartwarming male-male bonding in the face of—what else?—a common enemy.

In restructuring our image of the enemy, it helps greatly if that image is clear and unambiguous. Thus, most Americans have been quite willing to accept a new image for the former Soviet Union, partly because those Russians who have gained access to U.S. media have been so gracious and even abject in admitting their weakness, so forthright in acknowledging their errors (e.g., in Afghanistan), and so fulsome in their admiration for capitalism and democracy. There is some similarity here with the "rehabilitation" of Germany and Japan, which had been helped by the fact that those countries had been clearly and unambiguously defeated, hence more likely to evoke sympathy than shivers of fear. Among the great majority of postwar Germans and Japanese as well, there was never any serious question about whether they really lost the Second World War and whether it was time to turn a new page in their lives: They did, and it was. Similarly, relatively few Russians dispute the fact that they "lost" the Cold War, or, at least, that their system failed to deliver on its promises.

Compare this with the experience of Germany after World War I when Kaiser Wilhelm's armed forces had not been unambiguously vanquished on the battlefield. The Versailles Treaty was widely seen throughout Germany as a "stab in the back," a "defeat" that was particularly hard to swallow because it had never clearly taken place. The Germans nursed their grudges for two decades, only to strike again at their unresolved enemies.

Then there is the Vietnam War: The Vietnamese won, and have long been ready to let bygones be bygones, but the United States has had a terrible time forgiving them for beating us. In short, the enemy goes away when defeated. It is relatively easy to be magnanimous in victory. But in the aftermath of a debatable and disputed defeat (for example, France after the Franco-Prussian War, Germany after World War I, the United States after the Vietnam War) the bitterness and the continued enmity linger on.

With this in mind, we might indeed want to be especially concerned about what transpires within and among the republics of the former Soviet Union now that the Cold War is over—a "war" that was never actually fought, and whose aftermath might well lead to dangerous bitterness. Maybe the stubborn cold warriors are correct after all. Or maybe we should rewrite Pogo's observation yet another time: We have met the enemy and he has gone away, at least for now, until he reemerges, or we find—or construct—a new one.

But here is an odd question: How can we tell where we end and our enemy begins?

The Question of Boundaries

It must be nice to know for sure, and thus to confront the world with the definite knowledge of what is right and what is wrong, who represents god and who the devil, and to have the fundamentalist's certainty of good and bad, the saved and the damned. But some of us are cursed with a more nuanced sense of reality, especially when it comes to identifying friends and enemies. A case in point is the weightlifter, straining to raise a barbell weighing two hundred pounds. His face contorts with the effort, his muscles quiver, he sweats and grimaces and grunts loudly. He feels genuine discomfort, and even pain. ("No pain, no gain," we are told.) An observer from another planet would have no doubt that the barbell is the weightlifter's enemy, and at times, the weightlifter might even agree. But this characterization would be misleading. After all, the barbell makes him stronger, so it is also his friend.

Our enemy "strengthens our nerves and sharpens our skill," according to the eighteenth-century political theorist Edmund Burke. "Our antagonist is our helper."[14] Moreover, the weightlifter actually sought out his particular "enemy," and might well be paying genuine money for the pleasure of encountering his foe on a regular basis. And he rewards himself not by ceasing the confrontation, but by enhancing his "enemy," perhaps a few more pounds next time.

"Who goes there, friend or foe?" we hear the age-old cry of the sentry. (About 3,300 years ago, Joshua met a man wielding a sword on the outskirts of Jericho. He greeted the man as follows: "Are you for us or for our adversaries?" [Joshua 5:13] But the answer may not be as simple as the question implies. They can be strangely indistinct, those barbell boundaries between friend and enemy.

Boundaries can be made uncertain not only by the diffuse melding of friend and foe as in the case of the weightlifter, but also by doubt as to where the self leaves off and the opponent begins. With the

Cold War over, international economic rivalries have begun to take center stage. The players seem obvious enough: Germany is Germany and Britain is Britain. Japan is Japan and the United States is the United States. East is east and west is west, as Kipling assured us, "and never the twain," and so forth. But multinational corporations often cause all sorts of strange meetings. They introduce great uncertainty into the question of who is the "Other," the enemy, in large part by casting doubt on who is "us." For example, Taiwan's largest exporters include AT&T, RCA, and Texas Instruments. Furthermore, Taiwan has a large trade surplus with the United States, and AT&T, RCA, and Texas Instruments make up fully one-third of this surplus, through items they produce or purchase in Taiwan and then sell to the United States. But if these manufacturers are Taiwanese, what is an American corporation? Moreover, a controlling interest in RCA is now owned by a Japanese conglomerate.

We have already considered, albeit briefly, that there is no simple answer to the question: What do we want from our enemies? (As suggested by Sisyphus, Tycho Brahe, and much of human history, our goals are probably more complex than that these enemies should simply be defeated or "go away.") The purpose of this section is to suggest that even the very meaning of "enemy" is in many cases also subject to debate and likely to surprise us. The question "Who is our enemy?" is no more straightforward than the question "Who are we, really?" Moreover, the two may be inseparable. A close look at the phenomenon of enemies leads inexorably to a closer look at ourselves, in part because we often define ourselves by who (or what) we are against. Thus, closer examination cannot help but illuminate who (or what) we are. In some cases, as we shall see, if the enemy is removed, precious little is left of ourselves, and this simple but disturbing fact may well prove to be among the most demanding issues of modern life.

The question of self-definition (with or without enemies) may seem abstract and irrelevant to daily life; subsequent chapters will seek to show that it is, in fact, very concrete and painfully relevant in our personal and social lives, our relationships to each other, and to life in general. Beyond this, by raising the question of enmity and alliance, friend and foe, we raise another series of rich and complex issues: What are we after? Why do we do what we do? What does it take to be happy? What responsibilities, if any, do we have to others, and to ourselves?

One thing that seems simple enough is that most people want to get the best deal possible for themselves. And to achieve this they have to interact, often in complex ways, with other people who likely have their own interests in mind, or other things, which, like a barbell, may simply exert more passive resistance. In many cases, getting the best deal for ourselves requires becoming aware of the needs of our opponent, so that both parties become collaborators of a sort, playing against the house instead of against each other. In the process, there can be a breaking down of the seeming boundary between our own best interest and that of the other guy. For a revealing example, think about the Prisoner's Dilemma.

Prisoner's Dilemma

This is an ancient conundrum, a frustrating challenge to our logic as well as our ethics and sense of fairness. The idea is that two "players," call them A and B, are in a position to benefit, together, if both of them cooperate and to suffer—also together—if both are nasty to each other. So far, there is no dilemma, and in a sense, neither is a prisoner. The path for each of them would seem simple enough and should be freely chosen: Both players, in short, should cooperate (or as mathematical game theorists put it with disarming simplicity, they should be "nice") because if they are, both will gain. But unfortunately, things are often more complicated.

What makes the so-called Prisoner's Dilemma especially difficult as well as interesting is the following twist: Imagine that while one player is being nice, the other decides to take advantage of the situation and be nasty. Imagine further that if this happens, the nasty player winds up getting the highest payoff of all, while the nice one is a big loser. In fact, let us make the additional assumption that in this case, the nice guy (aka the "sucker") gets the lowest pay-off of all, even worse than if he and the other player had both been nasty and uncooperative in the first place. (These are reasonable assumptions in a world of "zero-sum games," in which, for example, there is only a limited amount of pay-off available, so that anything gained by individual A is lost by B, and vice versa.)

Given these conditions, let's listen in on player A trying to decide what to do, whether to be nasty or nice: "B can choose, like myself, to be either nasty or nice. If he chooses nasty, then I had better be nasty also, since if I choose nice I'd be a sucker and get a rotten pay-off, while B gets the highest return. So in case he decides to be nasty, I should be nasty too. But what if B chooses to be nice? Well, in that case, of course I could be nice, too, and get a pretty good pay-off: exactly the same that he gets, since the two of us would be cooperating in a sense. But wait a minute! If B chooses to be nice, then I have a better choice yet. I could be nasty, in which case I get to take advantage of him—just as I had feared that he might take advantage of me—and I get the highest return, while he gets suckered. Either way, therefore, no matter what B does, I protect myself and come out best by being nasty."

A's logic is impeccable (even though it may be immoral), and we can expect that B, reasoning the same way, would come up with the same answer. The resulting dilemma, then, is that both players find themselves compelled by the logic of the "game" to be nasty, and so they both get lower pay-offs than either would get if they had only been able to cooperate with each other—to treat each other as partners instead of enemies—and behave nicely.

Psychologists, ethicists, economists, political scientists, and logicians have devised numerous ways of testing the Prisoner's Dilemma, and they consistently find that people tend to behave as though their goal is to avoid being suckered, and to minimize the other's return, rather than to maximize their own. Like our hypothetical player A, participants typically find themselves entangled in the logic of a competitive system, prisoners in a dilemma of their own making. The point is that in situations like the Prisoner's Dilemma, people don't *have* to be enemies. There is no reason why they couldn't cooperate and each reap the rewards of doing so. However, they find themselves so worried about being a sucker and at the same time so eager to take advantage of the other player that they transform the Other into an opponent rather than a partner; as a result, both wind up being nasty, and hence, both wind up being worse off.

The Prisoner's Dilemma can be considered a simplified model for many things in modern life: nuclear disarmament, for example, in which each side fears to be nice (disarm) because it may be suckered if the other is nasty (keeps its weapons or builds more). So both wind up being nasty, stuck in an arms race, to the disadvantage of all concerned. We and the Soviets were long accustomed to exactly this system, with both sides receiving a negative pay-off, measured as the costs of hostility, distrust, wasted national treasure, and unmet domestic needs. Fortunately, however, the Cold War is now over, although it is taking some time for the implications to filter down to the many political prisoners of our longstanding superpower dilemma.

At the same time, many of us are fighting cold wars in our personal lives, prisoners of our own, private dilemmas. There are tugs-of-war between spouses, between parents and children, between worker and boss, between neighbors, in which each side would love to let go, but fears that it cannot afford to do so because the results will be embarrassing if not downright disastrous. And so, they settle for an ongoing standoff, in which both sides continue to struggle, and pull: to be, in a sense, nasty, although it feels more like being self-protective. Backs aching, hands bloody and raw, each receives the mutual punishment of a stiff-necked (but thoroughly logical) commitment to "winning," as each defines the other as its enemy.

Fortunately, there are ways out. In the movie *WarGames*, the computer advised that the only way to win the game (in the case of nuclear policy) is not to play at all. When it comes to tug-of-war, the easiest way to win is to let go. And even when it comes to Prisoner's Dilemma, the seemingly irrefutable logic of eternal, mutually punishing nastiness can, in fact, be sidestepped. Mathematically inclined students of the Prisoner's Dilemma have confirmed that nice guys don't necessarily have to finish last, especially if the dilemma in question is a continuing, repeated series of interactions rather than just a one-shot deal.[15] When the possibility exists for repeated interactions, when—as one theoretician has put it—the "shadow of the future is long," it can actually pay to be nice, since nice guys can set up reciprocating partnerships and avoid the costs of everyone being nasty and inflicting pain on one another.

It also appears that the only "winning"[16] strategy must include forgiveness. Thus, even after a treacherous opponent has recently double-crossed you, the strategy that is ultimately most successful is to cooperate—that is, to be forgiving of his or her past trespasses—so long as the opponent switches back to cooperation. The surest sign of repentance is benevolent cooperation, and the only "winning" response is to accept the other's apology graciously.

No one knows which form of the Prisoner's Dilemma is more important in human life: the nasty-making system of mutual punishment, based on distrust and prolongation of enmity, or the cooperation-inducing pattern of mutual niceness that allows us to behave not only ethically but even in accord with hard-eyed calculations of how to maximize our personal return. We do know, however, that when someone chooses to be nasty to us rather than nice, we are likely—and in a sense, justified—to consider him an "enemy." And furthermore, we are also likely to respond by being nasty ourselves, the next time we get the chance.

In any event, by the late 1980s the Soviet Union began to play differently, although presumably more as a consequence of economic and political necessity than after consulting their specialists for the latest advances in mathematical game theory. They began cooperating, often unilaterally: withdrawing from Afghanistan and Eastern Europe, accepting one-sided arms reduction agreements, acquiescing in the U.S.-led war against Iraq, helping to convene an Arab-Israeli peace conference, and so forth. And it is not at all clear that they have been stuck with the sucker's pay-off that traditional game theory would have predicted. Nor is it clear that we have been getting a higher pay-off because of their greater cooperativeness in the face of our own, often stubborn intransigence. Maybe the Prisoner's Dilemma model simply doesn't apply any longer to what had been called the Cold War, since the Soviets—now, Russians—have changed the game.

Maybe it doesn't even apply all that well to our private lives either, although there is some reason to suspect that in many cases, it does. If it doesn't, so much the better. And if it does, then the possibility exists that enlightened self-interest will help us to recognize that the solution to the dilemma lies in recognizing that it is shared. It might be useful to move the apostrophe and to rewrite the phrase "Prisoner's Dilemma" as "Prisoners' Dilemma," emphasizing that it is a shared problem that requires a cooperative solution. Or—another way of looking at it—the way out of such dilemmas may lie in considering that the other player is a fellow participant, maybe even an ally, and not necessarily an enemy.

The Faces (Human and Otherwise) of the Enemy

The "game" of identifying and responding to our enemies has been changed many times in American history. Consider this less-than-friendly description of a foreign country, by one of the great leaders in U.S. history: "We concur in considering its government as totally without morality," wrote Thomas Jefferson,

> insolent beyond bearing, inflated with vanity and ambition, aiming at the exclusive domination of the world, lost in corruption, of deep-rooted hatred towards us, hostile to liberty wherever it endeavors to show its head, and the eternal disturber of the peace of the world.[17]

The subject of this intense enmity? Great Britain, for many years now our good and great friend, with whom a "special relationship" is often acknowledged. After Great Britain, Mexico became our enemy, even Canada for a time, and, of course, the Native American "savages." For more than two centuries, there was an additional enemy, abstract and almost faceless, but nonetheless real: the North American wilderness and the western frontier.

Students of American history—notably Frederick Jackson Turner —have emphasized the impact of the closing of the frontier on the American mind and on our subsequent behavior as a people. In a sense, the frontier served as a beloved enemy for the restless, energetic, expansionist Americans of the eighteenth and nineteenth centuries. It was widely considered to be "nasty," and required us to be nasty in return, or, at least, it justified behavior that was often violent and brutal. We permitted ourselves to treat the North American continent as an enemy, and had little difficulty condoning an appalling amount of nastiness. Of course, the frontier was not simply a wasteland, a vast expanse of dangerous territory populated with hostile aboriginal people, although to many Caucasian Americans at the time, it was precisely and narrowly this. It was also an immense opportunity, a vast playing field against which we could pit our strength and measure our worth. If the Battle of Waterloo was won for the British on the playing fields of Eton, the battle of the American psyche was won on the western frontier.

It is worth noting that by contrast, the European sense of a "frontier" is quite different and far more sinister, a place of barbed wire and—until very recently—great danger, of armed guards and looming strangeness. Occasionally, it offered hope (in the sense of escape from totalitarianism), but it was generally to be avoided, or at most to be crossed hurriedly and on a moonless night, fleeing one's home. In any event, it was not something to test one's self against or within which to grow, nor was it someplace to linger, or a challenge to tame. The European "frontier" is a line, whereas the American frontier had two dimensions; it was an area, a place to explore, and often, to overcome.

It is probably more than a coincidence that with the closing of the American frontier in the late nineteenth century, America turned in earnest to the question of its place in the world. We fought our first overseas war of colonial ambition (the Spanish-American War), and ultimately joined in a major, bloody European fray (World War I), while in the process going against nearly 150 years of isolationist tradition. Deprived of our beloved frontier friend/enemy, we sought and found all manner of enemies overseas.

When most people think of an "enemy," they conjure up a group of people: Communists, Red Chinese, Nazis, Iranian fundamentalists, and Nicaraguan Sandinistas or contras (depending on our ideological bent). Even more often, we personalize the enemy image by focussing on a specific individual: Hitler, Stalin, Mao, Khomeini, Castro, Noriega, Saddam Hussein, or maybe that irritating neighbor who won't keep his dog quiet at night, a cantankerous and hypercritical in-law, the drug dealer down the block, or the fellow with the crazy look in his eye who sits in his house and plays with assault rifles all day long. Following a U.S.-Soviet summit meeting in Washington, D.C., in 1990, President Bush pronounced that the enemy was no longer the USSR, but rather, "instability and unpredictability." But instability and unpredictability themselves are too formless, unstable, and unpredictable to be adequate enemies. As political commentator Marianne Means complained about Bush's formulation: "The symbolism is too diffuse. It isn't us against them, its us against—who? Chaos has no single human face and no uniformly controlled troops or missiles on which our fears can be focussed."

In short, not only do we need an enemy, and not only do we tend to exaggerate this enemy and dehumanize it, but we also insist that this enemy have at least a recognizable face, typically the face of a leader through whom national identity—and antagonism—is filtered, and in whose image a complex welter of aspirations and antagonisms are congealed and personified. The frontier served us for a while, but it seems that we need people—better yet, specific individuals—upon which to focus.

In the world of nation-states, no less than of backyard neighbors, it is downright comforting to think that the problem really lies in one or a small number of especially noxious bad guys: the Kaiser during World War I; Hitler, Tojo, and Mussolini during World War II; Mao Zedong during the Korean War; Ho Chi Minh during the Vietnam War; Serbia's Slobodan Milosevic, and so forth. There is much consolation to be had in the reassurance that it isn't the Vietnamese who we detest, just a particular Communist or two; not Arabs or even Iraqis in general, just Saddam; not all Somalis, just that nasty "warlord," Mohammed Aidid, and so forth. Thus are we absolved from hating large numbers of people—who, deep in our hearts, we know to be scarcely more evil than us—while also setting ourselves up as the potential saviors of the evil ruler's oppressed countrymen, suffering as they are under the heel of such a villainous overlord. Moreover, once the focus of evil is pinpointed in a single foreign leader or a small cadre of ne'er-do-wells, it seems reasonable to hope that when he (rarely she) is overthrown, peace and justice will reign.

Although prone to error, our personal antennae are generally well-tuned to receive transmissions from such human enemies, even as we often distort and magnify the signals. But ironically, we are much less sensitive to other dangers, enemies that are real enough but faceless, and thus difficult to grasp and to oppose. There is no single visage, no simple enemy image, for overpopulation, resource depletion, poverty, the greenhouse effect, wildlife extinction, the denial of human rights, or the danger of nuclear proliferation. Even our own personal, private death is oddly elusive. And even mastery and success has its price. Frontiers—at least, the American version—are eventually tamed and plowed under, while individual foreign enemies (Mao, Ho Chi Minh, Khomeini, Stalin) either die or, like Castro, Qaddafi, or even Saddam Hussein, become less threatening. Only rarely, however, do we seriously consider our own role in the process, the degree to which we may have created these enemies by our own self-righteous insistence that we are right and they wrong. Even more rarely do we recognize that by playing "nasty" in public or private games of Prisoner's Dilemma, we may have helped produce enemies that need not have existed in the first place.

It is tempting, instead, to see ourselves as isolated, beleaguered soldiers, surrounded by enemies, manning the solitary outposts of our lives, standing by our watchfires, ever on guard against opponents who exist "out there," independent of ourselves. But the next time the sentry within us demands "Halt," and then cocks its rifle while asking "Who goes there, friend or foe?" we might want to consider that the question is not so easily answered. We might ask ourselves, as well, whether we oversimplify and thus mislead ourselves (as well as others) by aggressively broadcasting a simple yes-or-no, either/

or question into the darkness around us. And we might also consider that just maybe we are part of the answer.

*   *   *

We explore next the three primary levels at which we feel the presence of enemies—and their absence—so strongly. Beginning with biology, the most reductionistic, we progress in turn to the human mind (psychology), and then to society as a whole.

Notes

1. Francis Fukuyama, "The End of History." *National Interest* 16 (1989): 3–18.

2. An article in the *Seattle Post-Intelligencer* newspaper, on February 17, 1992, described the "new mission" for locally based fighter-interceptors as follows: "Although the threat from the Soviet Air Force vanished from the skies within weeks after the failed Moscow coup last August, the F-15s here are still on alert. But now, they focus on different enemies. 'What's keeping us alive here is the drug war,' said Oregon Air Guard Maj. Gaylord 'Lordy' Dawson, commander of the F-15 detachment. . . ."

3. It seems likely that a comparable process has been going on in the independent former Republics of the USSR, although most of their substitute enemies are found among the other Republics themselves; i.e., Georgians worried about Abkhasians; Uzbekistan anxious about Kazakstan; Armenians and Azeris at each other's throats; and everyone concerned about Russia.

4. Russian elections in late 1993, in which the party of ultranationalist, pro-Fascist Vladimir Zhirinovsky did better than any of his competitors, suggest that such fears may be at least somewhat justified.

5. The loss of the United States and NATO as enemies has also caused some problems for the Kremlin, problems that may be troublesome for the rest of the world as well. Thus, it appears that literally thousands of highly trained post-Soviet nuclear scientists are looking for jobs, and possibly willing to sell their expertise to the highest bidders. Furthermore, the economic and social dislocation initially caused by even modest efforts to reduce military spending in the United States

is likely to pale compared with the "threat" that peace poses to the formerly Soviet military-industrial complex, which was—relatively speaking—far larger than ours.

6. Samuel P. Huntington, "The Clash of Civilizations?" *Foreign Affairs* 72 (1993): 22–49.

7. The Bedouin, incidentally, are no slouches when it comes to enemies, either, having dozens of words for "sword."

8. Douglas MacArthur, *A Soldier Speaks* (New York: Praeger, 1965).

9. Abraham Kardiner, *Psychological Frontiers of Society* (New York: Columbia University Press, 1963).

10. See, for example, Haynes Johnson, *Sleepwalking Through History* (New York: W. W. Norton, 1991).

11. Some of us do, in fact, derive a perverse pleasure from the fact that the buffalo are coming back, while the railroads become extinct.

12. Charles Osgood, *Seattle Post-Intelligencer*, December 11, 1991.

13. Joseph Schumpeter, "The Sociology of Imperialism," in *Two Essays by Joseph Schumpeter* (New York: Meridian Books, 1955).

14. Edmund Burke, *Reflections on the Revolution in France* (Amherst, N.Y.: Prometheus Books, 1987).

15. R. Axelrod, *The Evolution of Cooperation* (New York: Basic Books, 1984).

16. This word belongs in quotation marks because it wins in only a unique sense: it cannot be exceeded by any other. In every contest, however, it never does any better than its "opponent."

17. P. L. Ford (ed.), *The Writings of Thomas Jefferson*, vol. 9 (New York: Putnams, 1848).

2

Biology

The story is told of the renowned astrophysicist who had been delivering a public lecture about the origin and structure of the solar system. The lecture was a stunning tour de force, employing data, models, photographs, and mathematical equations, impressively orchestrated with the full weight of modern science, and interpreted by a brilliant mind. But when it was over, a woman rose from the audience and said that she didn't believe a word of it. The Earth, she announced, was balanced on the back of a gigantic elephant, which, in turn, sat upon an immense turtle. "Well, then," asked the scientist, "what does this turtle rest upon?"

"Another turtle," was the response.

"And what does *this* turtle rest upon?"

"Oh, no, professor, you can't wiggle out that way," exclaimed the woman, triumphantly. "It's turtles, turtles, all the way down!"

Our goal in this book is to explore the enemy system, not the solar system. To begin our journey, nonetheless, we shall follow the turtles, all the way down, all the way to our genes and our dimmest Darwinian stirrings. First, let's consider some animal stories (all true), in order to set the stage. They speak about the role of enemies in the lives of animals, with implications for our own lives as well.

A Tale of Two Marmots

Stumpy was an adult male Olympic marmot.[1] He lived in a small social group of Olympic marmots, in a glorious alpine meadow high in the unspeakably lovely mountains of Olympic National Park, in the state of Washington. The year was 1967, and I—a graduate student conducting research for my Ph.D. in zoology—had just begun observing Stumpy and his associates. I would sit, unobtrusively, about fifty yards from these animals, with notebook and camera, a scientific voyeur in their airy mountain world. This particular group consisted of Stumpy himself, two adult females, their various offspring, and another, younger adult male, that I called Yellowtail.

Stumpy was a vigorous animal, in his prime, the undisputed boss of his (admittedly limited) social world. He had lost the greater part of his tail some time before, perhaps—I liked to think—in amorous pursuit. In any event, Stumpy did a lot of pursuing. He mated with the females, patrolled the perimeter of his domain, ever-watchful for predators and other intruding marmots, and he did his best to hasten the departure of his sons when they grew old enough to challenge his authority and sexual suzerainty.

Stumpy also spent a lot of time watching Yellowtail, the other adult male, and chasing him whenever possible, especially when Yellowtail got too near the females. Because they live so high in mountains that are snow-covered most of the year, Olympic marmots hibernate from October until May. Their brief period of activity begins with the mating season in late spring and ends when their alpine meadows no longer offer nourishment and the snows are about to fall. Within a few days of awakening from hibernation, Stumpy simply couldn't abide Yellowtail. When he wasn't attending the lady marmots, or watching for other males, or (rarely) eating, Stumpy could be found looking out for his nemesis, Yellowtail. And Yellowtail, when he could be found at all, was always as far from Stumpy as he could get.

But as the breeding season passed, so did the season of marmot enmity. The springtime of their discontent was quickly followed by a summer and early autumn of indifference, even a kind of fondness. As his hormone level receded from the roaring flood stage of early spring, Stumpy apparently didn't consider Yellowtail such a bad fellow after all. And Yellowtail, similarly mollified, saw no reason to escape his former tormentor. By mid-July, their enmity forgotten, the two previous rivals foraged peacefully among the bright flowers, warmed by the dazzlingly intense, mid-summer alpine sun. They dozed side by side on the soft dirt porches outside the comfortable underground burrow that used to be Stumpy's alone, but was now shared by both. Several times, when Yellowtail ambled over to sniff noses with the adult females—once so tantalizing in their availability, so infuriating when approached by another adult male, so worth fighting over— Stumpy merely glanced at the unfolding scene, after which, like a miniature Ferdinand the bull, he went back to contemplating the flowers.

Then came the long winter's sleep. I was back the next spring, and so were Stumpy and company. No sooner did Yellowtail and Stumpy poke their heads above the lingering spring snow, they forgot all about their seasonal truce. Once again, they couldn't stand each other: more chasing, avoiding, anxious watching, snapping, and snarling. And, then, right on schedule, after their vigorous renewal of unstinting animosity, there followed yet another season of reconciliation and bland indifference, culminating once more in the usual casual friendship.

The spring after that, my third year of observing, Stumpy didn't awake from his hibernation. Yellowtail emerged in the spring of 1969 in solitary splendor, the only adult male Olympic marmot in his colony except for a two-year-old juvenile who had been born that initial summer of 1967 when Yellowtail had first earned his spurs dodging Stumpy's aggressive sorties. This "teenager" hung around the place of his birth and showed (as far as Yellowtail was concerned) an inappropriate interest in the adult females. To the upstart adolescent, however, these females had somehow become infinitely fascinating, deliciously sexy, and—it goes almost without saying—worth fighting over. And so it was that Yellowtail, former number two marmot now promoted to number one, spent his spring and early summer chasing, instead of being chased. As Yogi Berra once said, it was "déjà vu all over again."

And now, two more animal stories.

The Coyote and the Goose, and Travails of Trout

The coyote burst suddenly out of the woods at the edge of the clearing. The goose turned and started to run across the grass, flapping its wings in a desperate effort to get airborne. But the coyote was too quick; it leaped at the goose and the two did a complete somersault as they collided a few feet off the ground. A pinwheel of goose feathers and yellow-brown fur disappeared behind a bush and then, ten seconds later, the coyote emerged, carrying what looked like a limp white sack. Only a few wisps of ragged, startling white, like an early snowfall, were left behind, ruffled here and there by the wind in the bright green grass.

In a fast-flowing stream not far from where the goose breathed her last, a dozen tiny fingerling trout struggled to maintain their position against a swift springtime current. They didn't seem to worry very much about each other; almost certainly they didn't even recognize one another as individuals. In general, they got along just fine—with each other, that is. "Getting along" in the world, on the other hand, was a different matter. Food was scarce. It consisted largely of insect larvae and the occasional flies (some of them cast by fishermen) that alighted on the surface of the stream. When a morsel appeared, it was quickly snatched up by whichever young trout happened to be closest. Because of the shortage of food, these trout grew slowly, although they were not sick or stunted. Had there been more food, on the other hand, they would have grown more rapidly. As it was, three of them soon became large enough to breed, and they did so, a full year earlier than the others.

These true-life stories, one of them unfolding over a period of three years in an alpine meadow, the other two playing themselves out in my neighbor's field, inspire us to wonder about the ultimate meaning of enemies. Was Yellowtail Stumpy's enemy? Insofar as only one of them could inseminate the colony's resident females, he was. Was the coyote an enemy of the goose? That depends. In general—seen from a detached, scientific distance as well—predators are not really the enemies of their prey. Ironically, they are actually less inimical to each other than two male marmots, even though the latter are members of the same species. Mountain lions and wolves, for example, tend to kill deer and elk that are old and sick, thereby culling the natural populations and keeping the numbers down to healthy levels. Without natural predators, prey populations often overbreed and destroy their habitat, to their own eventual disadvantage. On the other hand, if you were to interview the unfortunate goose-victim, or a doe breathing out her life in the jaws of a cougar, you would probably get a somewhat less enthusiastic testimony to the marvelous "balance of nature."

    For its part, the coyote almost certainly didn't consider the goose to be an enemy, although the goose would likely disagree. To the coyote, the goose was dinner, neither more nor less, although most coyotes would probably volunteer that geese tend to be a bit more cagey, quick, or vigorous in their own defense than the coyotes would prefer. As mathematicians might say, enemies are not commutative: X may be the enemy of Y, but this does not necessarily mean that Y is the enemy of X.

And what about the trout? Are they enemies? They lived in close proximity, and may have established a very loose social relationship, in which the smaller deferred to the larger. But in general, they went about their lives independently, neither close friends nor sworn opponents. They were not entirely independent, however, since these trout went through most of their lives hungry, a condition that could only be ameliorated, to some extent, by depriving their fellows. Every caddisfly larva eaten by trout X meant that one less bit of food was available for trout Y.

What about other kinds of enemies? Certainly, snowstorms and heavy rains can be the enemies of wildlife no less than of people, and yet without winter snows and spring rains there may not be enough water in the streams to float a trout, slake a goose's thirst, or nourish the forage on which depend small rodents and deer and in turn, coyotes and cougars. Goose and marmot, by contrast, would almost certainly agree that—on certain occasions, at least—their enemies include other geese and other marmots. The key here is competition, and it is to competition that we must turn in our pursuit of the biological origins of enmity.

Competition: The Key to Enmity

Competiton has a noble history in modern biology. It is one of the foundations of natural selection, worked out by Charles Darwin as follows: All living things are capable of producing enormous numbers of offspring, if they did so without restraint. Take even the very slow-breeding elephants, for example. If a single pair reproduced successfully and then each of their offspring did likewise, in a few hundred years every square foot of land would be occupied by elephants.

Clearly, this doesn't happen, neither for elephants nor even for more prolific creatures, such as human beings or bacteria. Despite the undeniable capacity (at least in theory) of living things to reproduce in vast numbers, the actual count of most plants and animals have remained more or less constant through time. This suggests that certain other factors are operating. Long before our hypothetical elephants begin crowding themselves to oblivion they bump up against other constraints. They die of disease, or (rarely) from lions, or (more recently) poachers, or they don't get enough food or water, or they have trouble finding a mate, or they experience difficulty breeding or caring adequately for their offspring, and so forth.

Darwin went on to develop the principles of natural selection from this deceptively simple but hugely important contrast between the capacity of life to overproduce and the reality that in most cases, the numbers of living things remain relative stable. In a sense, he reasoned that there must be severe competiton between all those elephant "wannabes" and the relatively few that actually get to exist. This is because there is only a limited amount of "elephant space," "coyote space," "goose space," or "trout space," with "space" referring not just to physical dimensions but to all aspects of the available ecological elbowroom that every creature requires in order to live and prosper.

Every living thing that reproduces sexually relies on other members (or at least, one other member) of its species to reproduce. But ironically, most living things also compete with special intensity against others of their own kind. And it is out of this competition, at the fundamental biological level, that enmity arises. (An important biological principle, known as Gause's Law, states that competition is greatest between species whose needs are most similar. Gause's Law can be extended logically, and correctly, to its limit such that competition is greater among members of the same species than between different species.)

Competition takes several forms. The simplest and least direct occurs without the competitors necessarily even meeting each other. Rather, they compete indirectly, by trying to gather up as much of a particular resource as they can. In a finite world, more for individual 1 means less for individual 2, and so they are competing, even though they may not know it, and may not even act as though their interests are in conflict. Hungry trout, competing for a limited supply of caddis fly larvae, would be a good example, participants in what ecologists call "scramble competition."

Scramble competition is like an Easter egg hunt: There are limited amounts of a coveted resource to be gathered, and the contestants (whether animals or people) try to collect as much as they can. They don't spend much time trying to interfere with each other; rather, each works on its own, scurrying to accumulate as many Easter eggs as possible. The "contest" is decided later, when everyone compares baskets to see who gathered the most eggs: in evolutionary terms, who produced the most surviving offspring and other descendants. So, rabbits living on opposite sides of a river, for instance, compete with each other to eat grass, avoid hawks, and make more rabbits, even though the bunnies in question may never meet and may not even feel like enemies.

Of course, an especially competitive Easter egg hunter might attempt to steal another person's eggs for him or herself. But even though most people play by the rules, they are nonetheless competing. If there was an infinite supply of eggs, or if people's desire for Easter eggs was readily satisfied, then the event would be more relaxed. And even though most children on Easter egg hunts do so with a cheerful and friendly attitude, it is sobering to note that this pastime has many of the characteristics of Darwinian competition, although on an impersonal scale.

Instead of competing to collect Easter eggs, trout compete to "collect" insect larvae, deer compete to "collect" forage (especially in winter, when the supply is limited), and even trees compete to "collect" photons, struggling to shade each other into oblivion. In the process, they become enemies of a sort. But they act only indirectly and impersonally upon their enmity.

Another, more obvious form of competition takes place when two male bighorn sheep, for example, butt heads to determine who gets breeding rights to the herd of waiting ewes, or when—as we have seen—two adult male marmots struggle over control of a colony. Here, the pay-off is achieved by besting the opponent, directly, head-to-head: not by scrambling independently to accumulate Easter eggs or some other biological currency, but by being crowned #1 (or even #2, in some cases). As in the case of the marmots I named Stumpy and Yellowtail, two males may compete for females. In these and other examples (elk, gorillas), males don't simply scramble, in solitary splendor, to gather together a bevy of mates; rather, they engage in a variety of aggressive contests with each other, and then the pay-off—in this case, the females—is parcelled out as a result of who won and who lost.

The point is that whether scrambles or contests are taking place, the competitors are, in a sense, enemies. But only in contest competition do these enemies "act like enemies." Unlike the gleeful "scrambles" of children at an Easter egg hunt or of fingerling trout grimly seeking, each on its own, to get as much as possible of whatever is in short supply, these involve direct head-to-head contests between two or more individuals. Sometimes the contests are subtle and understated. Sometimes they are filled with bluff and bluster. Sometimes they are lethal. But they are always real, and those who engage in them can accurately be described as enemies.

This form of highly personalized competition is most pronounced, and best understood, in the context of sexual reproduction and the biology of maleness and femaleness.

Gonads and Gametes, Males and Females

It is no accident that in our tale of two marmots the two animals who spent so much time chasing and threatening each other were both males. Or that the bighorn sheep with the biggest horns are always males. Or that among our own species, it is overwhelmingly the men who threaten, fight, and kill each other. The pattern of enmity is heavily supported by a pattern of male-female differences, and a bit of biology will help show why. It will also show why the "battle of the sexes" is largely a battle *within* the sexes, especially the male.

It doesn't take a professional biologist to distinguish a man from a woman, or even a boy from a girl, or for that matter a male giraffe from a female. But what about a male versus a female robin? Or hummingbirds? (Note that among most birds, neither males nor females possess external genitalia.) Or for that matter, what about oysters, in which there are no consistent differences in color pattern or outside anatomy between the sexes?

The defining difference between male and female is not the possession of penis versus vagina, or who has the breasts, or anything else so trivial and superficial, but, rather, the deeper issue of eggs versus sperm. Most living things that reproduce sexually are specialists, experts in producing either a very large number of reproductive sex cells (or "gametes"), or a very small number. If the former, then each gamete is likely to be exceptionally tiny, and—perhaps to compensate for their size—they are generally churned out in very large numbers. These abundant, miniature gametes are called "sperm," and the creatures that produce them are defined as "male."

Similarly, individuals that specialize in producing relatively large gametes are limited in how many they can make. And so, they produce fewer of them, but are able to invest more heavily in each gamete. We define these richly endowed gametes as "eggs," and their creators as "female." In the case of mammals, whose eggs are inconspicuously small, females provide much additional investment in their offspring, by virtue of pregnancy and then, lactation.

As a result of all this, a single male can fertilize many females. The limiting factor for the evolutionary success of most males is therefore set by their success in inseminating females. For females, the situation is different: Only rarely does it profit a female to mate with numerous males, since males are specialized to produce enough sperm to fertilize the limited number of eggs that most females produce in any case. Rather, females are best served by choosing carefully among potential mates, and then investing heavily in their own offspring. The stage is therefore set for an asymmetric competition: Males compete with other males to employ their cheap, abundant sperm to fertilize the valuable, relatively rare eggs produced by females.

In a now-classic bit of research, biologist A. J. Bateman set up many different worlds, each consisting of four male and four female *Drosophila* (fruit flies).[2] Each individual carried a distinct genetic marker so that his or her offspring could be identified later, and each one attributed to its particular parent. Two of Bateman's findings are especially relevant for our purposes: First, he discovered that the reproductive success of the males was much more variable than that of the females. Whereas the females didn't differ very much in terms of their number of offspring (pretty much every female got all of her eggs fertilized), there were substantial differences among the males. Some males fathered most of the children, whereas others were notably less successful.

Second, Bateman found that when a male copulated with an additional female, this tended to increase his chance of fathering offspring—until such time as all the eggs of all the females had been fertilized, of course. By contrast, so long as a female had already copulated at least once, additional matings did not contribute substantially to the chance that she would be a mother.

Here is another way of looking at it: The success of a male

depended on his access to females, and it occurred at the expense
of the success of other males. (This is because once a female's eggs
have been fertilized by one male, they cannot be fertilized by another.)
Bateman's simple bit of research helps to illuminate a fundamental
characteristic of the biological world, namely, the implications of being
male or female.

To make a long evolutionary tale into a very short story, among
most species of animals, the males tend to be relatively large, tough,
and aggressive, and/or bright, loud, and show-offy, in the former
case to defeat other males directly and in the latter to do so indirectly,
by winning the hearts of females. Either way, males are especially
likely to see other males as their enemies, and to behave accordingly;
hence, Stumpy's seasonal aggressiveness toward Yellowtail and, in
turn, Yellowtail's comparable intolerance of the juvenile male (who,
incidentally, was almost certainly Stumpy's offspring).

For another example, consider elephant seals, behemoth pinnipeds
that annually drag themselves onto islands off the California coast
in order to breed. The males are enormous—elephantine, in fact—
while the females are almost dainty in comparison. Males compete
violently with other males to control a harem that may consist of
fifty females. A successful harem-master obviously experiences great
evolutionary success, whereas since there are roughly equal numbers
of adult males and females, there must be forty-nine unsuccessful,
bachelor bulls for every such victor in the evolutionary competition.
Not surprisingly, bulls fight hard to be successful, and only those
who win get to project their genes—including, not coincidentally,
those genes which led to such success—into the future.

By contrast, nearly every sexually mature elephant seal cow is
reproductively successful. Each one produces a young pup every year.
Whereas it makes a great difference to each male whether he becomes
a harem-master, it makes much less difference to the females. Whoever
the victorious male may be, the biological success of every female

is pretty much assured. They congregate closely together, each associated with her pup, while the unsuccessful bachelor males hang out some distance away, squabbling with each other, resentfully eyeing the harem-master, each waiting for a chance to replace him. For a male elephant seal, every other male is a reproductive competitor, and thus, in a very real sense, an enemy. Female elephant seals, not surprisingly, are much less competitive, and less violent among themselves.

Consider another example: a little-known parasitic worm that lives in the intestines of rodents and pigs.[3] These creatures come in two kinds, males and females, just like other, more "respectable" animals. Their courtship is rudimentary: When male encounters female, sperm is simply transferred from his genital opening to hers. Then comes a secretion from his "cement gland," which keeps the sperm from leaking out (while also keeping another male's sperm from getting in). Of particular interest is what happens when male meets male. In this case, the one initiating the contact becomes the aggressor, using his cement gland to plug up the genital aperture of his victim. We know that this pattern of "homosexual rape" is specifically directed toward other males, and not just a case of mistaken identity, because in the case of male-male encounters, only the cement substance is transferred, and no sperm.

Stick with this example for another moment. Consider that when female meets female, no cement substance is transferred. Indeed, nothing much happens at all. This, once again, is consistent with the general biology of femaleness as opposed to maleness: The evolutionary success of a female parasitic worm is not likely to be diminished (at least, not very much), by the success of another female. Indeed, the cost of trying to interfere with another female's breeding would probably be greater than any benefit that might result. And so, females of this species do not treat other females as enemies. Not so for males: Every male whose sperm duct is cemented shut means one less competitor and thus an increased chance that the remaining intact males will get to breed successfully with the females.

Males are on something of a reproductive seesaw (or a zero-sum game) since the success of one typically diminishes the likely success of another; by contrast, females are generally less threatened by each other's reproduction, since their own prospects are not necessarily diminished just because another female's eggs have been fertilized. Even without the unique nastiness of cement glands, one very successful male—in virtually any species—can fertilize a large number of females, thereby effectively castrating his competitors. On the other hand, the success of one female generally does not greatly diminish the success of another, since there are usually lots of sperm to go around. So, sisterhoods are somewhat more cooperative than brotherhoods.

For females of most species, the definition of "enemy" is more subtle than that of males. However, it seems to be no less real. Take lions, for example, in which cubs often die of starvation. In such cases, the success of a female's cubs is enhanced if she is the only one in the pride bearing a litter; lionesses, in turn, are notorious for their almost insatiable sexual appetites, combined with the fact that they do not give the males any clear sign of exactly when they are fertile. During her prolonged heat, a lioness may copulate a hundred times or more per day. As a result, a breeding female monopolizes the sexual attention of her mate, effectively preventing other females from being inseminated by him at the same time. Therefore, under conditions of potential food scarcity, it is unlikely that more than one lioness will be giving birth at the same time, so the mother's brood will have less competition than would be the case if the lioness did not treat others as her enemies through sexual rivalry.

Other aspects of female-female competition have been observed among animals. It has long been known, for example, that female monkeys of many different species are particularly attracted to newborn babies, jostling one another to handle the youngsters. Traditionally, this behavior was described as "aunting," and interpreted as child-care practice for the adults as well as a kind of baby-sitting service for the new mother. More recently, such activities have been reinterpreted as considerably more aggressive, following upon the recognition that the "baby-sat" infants are often injured in the process.

Among many birds, males jostle with each other to acquire territories, which in turn are attractive to females because of the resources (food, nest sites, etc.) that they offer. But the females are not simply passive bystanders and comparison shoppers. It is often disadvantageous for a female to share "her" male with other females, since this means that she must share the resources that come with the territory, as well as possibly having to share whatever paternal assistance the male might offer. And so, biologists are increasingly discovering that many females try to keep other females from joining their reproductive network.

As a general rule in the animal world, however, female-female competition is less violent and more subtle than its male-male counterpart. Indeed, for years, biologists hardly even noticed that females competed at all. And even now, with our eyes opened for the possibility of female-female competition, there seems little question that females are less likely than males to consider other same-sex individuals to be their enemies. Add to all this the fact that among many species, males have a special role in defending the family group against predators (as well as against other, marauding males), and the stage is set for males to have a special awareness of, and intolerance toward, enemies. It is not just that they are more attuned to enemies; they actually have more of them.

Aggressive Neglect

Murphy's Law states that if anything can go wrong, it will. Murphy may have been an evolutionary biologist. Thus, natural systems are just too complex to operate smoothly. Things get out of whack. Among elk, for example, a few bucks get so caught up in aggressive challenges and actual fights with competing bucks that yet others—sometimes even males that are rather small and unimpressive in their own right—get to the females while the "lord of the harem" is off defending his conjugal rights. And certain birds (again, males) have been found guilty of "aggressive neglect" in which they spend so much time patrolling their territorial boundaries and displaying their prowess to their equally combative neighbors that their own offspring die of hunger or exposure.

Human beings are also subject to a kind of aggressive neglect. When it happens on a grand scale, we might call it the "Caspar Weinberger Disease," for Ronald Reagan's secretary of defense who presided over the hyperexpansion of the U.S. military budget during the 1980s while domestic services were allowed to wither. It may well be a syndrome to which men—perfectly biological males that they are—are especially prone. President Dwight Eisenhower was actually talking about the Caspar Weinberger Disease several decades ago, when he warned that

> Every gun that is made, every warship launched, every rocket fired signifies, in the final sense, a theft from those who hunger and are not fed, those who are cold and are not clothed. The world in arms is not spending money alone. It is spending the sweat of its laborers, the genius of its scientists, the hopes of its children.[4]

Two hundred miles east of Seattle, residents around Hanford, Washington, have recently learned that for many years they were exposed to massive releases of nuclear radiation in the name of "national security." Uranium miners were similarly subjected to the ravages of aggressive neglect, as were "downwinders" in Utah and Nevada. The *Seattle Post-Intelligencer* ran a series about the likely impact of a nuclear weapons accident on the state of Washington. With unintended irony, one of the articles was headlined "Public Safety Takes a Back Seat to Security."[5]

It is a personal decision no less than a national one, this obsession with "security" at the expense of individual safety. And it is not limited to *Homo sapiens*. Thus, we can readily imagine a talkative elephant seal or parasitic worm explaining why maintaining their sexual security warrants running risks with personal safety (if they are males, that is). Insofar as it reflects a kind of hyperawareness of potential enemies, of competitors posing uniquely unacceptable threats to one's personal success, threats to "security" may well resonate especially within the male psyche because of those aspects of the biology of maleness that we have just reviewed.

By the same token, it is likely no accident that soldiering is almost inevitably a male occupation, throughout history, and around the globe. Cultural tradition alone would scarcely explain the virtually unanimous, apparently independent insistence on male soldiering, encompassing people as diverse as humanity itself, from New Guinea to the African Bush to the Amazon Basin, the North American Plains, Europe, and Asia. Indeed, in every known society—now and at any time in the past—it has been men and not women who were primarily expected to deal with enemies. To some extent, male militarism, and the aggressive neglect that often accompanies it, may be a simple result of the fact that men are somewhat larger, more muscular, and more prone to violence. But then, if we ask why this is so—*why* men are consistently larger, more muscular, and more prone to violence—we are once again confronted with the effects of biology, and of the sexually asymmetric consequences of our enemy system.

The "Men's Movement"

I am not suggesting that the male fondness for militarism—with all its troublesome consequences for modern life—derives simply and directly from biological factors connected to competition and the meaning of enemies. Cultural traditions and social expectations also loom large. But there seems little doubt that maleness is intimately connected to our enemy system, and little doubt, also, that the complex combination of maleness, our enemy system, and recent developments in society and technology has yielded a dangerous and difficult brew. In a modern technological world in which our enemies no longer lurk just beyond the illuminated circle of the nearest campfire, the peculiar male focus on personalized enemies can also be a distinct liability. But ironically, even as too much enemy awareness is a problem, so, perhaps, is too little, not just because some enemies continue to exist, but also because men might well possess a psychological need to discharge enemy-oriented energy. Deprived of their enemies, they may be deprived of part of their maleness, even, perhaps, part of their humanity.

In addition to the relatively solitary, me-versus-them competitiveness promoted by male biology, there is also an affiliative component. Male baboons, for example, who compete aggressively with each other over sexual access to the females within their group also collaborate with other males in defense against leopards and against other groups of baboons. They clearly have an *ability* to buddy up with their erstwhile internal enemies against other, external enemies; along with this ability, they may also have a need. Our own species apparently spent a large proportion of its early evolutionary history living in small bands, much like baboons, on Pleistocene savannahs, not unlike those occupied by baboons today. It seems likely, therefore, that a penchant for male bonding—in human beings as well—has also been generated by our ancient enemy system, through the advantages of participating in socially oriented defense of the group. We clearly have an ability to engage in "male bonding." Do we also have a need?

There appears to be a painful void in the lives of many American men, a kind of psychological vacuum that comes not so much from the lack of an immediate, identifiable enemy as from the lack of an ally, specifically the steadying, mentoring alliance with an older man, ideally each young man's father. Poet Robert Bly has been especially eloquent and effective in describing and decrying this problem, and—by calling attention to it—helping men overcome the deficit.[6]

True, men have a propensity—likely rooted at least partly in their biology, as we have seen—for bluff, bluster, and aggression, and for avoiding intimacy and denying their vulnerability. But there is a flip side to this macho inclination: a need for connectedness that is often revealed by a fondness for male-male bonding in the form of fraternal clubs, bowling leagues, and regular Thursday night poker games. Unfortunately, such activities often fall short. Rather than satisfy the deep male longing for connection (especially with the father, who is often either emotionally or physically inaccessible), they may, ironically, only reinforce the hardened isolation of men from other men, and from their own deeper needs.

Into this impasse comes the allure of military life, and especially war itself, with its offer of intense, meaningful bonding between men. The military gives these modern-day savannah baboons the opportunity to share their union no less than their enmity. Listen to this account, for example, from World War II combat veteran J. Glen Gray:

> We are liberated from our individual impotence and are drunk with the power that union with our fellows brings. In moments like these many have a vague awareness of how isolated and separate their lives have hitherto been. . . . [W]ith the boundaries of the self

expanded, they sense a kinship never known before. Their "I" passes insensibly into a "we." . . . At its height, this sense of comradeship is an ecstasy.[7]

Or to Shakespeare's *Henry V*, rhapsodizing about the pleasures of sharing glory and danger with his men:

> we few; we happy few, we band of brothers;
> For he to-day that sheds his blood with me
> shall be my brother. (Act 4, Scene 3)

It is no surprise that these sentiments span many centuries.[8] For countless generations (and probably longer than recorded history), war has provided the pinnacle of what anthropologists call "rites of passage," through which men prove themselves, showing their worthiness to serve under senior father-figure commanders, who, in one language or another, have always been called the "old man." At the same time the younger men forge those longed-for connections with others, men of their own age upon whom to rely and with whom to belong.

This longing for acceptance and connectedness also helps make sense out of an otherwise surprising discovery by famed military historian and U.S. Army General S. L. A. Marshall. After exhaustively interviewing many combat veterans of World War II, Marshall concluded that the primary motivation for individual U.S. servicemen to fire their guns during battle was not fear for their own lives, or patriotism, or desire to help end the war, or hatred of the enemy, but rather the potent feeling of solidarity with a small group of buddies.[9]

In a nation at peace, being part of a team, any team, can provide much of the buddy-ship. And this remains true even if "membership" in the team is expanded to include merely being a fan. But, for example, as useful and important as the Chicago Bears football team is to fans of its archrival Green Bay Packers (and vice versa), deep inside everyone knows that these allegiances are in a sense trivial compared to the profoundly satisfying bonds evoked by a shared national enemy.

This is one reason why communism in general and the Soviet Union in particular have been so valuable. For decades, they provided American men—so many of them suffering from a deficit of male-male bonding and a virtual absence of meaningful initiation rituals—with a validation of their manhood and an excuse for joining together with other like-minded men in just the way that men have joined together since the Trojan War, and undoubtedly long before.

It is not a new problem, this need for men to learn from each other, to lean on each other, and validate themselves in the process. And it is unlikely that previous generations of young men found the process much easier or less strewn with socially imposed impediments than they do today. But nonetheless, it is just possible that if our father-son and other male-male patterns were more integrated and healthy, we would feel the recent loss of our enemies less acutely.

The Flush Toilet Model

The previous section glided too quickly over an important assumption: that men in particular and human beings in general may carry around an actual *need* to have enemies and to respond—often aggressively—to them. This assumption may or may not be valid. Certainly, it is consistent with common sense. It also fits an unprepossessing but nonetheless influential scientific concept, which might be dubbed the "flush-toilet model of behavior." According to this model, energy for a particular kind of act (e.g., eating, sleeping, sex, aggression, etc.) builds up within an individual, like water spilling into a holding tank. When the opportunity presents itself, the tank flushes, the water flows, and the behavior happens. Then, the tank starts filling all over again and the process is ready to repeat itself.

This basic model, simplistic as it may seem, was first proposed several decades ago by a Nobel Prize winner, ethologist Konrad Z. Lorenz. Although it is not taken literally by biologists today, it still has widespread appeal. It coincides with common-sense notions about "getting the anger out," even fitting some curious observations ethologists have made over the years.

For example, careful observers of animals have long known that when living things are in a difficult conflict situation, they often do something totally unexpected and seemingly irrelevant. A herring gull, arguing with her neighbor about the territorial boundary that divides the two animals, may suddenly begin pulling up grass with her bill. An avocet (a graceful shorebird with long legs and upturned beak) will interrupt a squabble by tucking head into wing and appearing to go to sleep. A human being, sitting nervously in a dentist's office, anxious about what is about to transpire, taps her foot. Or a student, trying unsuccessfully to conjure up the answer to an exam question, scratches his head, or twists a shirt button.

These "displacement activities" fit the homey (if inelegantly named) flush-toilet model. Energy has built up, the animal or person is itching to act, to do something to discharge that energy, but is inhibited from doing so. The gull is ambivalent: It wants to attack its rival but it also wants to run away. Reluctant to do either, it pulls on some grass, at least doing something and therefore (we presume) feeling better. Deep in her heart, the dental patient might like to punch the smiling receptionist in the nose, and/or burst out of the waiting room and run for dear life. But she, too, is reluctant, so she nervously wiggles her foot. In all these cases, the energy—whatever it may be—is released, which somehow eases the tension.

There are even "vacuum activities," when an individual who has been deprived of the opportunity to do something proceeds to do it even without the usual stimulus. Lorenz tells the following story about one of his pet birds. It seems that this animal was regularly given food in its tray instead of being let free to catch dinner on the wing. One day, Lorenz saw the bird in the middle of his living room, hovering in the air and snapping vigorously. The great specialist in animal behavior climbed onto a sofa and looked carefully: lots of beak-snapping, but positively no insects. Deprived of the satisfaction of snapping at its natural prey, yet awash with energy for doing so, Lorenz's bird had apparently proceeded to snap at the air, in a sense flushing the behavior out of its system.

Once, at the zoo in Seattle, an ocelot was stubbornly tearing the hair from its body. Now it happens that free-living ocelots dine especially on birds, which they pluck before eating. But this zoo-dweller was regularly given horsemeat instead: nutritious, but unsatisfying. Eventually, the zookeepers were prevailed upon to substitute an occasional dead chicken—feathers and all—whereupon the happy cat proceeded to meet its needs by plucking its food instead of itself.

Do we have a need for enemies, like the ocelot's need to pluck? Do we build up emotional tension—what Lorenz would call "action specific energy"—and does this energy demand release in one form or another, like an insect-eating bird who may be reduced to snapping at thin air? Most social scientists would say no. But most ordinary people would say yes. They send their children outside to "let off steam." They may slam the door when they are angry, or kick the cat, or talk with a therapist about acceptable ways to "get the anger out." Deprived of an outlet, their accumulated frustration may lead to high blood pressure, ulcers, rashes, or a host of other psychosomatic ailments which are no less real for having been generated internally instead of by "germs." One psychologist interviewed in the course of writing this book was so vehement about the fact that people had no special need to express their anger or to confront enemies that he pounded his fist on his desk while making this point!

Let us take the biological claim that we might have a need to discharge energy against enemies and recast it in modern terms, relegating "action specific energy" to where it probably belongs, with such other unlamented, unverifiable concepts as "caloric" or "phlogiston." Instead, consider that throughout human evolutionary history, we have had to overcome enemies of all sorts: animals, forces of nature, other human beings. Having evolved in a context of enemies, it would not be surprising if something in our emotional and intellectual makeup depends on them for normal functioning and development, just as our eyes, for example, require the stimulation of light in order to develop a normal retina. Perhaps our psyches require the stimulation of enemies in order to develop a normal personality. If so, it would not be surprising if we "need" enemies, to the point of actually seeking them out when they are lacking.

This line of thinking leads to yet another, troublesome possibility. Our deepest, innermost biological selves, our most private and fundamental human nature, may well have been formed in recognition of and response to those old friends, our enemies. Or, to rewrite Pogo's dictum, "We met the enemy, and that's how we became us."

Enemies, Evolution, and Human Nature

As strictly biological creatures, *Homo sapiens* are not especially noteworthy. It is true that we are outfitted with a uniquely opposable thumb, but the aye-aye of Madagascar (another primate) also has an extraordinary modified finger, this one for extricating grubs from holes in trees. We are unusual in being relatively hairless, but then there is the naked mole rat of Ethiopia. On balance, in fact, we are perfectly ordinary mammals except for one remarkable feature: our immense brains. The rapid evolution of large brain size among our Pleistocene ancestors is what made us uniquely human, and the forces that propelled this rapid evolutionary change remain among the most intriguing mysteries of human evolution.

For evolution to have increased the size of our ancestors' brains, natural selection would have had to favor big-brained individuals, who in turn must have had more offspring. This process, over time, would have produced a population of larger-brained specimens. In short, individuals who had larger brains—and who we therefore presume to have been somewhat smarter than their smaller-brained colleagues—must have been more successful than the various smaller-brained individuals with whom they competed or cohabitated. There are many ways this could have taken place, but one of the most plausible scenarios begins with primitive proto-humans eeking out their survival on the Pleistocene savannahs of Africa. There, they competed with other proto-humans. It is certainly possible that this competition went beyond eating the same foods and trying to monopolize the same cozy sleeping caves. It may well have become direct, personal, and even downright nasty. Something equivalent to primitive war (complete, perhaps, with head-hunting and cannibalism) would have made it especially valuable for early human beings to be smart.

This is because within any given band or group, the less intelligent (not surprisingly) were probably more likely to do something stupid or to refrain from doing something smart; hence, they almost certainly were "selected against." In the inexorable logic of natural selection, the likelihood is that being killed by your enemy diminishes the chances that your genes will be passed along to succeeding generations. In addition, intelligence would have conveyed a substantial pay-off in competition between groups: planning strategies, recognizing opportunities, employing weapons and tactics, or simply just being able to communicate adequately with other like-minded individuals.

So, our early involvement with enemies may have made us what we are today. (This is equally true, by the way, whether the primary agent of selection for intelligence and brain size was warlike competition with other primitive humans, or somewhat more peaceful competition with nonhuman predators, or even competition with nature itself over sheer survival.) A pessimistic notion? Perhaps. Put another way, however, it is not quite so dismal. Unlike a highly specialized type of claw, tooth, or antler, which might have operated like a key that opens only one type of lock, large brains and resulting intelligence are flexible and adaptable. After all, this is part of the definition of intelligence. Moreover, our uniquely human adaptation was not a penchant for automatic, mindless aggressiveness, but an ability to adjust to circumstances. There is, therefore, no reason why our marvelous human intelligence could not be directed toward new enemies, such as pollution, greenhouse warming, hunger, AIDS, over-population, poverty, illiteracy, and so forth—perhaps even against war itself. Finally, even success in fighting and warmaking required a sophisticated ability to coordinate a response, to cooperate with our fellows, to identify allies no less than enemies. So, maybe this aspect of our biology isn't such bad news after all.

In any event, we are a very social species, and have been so for a very long time, probably millions of years. Our ancestors were doubtless highly social, as were their ancestors before them, leaving an indelible (if sometimes illegible) record on our brains and behavior. To understand ourselves, as well as many other creatures alive today, we must look, therefore, to sociality. And when we do, we find additional signs of the role of enemies.

The Selfish Herd

To the surprise of the anthropocentric, many animals experience a rich and varied social life. Accordingly, their experiences of "friend" and "enemy" are equally diverse. To witness one of the simplest forms of animal sociality, barely deserving of the term, turn on an outdoor light bulb on a warm spring night and settle back to watch. The moths and other insects gathering and fluttering round aren't really responding to each other; rather, each is reacting separately to the stimulus provided by the light. Considered as separate individuals, each moth would be there even if the others weren't. But nonetheless, their shared attraction results in a kind of collectivity, an amalgamation of individuals that exists because each is responding *to* the same thing.

Now, consider a school of fish. Oddly, we still don't understand exactly why so many different species of fish form themselves into schools. But it seems clear that this, too, is a simple level of sociality, although one that operates on a somewhat higher level than the case of moths around a light bulb. Mackerels or minnows, bluefish or bonitos, all are positively orienting themselves with regard to the rest of the school. Instead of a light bulb providing the stimulus, others of their kind are doing so. Remove all moths in the world but one, and that one will blissfully flutter against a brightly illuminated surface; remove all fishes but two and the pair would likely swim together.

Clearly, fishes orient to each other. But why? Is it mutual appreciation, loneliness, love? Many possibilities have been suggested, and of these, one of the most intriguing was first proposed in a technical article with the odd title "Geometry for the Selfish Herd."[10] It conveys the following idea: Imagine that you are a relatively helpless herring, swimming in the cold seas of the North Atlantic. Any moment, you might be swallowed by a hungry tuna. There isn't much you can do about it, except hope for the best. Or is there? What if you swim alongside another herring? If that hungry tuna sidles up, maybe it will snatch your neighbor rather than yourself, and furthermore, maybe after eating your neighbor the predator won't be so hungry anymore. Of course, herring number two "reasons" similarly, and sees no harm in the arrangement, since maybe you will constitute the tuna's dinner instead; proximity therefore benefits both of you.[11] The same applies to herring numbers 3, 4, and so forth Indeed, as the numbers swell, the cost to each declines while the benefit increases (since it becomes more likely that someone else will get eaten). And so, with a great show of love for their fellow herring, these fish cheerfully swim alongside each other, forming a primitive social group.

The basic geometry of spatial proximity, combined with the simple fact of having a shared enemy, may thus have contributed to some animals, at least, joining together instead of living on their own: "If one of us is going to be eaten, it might as well be you." When everyone calculates in such a selfish way, the result, ironically, is a fundamental kind of social harmony and apparently altruistic benevolence.

The next step, perhaps, in the evolution of sociality would have been for individuals to derive some direct and ongoing benefit from interacting positively with others in their group. There are many ways this could have happened. For example, animals that were prey as individuals might have discovered the proverbial strength to be found in numbers. A single baboon, for example, cannot do much when set upon by a leopard, but a troop of baboons can make the cat run for its life. Groups may also provide more eyes and ears, more potential sentinels to warn of approaching danger. Ostriches, for example, don't really stick their heads in the sand; however, they do put their heads down to eat savannah grasses, at which time they are vulnerable to being surprised by a stalking lion. This appears to be the reason why ostriches tend to travel in groups; the larger the group, the more time each animal gets to spend eating, while still being protected by the simple fact that in a big group there is always someone likely to be on guard for danger.

The benefits of togetherness are not limited to vulnerable would-be prey. Even some predators have found that they do better when they hunt in packs. An individual wolf, for example, is no match for an adult moose. When wolves get sociable, on the other hand—as many, but not all wolves are—the situation is reversed. If the prey is sufficiently large, such as a moose, the disadvantage of having to share is outweighed by the advantages of having something to share. (Wolves aren't especially sociable, by contrast, when hunting meadow mice.)

As social living evolved further, other benefits became apparent: communication and coordination among group members, specialization and division of labor, and then, as organized groups became threats to each other (perhaps at the dawn of human evolution), the benefits of group living may, ironically, have become recursive, coming to center on an ability to survive the dangers posed by groups themselves or rather, by other groups. The benefits of sociality may thus have led, in turn, to some of the most cherished aspects of our own humanness, as we became enemies to ourselves; as the English political philosopher Thomas Hobbes suggested more than three hundred years ago, *Homo homini lupus*: "man became a wolf to men."

Enemy Genes?

Are there other possibilities, other ways in which the fundamental reality of social life—the fact of group living itself—may have been stimulated by enemies? Here's another one: Maybe we live in groups so as to help our relatives and hurt those with whom we do not share an evolutionary interest. Sociobiologists have discovered that living things achieve evolutionary success not only by surviving and reproducing, but also by contributing to the ultimate success of other relatives in addition to their own children.[12] After all, in evolutionary terms, an offspring is important to its parent because every gene that it carries has a 50 percent chance of being identical with genes from each parent. Adults therefore enhance their evolutionary success—their "fitness"—by reproducing and then caring for progeny. But any individual, whether or not a parent, may also have other relatives such as cousins, nieces, and nephews, and so forth, who also carry genes shared with that individual. It is just that the more distant the relative, the lower the probability that genes will be shared. In fact, this is what is meant by a genetic relative: a "close" one is somebody with whom we have a high probability of sharing genes, and a "distant" one is somebody with whom the probability of sharing genes is comparatively low.

Genes occupy preorganized places on chromosomes, as though each occupies a spot at a formal dinner awaiting a particular guest. At the level of an individual gene, there are two kinds of "enemies": genes that don't do their job or perhaps even injure the body in which they reside, and others that would, if given the chance, occupy the place-setting on a chromosome where copies of the ancestral gene in question might otherwise happily seat themselves. Seen from the perspective of the individual, a gene's-eye view of evolution suggests that an enemy is someone who either threatens to compete with or injure one's self (or a relative), or who carries a large proportion of different, unrelated genes. Among most animal species, such strangers are treated badly, often brutally. Among our own species, some of our less pleasant traits, such as racism and other manifestations of intolerance toward individuals who are different from ourselves, may also derive, fundamentally, from a tendency to treat relatives as "friends" and unrelated strangers as "enemies."[13] It may be significant that the word "hostile" derives from the Latin *hostis*, which originally referred to "stranger." Only by a social transformation does that "stranger" become an "enemy," but that "hostility" arises almost automatically, and it is also consistent with biology.

When it comes to some of the inclinations of our own genes, therefore, we have reason to be less than proud. Indeed, there is cause to think that especially in the modern world, many of these inclinations are out of touch with cultural evolution, and indeed, dangerously out of phase with morality as well as our own enlightened self-interest.[14] Nonetheless, the behavioral leanings of many living things—ourselves almost certainly included—seem to have been honed by evolution to favor our relatives, at least on balance.

Anthropologists have long searched for "cross-cultural human universals," things that all people, regardless of their local customs and social traditions, are likely to do. Nepotism (the favoring of relatives) comes as close as anything to filling the bill; it is found to some degree in all human societies, and in a remarkable array of animal cases as well. Through nepotism, we and many other living things can dispense benefits to our relatives, thereby, in a sense, aiding ourselves, or rather, our own genes within the bodies of others. Without social groups, nepotism would be virtually impossible, since it would be difficult for a solitary hermit-like creature to behave preferentially toward its close relatives. This leads in turn to the interesting possibility that perhaps one of the biological reasons for social grouping is to provide an opportunity for nepotism to take place.

Nonetheless, only rarely do people identify nepotism as one of the *reasons* they live in societies, or social groups. The presence of external enemies, on the other hand, is a socially acceptable and easily understood justification, a plausible excuse for banding together, even if and when other factors—including factors beyond our ken—may also operate. Maybe we actually fool ourselves, claiming that our groups are for defense when actually they are "for" a rather exclusionary kind of altruism toward our relatives. In any event, it is a curious fact that whereas only a very small proportion of human beings can describe the mathematical evolutionary biology of nepotism (technically known as "kin selection" or "the maximization of inclusive fitness") there exists not a single person who is unfamiliar with the fundamental calculus of enemies and how to thwart them.

In fact, for most people, avoidance of enemies and adherence to friends begins very early in life. This aspect of enemy awareness provides a suitable transition from biology to psychology, from the vast realm of evolution to the private province of the mind.

Stranger Anxiety and Early Development

Consider the case of Meghan, eight months old, a cheerful, outgoing baby who smiles readily, gurgles engagingly, and crawls enthusiastically wherever her pudgy arms and legs can carry her. She hasn't yet met her uncle Rick, an encounter to which Rick—as well as Meghan's parents—had been looking forward. But their first meeting was a disaster. "I don't understand what got into her," said her mother, shaking her head. "As soon as Rick came near her, she just burst into tears." Things didn't get much better throughout Rick's four-day visit. Moreover, Meghan started behaving equally "badly" with other newcomers to her life: the woman at the bank, the electrician, people at the post office.

Was something suddenly wrong with Meghan? Not at all. She was simply going through a typical, predictable, and normal behavior of young children: stranger anxiety.

Although commonplace, stranger anxiety is something of a mystery nonetheless. After all, why should a young child suddenly develop an aversion to strangers, to absolute newcomers she has never met before and who have never injured her? Psychoanalysts such as Rene Spitz[15] and Margaret Mahler[16] see stranger anxiety as the inverse of the child's connection to its mother. The mother has come to be all that is good, nurturing, protective, and dependable in the child's small universe. Strangers aren't scary because of who they are, but because of who they are *not*. Anyone who isn't the mother is different, wrong, frightening. In a word, an enemy. (We can extend the notion of "mother" as the sole source of security to include father, siblings, anyone to whom the infant becomes securely bonded.)

Another psychoanalyst, F. Fornari, described stranger anxiety as "the original emergence of the other as enemy." As he sees it, the stranger "is sensed as a bad presence which the child tries to eliminate as such." Fornari then goes on to proclaim that,

> Because the enemy first emerges in the child's stranger anxiety, without the child's ever having experienced an attack on the part of the stranger, the original establishment of the other as enemy is comprehensible only in terms of externalization onto the stranger of a bad internal object.[17]

We may bristle a bit at Fornari's use of the word "only," implying as it does that no other explanations may legitimately be entertained. But, making due allowances for the psychoanalytic penchant for dogmatism, there is something compelling about this portrait of infancy.

The argument goes as follows: Even the best mother (or other caretaker) is bound to be deficient, at least insofar as the infant's all-consuming needs are concerned. Occasionally the Little Dictator is disappointed, perhaps because it isn't fed exactly when it wants, or held long enough or just right. But the mother is also godlike and essential. Anger at her is therefore dangerous; rejection, unthinkable. So, according to this interpretation, the infant develops a "bad internal object," which it then projects or externalizes upon someone else: someone who is safe, a stranger who instantly becomes the enemy. In this way, the mother is kept inviolate, as befits a crucially important friend and ally.

There may be other things going on as well, all at the level of "intrapsychic conflict" that the descendants of Sigmund Freud consider so important. For example, as a young child begins to experience the world, he or she also begins to experience an increase in aggressiveness and assertiveness. And again, sensing that it may be dangerous to turn these new and feisty traits upon the mother, it may be that the child appropriately directs them against someone else, ideally someone who really is a stranger. "If I alienate this stranger," the child could as well be reasoning, "so what?"

Evolutionary biology, however, suggests another level of interpretation, one that does not contradict the suggestions of psychoanalysis but rather amplifies and further enriches our understanding. Consider normal social life among most nonhuman primates, including baboons and macaques. A newborn monkey is intensely connected to its mother, held tightly, nursed, and carried everywhere. As it gets older, the baby primate typically arranges for its own transportation, hanging down from mommy's belly. Then it progresses to riding, cowboy-like, on the mother's back. All the time, it is also beginning to wander on occasion farther and farther from parental protection. And here is where the monkey equivalent of stranger anxiety comes in: Among most primates, adult group-members are strongly inhibited from attacking a newborn. But as the baby graduates to being a juvenile, it finds itself increasingly at risk, in part because having grown larger, its safety is ironically more jeopardized since it has outgrown its immunity to attack from other, older individuals. In addition, as it becomes more mobile, the growing youngster is more likely to intrude itself into situations where it is not wanted or appreciated. As a result, a developing juvenile has every reason to be anxious about strangers: they are genuine threats; enemies, even.

In an eye-opening bit of research more than twenty-five years ago, psychologist Gene P. Sackett found evidence that this response to enemies may even be largely innate, independent of experience. Sackett kept young rhesus monkeys in isolation from birth, exposing them to photographs of trees, people, and geometric patterns, as well as other monkeys. Beginning at about two-and-one-half months of age, these young monkeys—which had never encountered other monkeys, let alone been attacked by any—suddenly began responding to photographs of threatening adults with fear and clear-cut "submission behavior."[18] The significance of such responses seems obvious: At this age, free-living young monkeys are beginning to encounter other animals, some of which are likely to be dangerous, and it is biologically adaptive (that is, likely to be favored by natural selection) for these individuals to begin automatically responding in a manner that tends to inhibit aggression on the part of older, larger, more dominant individuals . . . members of their social group, to be sure, but potential enemies as well.[19]

Back, now, to young Meghan and her stranger anxiety. Maybe, as the psychoanalysts say, she is externalizing a bad internal object. Maybe she is in the throes of intrapsychic conflict. Or maybe she is responding in a biologically appropriate way to the appearance of a potentially dangerous stranger. After all, an eight-month-old human is developmentally comparable, in some ways, to a two-and-one-half-month-old rhesus monkey: Both are becoming mobile enough to encounter threatening adults. Any way you look at it, however, she is meeting the "enemy" and setting the stage for her future, and everyone else's.

And so, here we are in the final decade before the twenty-first century, small Meghans about to encounter an army of terrifying, dangerous, unknown strangers, and—not surprisingly—less than enthusiastic at the prospect, like tiny tasty herrings in a vast, cold ocean, deriving a peculiar sense of security from being part of a group, whether a small unit such as a family or local community, or a large one such as a nation-state. (Only rarely do we seem to extend this group-orientation to include our entire species, or, for that matter, the whole planet.) It is widely assumed that nationalism, for example, is a learned sentiment, a result of education, family influence, government propaganda, and such; rarely is it considered that the tendency to associate in groups, and to prefer larger groups over smaller ones, may emanate from within ourselves, as a multitiered response to enemies. But just like our ancestors and our animal cousins, we still seek safety in numbers. We still associate with others, to benefit or to suffer as a result. We still avoid, and reject, strangers. We still threaten each other as well. And it may well be that for all this, in ways we are just beginning to glimpse, we can thank—or blame— our biology, as well as our enemies.

❖   ❖   ❖

We can explore the role of enemies in human behavior at various levels, each like one of those Russian dolls, nested inside another. Of these levels, biology is, in a sense, the smallest and most reductionistic. Let us now turn to the next level, one "turtle" above this chapter, to the arena at which inclination meets behavior: psychology.

Notes

1. Marmots are large rodents, of which there are a half dozen species in North America. The best known marmot is the woodchuck or groundhog, although our western mountains are home to several other species, including the yellowbellied marmot of the Sierra Nevada and southern Rockies, and the hoary marmots of the northern Rockies and Cascade Mountains. It has been rumored that some people do not share my unquenchable thirst for marmot-lore. To the others, I unblushingly recommend my own *Marmots: Social Behavior and Ecology* (Stanford, Calif.: Stanford University Press, 1989).

2. A. J. Bateman, "Intra-sexual Selection in Drosophila," *Heredity* 2 (1948): 349–68.

3. L. G. Abele and S. Gilchrist, "Homosexual Rape and Sexual Selection in Acanthocephalan Worms," *Science* 197 (1977): 81–83.

4. Dwight D. Eisenhowever, *Peace with Justice: Selected Addresses* (New York: Columbia University Press, 1961).

5. *Seattle Post-Intelligencer*, October 24, 1990.

6. Robert Bly, *Iron John* (New York: Addison Wesley, 1990).

7. J. Glenn Gray, *The Warriors: Reflections on Men in Battle* (New York: Harper & Row, 1967).

8. Perhaps we also shouldn't be surprised that such sentiments have been so quickly converted into rage at the possibility of admitting avowed homosexuals into the American military; especially for men who are insecure in their own sexuality, it may be very threatening to consider tinkering, however benignly, with the rigid, heterosexual, military bastion of male-male bonding.

9. S. L. A. Marshall, *Men Against Fire* (New York: William Morrow, 1947).

10. W. D. Hamilton, "Geometry for the Selfish Herd," *Journal of Theoretical Biology* 31 (1971): 295–311.

11. No conscious reasoning is here implied. Rather, natural selection could easily have performed the calculation, so that the individuals in question aren't necessarily any more aware of what they are doing, or why, than a rock is aware of Newton's Law of Gravitation, or a tree is aware of what season is best for it to flower.

12. The same biologist who gave us the selfish herd also gave us this insight: William D. Hamilton, "The Evolution of Social Behavior," *Journal of Theoretical Biology* 7 (1964): 1–52.

13. See, for example, David P. Barash, *The Whisperings Within* (New York: Penguin, 1980).

14. See, for example, David P. Barash, *The Hare and the Tortoise* (New York: Penguin, 1987).

15. Rene A. Spitz, *The First Year of Life* (New York: International Universities Press, 1965).

16. Margaret S. Mahler, *On Human Symbiosis and the Vicissitudes of Individuation* (New York: International Universities Press, 1968).

17. F. Fornari, *The Psychoanalysis of War* (Bloomington, Ind.: University of Indiana Press, 1975).

18. Gene P. Sackett, "Monkeys Reared in Isolation with Pictures as Visual Input: Evidence for an Innate Releasing Mechanism," *Science* (October 3, 1966): 1–3.

19. It is also interesting that one of the most common of these submission behaviors is the so-called "fear-grin," which is eerily reminiscent of the forced smile typically seen on a subordinate human being.

3

Psychology

Once, there was a Charlie Chaplin look-alike contest. On a lark, Chaplin himself entered. He came in third.

Once, there was a religious leader of Iran. He didn't like the United States, wouldn't return our hostages, and jacked up the price of oil. He called us the "great Satan," and we weren't any kinder to him. The chances are, however, that if the real Uncle Sam had entered a "great Satan" look-alike contest, he also wouldn't have done any better than third, even in downtown Teheran; similarly for the Ayatollah himself, on Main Street, USA.

The truth is ours to embellish—and to create. (This is what, in more elaborate phrasing, is known as "psychology.") When it comes to enemies, we give ourselves even more leeway than the judges at the Charlie Chaplin look-alike contest.

It would be misleading to focus upon our enemy systems only in the abstract, or in the distance, because in fact, enmity ranks among our most personal experiences. On an intimate, human level, "enemies R us"; or rather, the meeting, making, and even the losing of enemies is an experience that we all share. Since we encounter enemies (both imagined and real) so often in our own private, daily lives, in this chapter we shall intersperse psychological theory and generalization with examples of such lives. The names have been changed, and in some cases a few trivial details have been rearranged to protect the privacy of the individuals involved, but the situations are genuine, and are recounted precisely as they took place.

Images of the Enemy

Many psychologists and psychiatrists have studied the "image of the enemy," and they have concluded, among other things, that our images of the other side (whether visual or in words) tend to emphasize, exaggerate, and even create nasty traits, all the while literally "dehumanizing" the opponent. Thus, we find words such as "rats," "dogs," "vermin," "scum," and "pigs" applied to "the enemy" not just in the English language but also in German, Arabic, Japanese, Russian, Hindi, and Swahili, among others. Anthropologists have also noted that several isolated, nontechnological peoples—such as the Jivaro of the Amazon—employ the same word for their tribe as for human being. This is much more than a semantic detail; it is the stuff of life and death, because although most societies have prohibitions against killing other members of their tribe, the rules are much more lax—in most cases, downright encouraging—about killing members of other species, such as pigs, deer, or monkeys. So, when neighboring but other-tribe human beings are effectively dehumanized, they can be killed with impunity, even enthusiasm.

Psychoanalyst Erik Erikson observed that, "Man has evolved . . . in pseudo species, i.e., tribes, clans, classes, etc., which behave as if they were separate species, created at the beginning of time by supernatural intent."[1] As a result, each group developed not only "a distinct sense of identity, but also a conviction of harboring *the* human identity." In our enthusiasm to recognize the characteristics of our particular group as somehow embodying all that is good or noble—indeed, all that there *is*—in humanity, we err even more than did the judges at the Charlie Chaplin look-alike contest. After all, despite the inflated and inaccurate perception of what Chaplin actually looked like, the real Charlie Chaplin at least came in third. But when we set ourselves up to judge the humanity of our fellow human beings, the results may be even farther off, since we are likely to conclude that these "others," these enemies, aren't even people at all.

One needn't doubt the literal humanity of someone else in order to operate under similar unspoken rules. Famed anthropologist Clifford Geertz[2] emphasized the importance of "primordial alliances," whereby people define themselves and their allies while at the same time pointing with equal certainty to their enemies. Sigmund Freud wrote about "primary groups," within which the crucial concept, as he saw it, was "identification." Church members or soldiers, for example, identify themselves with the larger organization, its goals, its leaders, and its physical and behavioral traits.

We can go even further, and suggest that a kind of *negative identification* also takes place between different groups, emphasizing distinctions and creating handles by which enemies can be grasped. Thus, one of the underlying functions of groups is to identify members of *other* groups as different from themselves. It is tempting to say that they "misidentify," since they exaggerate any existing differences, partly in the service of getting a firmer grip on who they are themselves. Just as the yin defines the yang, the other—the enemy—becomes important as the not-me, which defines the me.

Freud also wrote about the "narcissism of minor differences," by which he meant the tendency of people to focus on those small features that distinguish their group from another.[3] Often, the greater the over-all similarity, the greater the need to magnify such minor differences as may exist, so as to have some basis for separating *us* from *them*. Much is made of details in religious belief, ways of pronouncing certain words, or food habits. In Jonathan Swift's *Gulli-*

ver's Travels, the Lilliputians and Blefuscudians fought over whether a cooked egg should be opened from the large or the small end. In what used to pass for the sovereign state of Yugoslavia, Greek Orthodox Serbs and Roman Catholic Croats are almost indistinguishable; they even speak the same language, known appropriately enough as Serbo-Croatian. But Serbs cross themselves from right to left and carry pussy willows on Palm Sunday, whereas Croats cross themselves from left to right and carry palm fronds. And each side carries guns, which are used against the other.

The notion of "enemy" turns out to be intimately bound up with a sense of ethnicity, and, on a larger scale, nationalism, perhaps because it is only by having a clear sense of *them* that we can get a clear sense of *us*.

The small island of Cyprus is another example of longstanding animosities, reinforced by seemingly trivial cultural badges. Psychoanalyst Vamik Volkan, a Turkish Cypriot by birth, describes the contending factions on that small Mediterranean island:

> During the British rule in Cyprus, and even into the early months of the republic, it was customary for the Greeks and Turks to take evening strolls into town. There were favorite spots for promenades. Although the two groups usually congregated according to ethnicity, there were also common areas used by both groups, such as the boardwalks of Larnaca and Kyrenia. To a stranger, the crowd of Greeks and Turks might look like a homogeneous group of Mediterranean people dressed alike and taking a common pleasure, but to the islander, differences among members of the crowd were obvious and important.
>
> Greeks and Turks could distinguish each other at a glance just by noticing such seemingly insignificant details as different brands of cigarettes, Turks preferring those packaged in red and white, the Greeks those in blue and white. In the villages, where usual masculine dress consists of baggy trousers and shirts, the Greeks

wore black sashes, the Turks red. In normal times, a breach of this color code might be tolerated, but when ethnic relations were strained, when group cohesion (and therefore individual integrity) were threatened, a Turk would rather die than wear a black sash and a Greek would be just as adamant in his refusal to wear a red one.[4]

Not surprisingly, the psychology of "us versus them" begins very early in life (consider the example of stranger anxiety, discussed in the last chapter). By the time they are teenagers, most people are vigorously at work defining themselves by a variety of cultural badges, which is part of the reason why teenagers are so notoriously focussed on peer groups and the trappings of group association. Normal adolescents develop a sense of "ego identity"—a deep-seated knowledge of who they really are—by the groups they associate with: the clothing worn, radio stations listened to, places they shop or just hang out, sports they participate in, flags they salute, and foods they eat, not to mention the more obvious indicators such as skin color, language, and so forth.

In early adolescence most particularly, the sense of ego identity (also commonly known as "self-concept") is closely intertwined with the choice of what psychoanalysts call "suitable targets for externalization," by which young people seek to reconcile internal contradictions through reference to external symbols. At this stage, the adolescent's self-concept may differ from that held by others important to him or herself. The result is frequently an "identity crisis," in which the young person turns all the more strongly to his or her peer group, showing particular fervor in identifying with it, and with its symbols. Shared commitment and identification leads to a sense of solidarity combined with confirmation of selfhood.

All of the above makes a kind of intuitive sense, especially our penchant for allies, our need to affiliate. It is less obvious, however, why we should have an opposite need—for enemies—until we consider that our early alliances, with all their psychological import, would be meaningless unless there were contrary alliances against which to identify and measure ourselves. It would mean little for a Greek Cypriot to wear a black sash unless there were Turkish Cypriots sporting red ones.

We cling to our various sashes, often with the desperation of shipwrecked sailors clinging to a life raft. And once again, it is no great surprise that young people do this with special fervor, because adolescence is a time of drastic changes and stormy seas, when we particularly crave consistency and connectedness, even as we strive for self-definition. Sometimes, however, we get thrown overboard, and when this happens, the experience can be not only bracing, but even amusing, at least in retrospect. The following is testimony of my own personal dunking.

An Education in the Transformation of Enemies, Courtesy of Sal Maglie

My first encounter with enemies and their transformation took place in the summer of 1956. It was the summer I grew up. It wasn't my first sexual awakening, or my first exposure to a great book, or my bar mitzvah. No, 1956 was far more dramatic, and painful. It was the year Sal Maglie was traded to the Brooklyn Dodgers.

Let me explain.

Sal Maglie had been a pitcher for the New York Giants. He wasn't just any pitcher, just as for me—a ten-year-old baseball fanatic— the New York Giants weren't just any team. Sal Maglie was Sal the Barber, an artist whose pitches were so controlled, so perfectly thrown that they could shave, precisely, a tiny sliver of home plate, wherever and whenever the Barber might command. (At least, so I was told as a child. Later, I learned the dark side of the Barber's reputation: To intimidate opposing batters, Maglie sometimes pitched so close to their heads that his fastballs nearly gave them a shave.) He was also "the Dodger killer," because Sal Maglie had a special knack for defeating the Giants' archrival, the Brooklyn Dodgers. (The Giants and Dodgers were such longstanding and useful enemies, incidentally, that when both teams later abandoned New York for California, the former went to San Francisco and the latter to Los Angeles, so as to continue—and to continue profiting from—their convenient enmity.)

There were lots of stars on the New York Giants during Maglie's salad days, notably Don Mueller, Alvin Dark, Whitey Lockman, and the incomparable Willie Mays, as well as extraordinary pitchers such as Johnny Antonelli, Hoyt Wilhelm, and Rueben Gomez. But Sal Maglie was different and special, at least to me. He seemed older, wiser, more poised and sophisticated than the young hotshots, just as the New York Giants seemed in every way superior to the Brooklyn Dodgers. To me, Sal Maglie *was* the New York Giants.

In any event, you had to grow up in New York during the 1950s to appreciate the intensity of the Giant-Dodger competition and to know how terribly important it was (for some of us) that the Giants beat the Dodgers, and the crucial role of Sal Maglie in doing so. The Dodgers were bad simply because the Giants were my team and for Giants to love Dodgers would be like dogs loving cats, or Macy's loving Gimbels. I knew that the Dodgers had done a wonderful and courageous thing by hiring Jackie Robinson, the first black baseball player in the major leagues, but my dislike of the "Brooklyn Bums" was such that I even blamed them for being admirable, or rather, for pretending to be good, for tinkering with my certainty that deep down inside, they were bad.

I will never forget the glowing, transcendent day that Sal the Barber struck out, in two glorious successive innings, the heart of the Dodger lineup: Pee Wee Reese, Duke Snyder, Gil Hodges, Carl Furillo, and Roy Campanella. That was happiness.

And I also will never forget when Sal Maglie, Dodger killer extraordinaire, was traded . . . to the Dodgers.

I couldn't believe it. I felt like I had been hit by a baseball bat. When, thirty-two years later, Iran's Ayatollah Khomeini announced to his citizens that he was making peace with Iraq's Saddam Hussein, and that doing so felt like "drinking poison," I understood at once, but I knew that it couldn't have felt worse than my own physical illness that fateful day when I learned that Sal Maglie would henceforth play for The Enemy.

I developed a fantasy: Maglie would refuse to report to the Dodgers. He would show them. Like the proud, unconquerable Iroquois warrior in Oliver Wendell Holmes's poem "As Red Men Die," who chooses death over the dishonor of sitting with the women of the hated Hurons who had captured him, Sal Maglie—the Barber, Dodger-killer, proud warrior of the Polo Grounds—would scorn those Bums from Brooklyn, would rather hang up his glove forever than switch and be dishonored with the detestable Dodger uniform.

Fat chance.

Sal Maglie was much wiser than I. He went on to pitch, and to pitch well, for the Dodgers.[5] To my amazement, the world kept spinning, seismologic stations throughout the country did not report any novel or extraordinary activity, and I was faced with a three-way choice: either the Brooklyn Dodgers had suddenly become good, Sal Maglie had become bad, or there was something wrong with my original perception of who and what the enemy really is.

The path to maturity may well be littered with the corpses of enemies revealed to be less inimical than previously thought, and, by the same token, with heroes now seen to be less heroic. But at the same time—and notwithstanding the True Tale of Sal Maglie—our enemy system is not just something that we eventually outgrow.

It occupies a deep and important place in the psychology of adults no less than children. And, as we shall now examine, it also organizes much of our behavior toward others: frequently, more than is good for us, and nearly always, more than we realize.

The "Dark Side"

C. P. Cavafy posed some prophetic questions in his poem "Waiting for the Barbarians":

> Why this sudden bewilderment, this confusion?
> (How serious people's faces have become.)
> Why are the streets and squares emptying so rapidly,
> everyone going home lost in thought?
>
> Because night has fallen and the barbarians haven't come.
> And some of our men just in from the border say
> there are no barbarians any longer.
>
> Now what's going to happen to us without barbarians?
> Those people were a kind of solution.[6]

If the barbarians have been a kind of solution, what was the problem? One thing we can state with confidence: it has long been within ourselves, and deeply so. When we encounter things that move us, but about which we rarely if ever think, the likelihood is that we are confronting aspects of our fundamental personality structures. Sigmund Freud, one of the pioneers in such confrontations, called our ravenous, selfish, often destructive unconscious core the *id*, from the Latin word for "it." Nothing so personal as the "I," mind you, or the "me," the "you," or even the "us," but *it*—something external, out there, distanced in some way from each of us. By taking an unpleasant aspect of ourselves and naming it "it," something apart from us, he made its existence more tolerable. In just this way, the existence of "barbarians" outside has made it easier for us to live with those other barbarians, inside.

It is an old trick.

Another founder of psychoanalysis, Carl Jung, discussed what he called our "shadow self." The image is significant. Picture yourself standing against a brightly lit wall, casting a shadow against it. The shadow, of course, is real, and it undeniably comes from you. Without you, it wouldn't exist. But even with you, the shadow is no more than a passing vision, an absence of something (light) produced when your substance blocks energy from a light bulb or the sun. According to Jung, this shadow self, the dark side of our own personality, is typically nasty or otherwise disreputable; many of us even have a hard time acknowledging its existence, not to mention accepting ownership or responsibility. Once again, it is "it," not us—maybe "you," almost certainly "them," but definitely not "me." And so, we take our shadow self and project it elsewhere, where it is more palatable: onto someone else—onto the barbarians, onto an enemy.

This is not to say that there aren't real barbarians, or to deny that people sometimes have real enemies. Certainly, our perception of an enemy may be based on more than "mere" psychology. But it is also true that our enemies are not merely "real." They are, at least in part, a product of our minds, our mental representation of complex internal and external events, as well as a reflection of reality. Inventive creatures that we are, we often make potentially bad situations worse, creating additional enemies and energizing their ranks with the special animosity that comes only from within ourselves. "He gripes about the smallest details," complains the fellow obsessed with precisely such details. "They only understand force," say those who are indifferent to all other means of persuasion. "You can never trust her," says someone who, in fact, has never been trusted, and—

not surprisingly—is not very trusting, or trustworthy. "Better attack them now, because otherwise, they are going to attack us first," warn those who, when given authority, have started some of history's most destructive (and otherwise preventable) wars.

There may be more than passing truth, therefore, in the old saw, "Peace begins with me." Like most old saws, this one still has a few sharp teeth: So long as people are conflicted, at war with a part of themselves that they refuse to acknowledge, they may well persist in creating enemies "out there." By taking those aspects of ourselves that we refuse to acknowledge and projecting them onto others, we free ourselves to criticize them, to accuse them of perfidy and all sorts of deviltry, and to know them for what they are—or rather, what we insist that they be—our enemies.

"If only it were all so simple!" wrote Aleksandr Solzhenitsyn, himself no stranger to the having of enemies.

> If only there were evil people somewhere insidiously committing evil deeds, and it were necessary only to separate them from the rest of us and destroy them. But the line dividing good and evil cuts through the heart of every human being. And who is willing to destroy a piece of his own heart?[7]

In short, we see, and often create, the enemy outside as a way of denying the enemy that is within us, and also as a way of justifying that interior demon. After all, once we are adequately supplied with enemies, we can aver that we are not really nasty, even though we may be doing nasty things; rather, we do those things reluctantly, only because we are forced into it—by the enemy. "How wicked these people are," Hitler is reported to have wept, reviewing films of the bombing of Warsaw in 1939, "to have made me do this to them."

But when the enemy is no longer available, either because he has been defeated, or has physically departed, or has perversely insisted on becoming a friend, we are compelled to look inside ourselves, to confront a disorienting loss of that self which existed largely in reflection. After all, if we have defined ourselves by who was against us, and then try to lean, as usual, against that someone only to find that he is no longer there, we are liable to fall over. Then, we might even have to encounter certain painful truths about ourselves: perhaps our own incompleteness, lack of purpose, or even our own "badness." With our enemies gone, we must look within, where we find—if indeed we find anything at all—yet more enemies. And to no one's surprise, these enemies look remarkably similar to those we had pointed to all along, projected on the wall, or onto others. It may feel new to us, but it is an experience as old as the human species.

Thus, in *Prometheus Bound*, Aeschylus asks,

> Prometheus, Prometheus, hanging upon Caucasus
> Look upon the visage
> Of yonder vulture:
> Is it not thy face,
> Prometheus?[8]

By clutching our enemies, we avoid self-awareness. We see, clearly enough—and hate, readily enough—the hideous, leering vulture that gnaws daily at our liver, but we fail to see our own face. And so, like Diogenes the Cynic, we search the streets at night, holding aloft our lantern and projecting our shadows everywhere, startled from time to time by the shifting apparitions of our own making, looking desperately for what we dare not find inside ourselves.

Walter and Ellen

"Please pass the salt." Rarely had such an ordinary, garden-variety sentence been uttered with such venom.

"I packed your clothes," announced Ellen, indifferently, five minutes later, after she and Walter had eaten in silence, except for the droning of the television news. Their television was perched on the dining room table, and was always tuned to the evening news during dinner, since otherwise Ellen and Walter would have felt obliged to speak with each other, or confront the painful fact that they would rather not.

"The suitcase is on the bed," Ellen elaborated, between bites. Walter still didn't answer, or even look at her.

Walter travelled a lot, attending meetings and sales conferences. Ellen was relieved whenever he was gone. She resented cleaning up after him when he returned, but she appreciated the money he earned. Ellen hated Walter for the way he ignored her, and for his single-minded focus on stocks and bonds. Walter had loved Ellen once— or so he seemed to remember—when they were first married, nearly fifty years before. But that was a long time ago, in feelings as well as in years. Now, they lived in the same house but not "together," in a state of continual but unspecified hostility. Walter couldn't stand Ellen's constant television-watching, her smoking ("Sometimes I can't even see the wall for the smoke"), and her obsession with keeping the house so neat that he felt himself a stranger there.

Then one night, while Walter was being drenched in a thunderstorm in sultry Miami, there was a sudden screech of brakes and the awful crunch of metal on metal on an icy road two thousand miles to the northwest, and Ellen was dead. Walter decided to retire, and to move in with his son Harold, a plump, cheery man who had somehow managed to remain unaffected by his parents' long silences punctuated by the tossing of pointed, verbal darts. In fact, Harold and his wife, Julia, looked forward to getting closer to Walter, and they hoped to make his life less lonely.

Julia didn't smoke, but she did like cashews. In fact, she ate them all the time. After living with Julia and Harold for a month, Walter commented, with some annoyance, "Sometimes I can't even hear myself think for the darned cracking of cashew shells around here." He also started complaining that the house wasn't clean enough, and that his grandchildren—whom he once adored—were spending more time with the family cats than with him. He insisted on keeping the television on throughout the day, including (maybe even, especially) during meals. And it was at just such a meal, with the TV news droning in the background, that one day Julia, Harold, and their children heard Walter hissing, through clenched teeth, "Please pass the salt."

The Most Intimate Enemy

Warning: if the following were a movie, it would probably be R-rated because of language. Specifically, the next few hundred words are about a very personal encounter well-known to each of us, absolutely unavoidable, and yet, rarely considered or even acknowledged. It concerns an enemy of sorts, a dark side so foul, so vile, that it is literally unmentionable in polite company. Its very existence is almost denied. And yet, it is fundamental to the human experience.

The subject is "shit," a more honest word than "excrement" or "feces"; so, if shit offends you, I suggest skipping ahead. In fact, shit offends just about everyone. And that is the point. However delicate and fastidious we may be, every one of us produces shit. Or, as the bumper stickers attest, "Shit Happens." We may eat alfalfa sprouts and totally organic tofu, the greasiest of pork rinds, or perfectly poached truffles in safron. Prince or pauper, duchess or drug addict, senator, surgeon, or seafarer, whoever we are and however we nourish ourselves, steamy, smelly shit comes out the other end.

What do these scatalogical reflections have to do with enemies? Just this: Almost everyone—excepting only very young children and certain very insane people—considers shit to be unpleasant, and goes to extraordinary lengths to separate him or herself from it. We flush it down the toilet, pretending whenever possible that it doesn't exist. Forced to confront it, we wipe it away, wash it off, disinfect, bury, and otherwise dispose of it as quickly as possible, generally holding our breath and often looking the other way. Even beyond the fundamental distinction between living and dead, that between me and not-me may be the most basic of all, and here, shit plays a prominent but rarely appreciated role: It italicizes the fact that the "me" is good and the "not-me" is filthy and smelly, even dangerous. It is bad and thus, at a fundamental level, an enemy. It divides the world into two camps, the shitters and the things shat. At the same time, however—and as much as we seek to avoid it—we must own this substance which is so intimately ours. It comes directly from us; like our own offspring, it springs from our bodies. It was once part of us. And yet it is rejected, and vigorously so.

The origin of the word itself is oddly revealing, derived from the German *skit*, which dates from prehistoric Indo-European *skheid*, meaning "to separate, divide, or split" (thereby providing an origin for such perfectly acceptable English words as "schism," the geologic term "schist," and "schizophrenia"). In any event, the basic idea is separation, expulsion from the body, just as an enemy might be expelled from the body politic.

Our encounter with shit is to some degree part of a deeper and even more difficult encounter with our own dualistic nature. On the one hand, we write poetry, compose symphonies, perform acts of philosophic and scientific creativity, think thoughts of sublime beauty, or engage in deeds of ethical perfection. We are, in some ways, like gods. But on the other hand, as Ernest Becker has written,

> Man is a worm and food for worms. This is the paradox: he is out of nature and hopelessly in it; he is dual, up in the stars and yet housed in a heart-pumping, breath-gasping body that once belonged to a fish and still carries the gill-marks to prove it. His body is a material fleshy casing that is alien to him in many ways— the strangest and most repugnant way being that it aches and bleeds and will decay and die. Man is literally split in two: he has an awareness of his own splendid uniqueness in that he sticks out of nature with a towering majesty, and yet he goes back into the ground a few feet in order blindly and dumbly to rot and disappear forever. It is a terrifying dilemma to be in and to have to live with.[9]

If shit is less terrifying than death, it is nonetheless even more prevalent. Death, at least, happens only once to each of us, something for which most of us can be grateful. But shitting is a (more or less) regular event. It forces us to confront, if only briefly, the fact that we are fundamentally dichotomous creatures, grounded in stuff that we would rather not acknowledge. For most people, their own shit is probably their first experience with an enemy. It is also an experience that we share with all other members of our species, a cross-cultural, R-rated encounter with our own "dark side." And unlike most psychologically oriented explanations of our enemy system, it is undeniably real, and it emanates, in its entirety, from each of us. No one else can be blamed, neither another individual, nor patterns of social learning or cultural tradition; not even "the system."

By contrast, psychologists—when they turn their attention to our enemy system at all—are inclined to emphasize the role of experience. And one of the most straightforward of these experiences is frustration.

Frustration

Psychological theories of enemies and enemy-making tend to focus on our own role in creating and maintaining enemy images, but they do not saddle the individual with sole responsibility. The likelihood is that Walter's behavior toward Ellen and then, after her death, his behavior toward his remaining family resulted from complex circumstances in his own life, perhaps beginning early in childhood. Part of the stock in trade of psychology is the recognition that the external world makes a generous contribution to all behavior, including our response to enemies as well as our creation of them. Walter and Ellen were deeply frustrated because of their unhappy married life, but it is likely that their troubled marriage was itself, in part, a reaction to other, more deep-seated frustrations felt by each of them.

The connection between frustration and aggression, and its role in creating enemies, has been well documented in animal studies.

Imagine, for example, that you are a rat. Not only that, you are a sexually deprived rat. Then, the lady rat of your dreams miraculously materializes only a few feet away, and her chirping and posturing—not to mention the alluring smells wafting in your direction—confirm that she is undeniably, scrumptiously, in heat. You run toward her, as quickly as your little ratty legs can carry you. Then, unaccountably, you run smack into a plexiglass wall, which has just been lowered between you and the delectable creature. What do you do? Not surprisingly, rodent Romeo, you get angry. If another rat is nearby, you are even likely to attack him, even though he may be just an innocent bystander. Variants on this theme have been confirmed by numerous experiments.

People, too, behave aggressively when they are frustrated, when—in the jargon of behavioral scientists who study frustration and its effects—there is "externally imposed inhibition of an ongoing goal-directed response." In 1939 Yale University psychiatrist John Dollard[10] and his colleagues developed the frustration theory of aggression presented rather dogmatically (even a bit aggressively) as follows: "The occurrence of aggressive behavior always presupposes the existence of frustration, and contrariwise, the existence of frustration always leads to some form of aggression." Empathizing with a frustrated, sex-starved rat, most of us can agree.

What does all this have to do with enemies and, specifically, with the internal factors creating enemies as well as the question of what happens when enemies disappear? Several things. For one, when frustration arises, so does enmity. A frustrating agent quickly becomes an enemy, whether this "enemy agent" is a spy, a plexiglass partition, an unloved or unloving spouse, a group of people, or a government whose aspirations run counter to one's own. Anyone else associated, even incidentally, with the frustration can similarly be tarred with enmity.

For another thing, the removal of a frustrating agent—the object of aggression, the enemy—can itself be frustrating. With the obstacle removed, the goal may readily be achieved, but even then, dissatisfaction may remain. Often, the most satisfying route is first to beat the frustrator over the head, *then* get the goal. This is because overcoming the frustration is often part of the goal itself. Or, as Cervantes put it in *Don Quixote*: *La senda es mejor que la venda* ("the path is better than the inn"). As a result, Khomeini haters found themselves bereft when the elderly Ayatollah went at last to embrace his Allah. And Commie haters are deeply frustrated (even to the point of internecine aggression) at the demise of the "communist threat."

"Why do the folks hate Saddam Hussein, a man they never heard of two months ago?" asked columnist Christopher Matthews. "Because Moammar Khaddafi is too daffy to hate, because the terrorists who blew up Pan Am 103 can't be found, because the Ayatollah Khomeini is dead." One of the most troublesome things that can happen, in short, is for our enemy—erstwhile source of frustration—to disappear. It can be downright frustrating.

At first glance, this is surprising. If enemies are simply imposed upon us from outside, we should be relieved but not otherwise conflicted when and if they disappear. As we have seen, we might be troubled by our inability to project our "dark side" onto others, but most of us should be able to function rather well without such projection. Unless, as we shall now explore, our enemies actually help us in other ways.

Hoffman's Law, or the Enemy as Whetstone

Many lives are given shape and substance by their orientation toward an enemy. Just as a knife blade can be honed razor sharp against a whetstone, the human personality can become similarly dependent on its encounter with worthy opponents. In her moving account of the immigrant experience, Eva Hoffman tells of the travails of her father, a man who survived the Holocaust and the horrors of war-ravaged Poland, only to be frustrated and laid low by the politeness and gentility of the very British inhabitants of Vancouver, Canada:

> My mother reminds herself and us that my father is the man whose resourcefulness has never failed him, who has never been in a situation he couldn't get out of. But for the first time, he can't find his nerve; he becomes anxious about making small decisions, and anxious that he has made the wrong ones. What has him so afraid, he who was apparently fearless in the face of literally deadly danger? It is, I think, the lack of danger. Without an enemy whom he can outsmart, without a hokum law at which he can thumb his nose, he is left at a loss. The structure of the space within which he moves has changed. It has no obstacles he can daringly jump over, no closed doors he can cleverly open. Everything seems to be open, but where is the point of entry? How do you maneuver when there seems to be nothing to maneuver around? How do you fight when there

seems to be no particular opponent confronting you? My father is used to battling fate; here, he is faced with seemingly unresistant amorphousness, a soft medium in which hard punches are lost. He needs more of a T'ai Chi technique, something in which you manage and control your own force, because there is no one else to do it for you.[11]

One of Sir Isaac Newton's laws of physics tells us that for every action there is an equal and opposite reaction. The laws of motion also inform us about the essential role of a much maligned force: friction. Thus, without friction to exert an equal and opposite pressure against the bottoms of our feet, we couldn't even walk across a floor; instead, we would be forever slipping and sliding, clumsy oafs in smooth-soled shoes trying to make our way across a skating rink. Hoffman's Law, named for Eva Hoffman's father, might state that just as physical movement requires a degree of mechanical friction, psychological and social movement (and perhaps even normal growth as well) demands another kind of useful opposition, the sort provided by an enemy.

Let's explore the argument. First, there is no doubt that enemies keep us on our toes. To be sure, spending too much time in this position can result in leg cramps, but there is something to be said for the process, if only because of the muscle toning it provides. Second, beyond the simple question of exercise and the benefit of moderate stress, there are other advantages of being pushed and challenged, urged to be more than we otherwise are. Maybe even "all that you [we] can be." (Is it merely coincidence that the U.S. Army, an institution predicated on the having of enemies, advertises with this slogan?[12])

Consider the case of Pibul, a young native of Thailand who grew up in Bangkok and then attended medical school at the University of Wisconsin. Much as he loved his home city, Pibul dreaded his annual trips back home because he inevitably became sick with the same fever, nausea, and diarrhea that often afflicts the average Western tourist going to Thailand for the first time. As a result of living in the United States, with our relatively clean water, inspected meat, and high level of public hygiene, Pibul's body had grown soft. It was no longer challenged by the various antigens—the myriad microbial enemies—that the average Thai encounters every day, and which induce the production of protective antibodies. His friends and relatives still swam with impunity in the stinking Menam River, with its flotsam of animal carcasses and human feces, just as he did as a child, but not Pibul. He couldn't even eat dinner with his family without getting embarrassingly ill. The answer, for him, was to confront and ingest regularly the various bacterial, viral, and protozoal enemies that make up the daily environment of Bangkok slum-dwellers. Pibul contrived to return home more often, and, as a result, he stopped getting sick when he did so.

Nietzsche claimed that anything that does not kill you makes you stronger, advice that is of dubious value. But when it comes to enemies, especially mild ones, Nietzsche may have captured a kind of truth.

This may be why noted psychologist William James wrote in his renowned essay "The Moral Equivalent of War" that militarism could only be eliminated if something equally exciting and rewarding took its place. Just as Pibul needed to be challenged by the biological opponents we call antigens, and just as Eva Hoffman's father needed strenuous social opposition, many—perhaps most—people, according to James, need to do *something*, often something vigorous, and against a worthy adversary, if their lives are to be fulfilling. In the past, James suggested, they have needed war, which is why, "The war against war is going to be no holiday excursion or camping party. The military feelings are too deeply grounded to abdicate their place among our ideals until better substitutes are offered." Both William

James and Eva Hoffman—as well as Pibul, now a successful physician back in his native Thailand—might well subscribe to the need for suitable substitutes, in daily life no less than in the larger, public realm of war and peace.

They would probably also agree, however, that in some cases, that need is carried too far. This is especially true when the search for enemies occurs in the service of meeting other needs. For some people, the bracing effect of enmity can go far beyond stimulating one's immune or muscular system, or keeping our social selves in trim. For a particularly unpleasant example, consider JoAnne.

The Joy of Enemies

JoAnne was unhappy. She had always been unhappy. She didn't like her job or her marriage or her children. She didn't like her parents, or her two brothers. In fact, she didn't much like anyone, and not a lot of people liked her. She was clever—or, rather, intelligent (she had a high IQ, but was, in many ways, not very *smart* at all)—and she had a successful and promising career as an advertising executive. Occasionally, she had affairs, especially when she went to out-of-town sales meetings and conventions, but she never had an orgasm or even much interest in the men she woke up with in various hotel rooms, and she started wondering if maybe she was lesbian or at least bisexual.

Even more than unhappy, however, JoAnne was angry. She was angry at her parents, who, she said, never had any time for her or interest in her. They had given her nearly one hundred thousand dollars, but she sneered at the money, pointing out that it was a poor excuse for parental love. Years ago, she had used a Dalkon Shield, had developed pelvic inflammatory disease as a result, and was permanently sterile. She received nearly one hundred fifty thousand dollars as part of an insurance settlement against the manufacturer, and adopted three children, all of them Asian-Caucasian.

She sued her husband for divorce and eventually entered into a long and difficult court case, which resulted in joint custody of the children. Then she sought therapy for herself because she was experiencing rage attacks against those same children and was worried that she might hurt them. She demanded antidepressants from her psychiatrist, then left treatment when he wouldn't prescribe the latest "wonder drug," Prozac, which, based on an article in *Time* magazine, she had decided was the cure for all her ills. She interviewed five more psychiatrists, finally settling on a psychiatric social worker, while at the same time beginning two new lawsuits: one against her attorney in the divorce case, for legal malpractice (she felt that he hadn't adequately explored the possibility of winning sole custody), and one against her employer for gender discrimination since she had just been passed over for a coveted promotion to vice president.

She seemed to be doing better for a time, especially while both lawsuits were proceeding through the judicial system: serving papers, giving depositions, engaging in strategy sessions with various attorneys, and the like. In fact, she felt challenged, energized, and generally "turned on" by the legal proceedings, and she spent a lot of time fantasizing about the discomfort her suit was causing the defendants. The lawsuit against her employer settled (for a few thousand dollars) out of court; the one against her previous lawyer did not, and JoAnne lost. She wanted to appeal but couldn't get an attorney to pursue the case. She tried to act as her own lawyer, bungled the paperwork, was forced to give up, went home and severely beat her youngest child (age ten months). Following the law in her state, which required that the police be notified whenever child abuse was suspected, her therapist informed the Criminal Enforcement Division of the Child Welfare Department, whereupon JoAnne attempted suicide, swallowing several handfuls of pills that she had stolen from the hospital when she was visiting the injured child (who she originally claimed had fallen down a flight of stairs).

JoAnne's unconscious body was discovered by her oldest child less than an hour after her overdose. So JoAnne survived, thanks to a prompt aid car and a vigorous stomach-pumping at the local hospital's emergency room. Now JoAnne was truly miserable, until she came upon a cheering cascade of thoughts: Maybe she could sue her therapist for not having intervened earlier in her potentially destructive behavior toward her children, and also the emergency room physician because the gastric tube used to pump her stomach had bruised her larynx, giving her voice a peculiar and rather annoying tone that might possibly impede her professional career. Not only that, but maybe she could also go after the aid car medics, because—according to her neighbors—it had taken nearly eleven minutes (three minutes more than the community standard) for them to arrive at her house, and also the hospital for making it so easy for her (obviously a depressed woman, clearly a danger to herself) to steal potentially lethal medications, and maybe she could also sue her previous psychiatrist, the one who had refused to prescribe Prozac (which "clearly" would have solved all of her problems).

The possibilities were endless, and delicious. JoAnne felt renewed, invigorated, and (at least temporarily) at peace. All was not lost. Her life was worth living. She had some enemies once again.

JoAnne had, in fact, more than her share of enemies, in part because of her own behavior. Unlike JoAnne, most people do not obviously relish their enemies. But as we shall now examine, many of us have nonetheless been unwitting accomplices in creating and keeping them.

Paranoia: The Making and Multiplying of our Enemies

There is a striking scene in Walt Disney's cartoon masterpiece, *The Sorcerer's Apprentice*. By dint of magical incantations unwisely invoked, Mickey Mouse, the apprentice, managed to cast a spell on his mop, which obediently proceeded to do Mickey's appointed work, carrying pails of water and emptying them into a large tub. But the enchanted mop did its job too enthusiastically. Water began overflowing the tub. The magic mop wouldn't stop, so the distraught Mickey hit it with an axe, splintering the rogue appliance into dozens of pieces. Rather than solving the problem, however, this only made things worse, because each splinter gathered itself up, grabbed a pail, and began carrying even more water, ultimately making a minor overflow into a disastrous flood.

Sadly, we do not multiply our enemies in fantasy alone. For years, oystermen on Long Island Sound used to chop up the starfish that they hauled onto their trawlers along with the sought-after oysters. Starfish prey upon oysters; thus, there is no love lost between oystermen and starfish. They are, in fact, enemies. After wreaking their revenge, the triumphant oystermen would throw the dismembered starfish parts back into the ocean. But after a while, it was discovered that the starfish population was actually increasing, whereupon marine biologists pointed out that starfish are capable of regenerating whole animals from a single arm (or is it a leg?). Like the Sorcerer's Apprentice, the starfish choppers who thought they were destroying their enemies were simply making more of them.

With this in mind, we shall now consider a progression of increasing enemy-making and progressive paranoia. First, take the case of Raymond. He was neither sorcerer nor apprentice. Raymond didn't even like oysters. What he *really* didn't like, however, was people trespassing on his property. But a bunch of kids were in the habit of doing just that, taking a shortcut through Raymond's backyard, in order to get to the bus stop. One day he counted eight little trespassers during a fifteen-minute period. So Raymond devised a scheme: He told his neighbors that he was putting little booby traps in his yard. Nothing dangerous, mind you, just holes covered up with twigs and dirt, and thin wire cables attached to firecrackers. He didn't even do it, just said he would. But it backfired. The neighborhood kids thought it would be a great challenge to try and make it safely through Raymond's homemade minefield. They even invited their friends, until one day, just a week after Raymond had triumphantly announced his anti-trespassing measures, there were seventeen—count 'em, seventeen—little trespassers, with at least another dozen eager to try their luck at the most exciting new neighborhood sport.

Next, there is Richard Nixon. When he was president, Nixon kept an "enemies list," which consisted of politicians, journalists, or activists who had the temerity to disagree with or criticize the man or his policies. To an extent rarely equalled in American public life, Nixon brooded about his enemies; similarly (and not surprisingly), he was notable for the enemies he had—and created.

Although Nixon was not psychotic, he was a starfish chopper. He also exemplified a paranoid style. It is no coincidence that he was called "tricky Dick," and that one of the most effective zingers tossed at candidate Nixon was "Would you buy a used car from this man?" And, significantly, the most memorable statement about Nixon the president was uttered by tricky Dick himself: "I am not a crook." Lacking inner peace and self-confidence—not to mention being, in fact, guilty—he often looked and sounded shifty-eyed and dishonest. His own distrustful attitudes, not to mention his despicable behavior, brought out well-deserved distrust and enmity on the part of others. Seeing enemies all around him, Richard Nixon made enemies aplenty.

Edgar, on the other hand, was paranoid. Not just a little, like Nixon; Edgar was a bona fide nut case, a paranoid schizophrenic. Edgar's enemies list was long indeed. He lived in a small rented apartment, and made ends meet with an annual allowance from his parents plus regular disability checks from the Veterans Administration. It was bad enough that he was convinced the FBI and Fidel Castro were both out to get him, and that malevolent foreign agents had implanted a radio receiver alongside his lungs, which proceeded to broadcast tempting—but bad—advice. Worse yet, Edgar even had conclusive proof that "they" were out to get him.

Case in point: Edgar hated going shopping, because he knew that his many enemies would take the opportunity to humiliate or assault him. But one day, he went anyhow (following, to his subsequent regret, the advice of his internal radio receiver). Sure enough, the carefully orchestrated plan began to unfold against him. Just as he wheeled his cart to the checkout stand, the clerk put up a "Closed" sign, forcing him to go to another line where "they" were waiting for him. They looked at him aggressively, trying to make him flinch, daring him to return his cans of food to the shelves from which he had defiantly plucked them. But Edgar had already steeled himself for the battle. He was mentally prepared. He manfully pretended not to notice. He even kept his cool—barely—when a young woman snuck in line ahead of him. But when a smirking, pimply-faced teenager brushed his grocery cart in a clear challenge to his adulthood and masculinity, Edgar could take it no longer. Verbal insults led to a fistfight, and Edgar ended up in the custody of the local police— and subsequently, as a psychiatric patient.

Edgar argued that he didn't need help, except perhaps in fending off his numerous and powerful enemies. And to some extent, he was correct: For some reason, he was no longer especially welcome at the local grocery store. His landlord began to wonder about this guy who regularly got himself arrested. Yes, people really did start looking at him "funny." Once again we see that even paranoids have enemies: real enemies. But they also follow a self-fulfilling prophecy, whereby they create (or at least, intensify) precisely what they most fear.

Edgar saw things differently, however. Anyone could see, he insisted, that he had gone, innocent as can be, to buy some groceries, only to be set upon by the forces of evil, a fiendishly well-organized anti-Edgar coalition, carefully planned and carried out, from the checkout clerk who diverted him to the prearranged line, to the provocative line-cutter, to the teenager who delivered the *coup de grâce*. It was all their fault. They were out to get him. He wasn't crazy. He had done nothing wrong. He may be tricky, but he certainly was not a crook.

"Imagine the vanity," wrote St. Augustine, "of thinking that your enemy can do you as much harm as your enmity." This saintly observation merits a closer look. Augustine is saying that the *perception* of having enemies—one's personal, psychic state of enmity—can be no less damaging than whatever harm those actual enemies can inflict. Presumably, this is because Christ told us to love our enemies; if, instead, we give ourselves over to hatred and enmity, we make a mockery of God's love. (While also, perhaps, making it that much less likely that we will ourselves be admitted into heaven, where presumably no one has any enemies.)

Augustine also used the term "vanity," suggesting that it is not only inaccurate but also self-serving to think that any of us is immune to the corrosive effects of enmity. He might also have suggested that enmity does not take place in a vacuum; hence, by behaving as though we have enemies, we are likely creating more of them in the process. From the Sorcerer's Apprentice through Richard Nixon to Edgar the full-blown paranoid, much in human experience would suggest that Augustine was on the mark.

It happens on the societal scale no less than the personal. For example, paranoia as a self-fulfilling prophecy has been especially potent in what used to be Yugoslavia. Overheated nationalist rhetoric was added to old-fashioned demagoguery to inflame fears and hatreds on all sides. Then, with the grisly process of "ethnic cleansing"— notably of Bosnian Muslims by Bosnian Serbs—the situation became increasingly resistant to solution. After having been told that they couldn't possibly live with the Muslims (despite the fact that, in fact, they had done so for centuries), Bosnian Serbs proceeded forcibly to evict, imprison, torture, rape, and murder their Muslim countrymen. As a result, should anyone really be surprised that these same Serbs now claim that, indeed, they couldn't possibly live with the traumatized and presumably vengeful Muslims who survived the carnage? There is no evidence prior to the recent Yugoslav fighting and atrocities that Serb, Croat, and Muslim could *not* have coexisted, and lots of evidence that they could.[13] But having responded violently to their leaders' trumped up claims of eternal enmity, there may finally be some justification to the pervasive fear that "Yugoslavians" really can no longer live peacefully with each other.

One of the points of this book is that the enemy system is a continuous thread connecting biological processes on one extreme to international affairs on the other, in the process running through interpersonal behavior and social patterns. Let us therefore turn back now to interpersonal behavior, looking for how family dynamics plays into the creation of enemies. We shall examine two phenomena that have recently attracted considerable attention from psychotherapists: first, codependency, and then, triangulation.

Codependent, Coenemy

It was time for them to leave. In fact, it was nearly a half-hour late, but it could as well have been three in the morning because Cindy could tell that they weren't going to make it, or that if they did, they'd regret it. Bob, it seems, was already drunk. Again. Not falling-down, blacking-out, throwing-up drunk, just inebriated enough that he couldn't be trusted to drive, although he would surely insist otherwise. As dinner parties go, this wasn't all that important, but Bob's supervisor and his wife would be there, as well as some new clients.

Cindy sighed, cursed softly, undid her pearl necklace, then made yet another phone call of the sort that she did so often and so well. This time she explained, with mock exasperation, how their favorite babysitter had backed out at the last minute: You know how teenagers are, must have suddenly been asked to a movie, and so forth.

Bob wobbled past, mumbled something about Cindy being a wonderful woman, gave up trying to master his necktie, and lay back gratefully on the bed.

Cindy told herself that she didn't complain much. After all, Bob was a good man and a loving husband, a devoted father (when he was home and sober), and a more than adequate provider. His drinking was nothing new, and besides, she had become an expert at covering for him. (She had gotten a laugh when Donald Regan, then Chief of Staff for President Ronald Reagan, described the job of correcting Mr. Reagan's misstatements as being like the crew that follows after the elephants in the parade, cleaning up with shovels and brooms. Cindy sometimes spoke of herself—although perhaps with as much bitterness as pride—as a "one-woman shovel brigade.")

She had recently confided to her mother that she didn't know how much longer she could take it. "But, if I left him, what would I do then?" she followed up, immediately. "How could I live without him? It would be awful for the kids. And what about Bob? He'd just fall apart." In fact, her life wasn't the "hell on earth" that her mother insistently proclaimed it, although it was far from heavenly.

It wasn't Bob's fault. Cindy was sure of that. He wasn't the enemy. Just like the self-help, pop-psych advice-givers say, you can love the person while hating the behavior. That was it: Bob wasn't the enemy. His drinking was. Cindy even knew why Bob drank: because his work was so stressful. They had even talked about Bob getting some counselling or treatment, but Cindy had been reluctant to push too hard, recounting the joke: "How many psychiatrists does it take to change a light bulb?" "Only one, but the light bulb has to want to change!"

Then, one Sunday morning when he woke with a headache so severe that he couldn't bring himself to help coach his daughter's soccer game, the light finally went on. Bob decided that he really did have a problem and that he'd better get serious about overcoming it. He also announced, as though it suddenly occurred to him for the first time, that he would need some professional help in doing so. Cindy was elated, or so she seemed. Together, they looked over the various options, and decided to see the therapist their doctor had recommended several years before. Bob also started attending AA meetings.

Cindy found herself doing a whole lot less shovelling. She spent more time with Bob in the evenings, and she noticed that he was much more involved with the children, especially on weekends. She had much less to complain about now. Bob was more energetic and healthier than ever. He was even a better lover, certainly a more available one. She began to wonder what she would do with her spare time, particularly now that Bob regularly took their daughter Becky to Campfire Girl meetings, and he was more successful than ever at work. She told herself this was an opportunity. Maybe she would take an aerobics class. She told her best friend that now with Bob no longer drinking, a heavy weight had been lifted from her shoulders. Maybe she would take up gardening. She told her mother that perhaps she would go back to school and finish her master's degree in music, just like she had always said she yearned to do. (Although of course, it was a long way to the university, and deep down, she wasn't sure she really wanted to compete with all those young, disgustingly talented, eager-beaver graduate students, and, well, it was also expensive.) She told Bob how proud she was of him. But she found herself feeling empty and even a bit lonely. She didn't go back to school or start aerobics or take up gardening. She even told Bob that he was so far recovered, he owed it to himself to have a drink or two after he got home, especially if it had been a really hard day, and not to worry if things went too far, because she, Cindy the wonder woman, could take care of everything. After all, he must remember, once upon a time she had been real good at cleaning up.

Why did Cindy find herself sabotaging her husband's efforts to cure his alcoholism? Cindy is increasingly well known to mental health professionals and the public alike: a codependent. The concept of codependency derives from advances in the treatment of drug abusers, especially alcoholics, and particularly from the recognition that often it is not only the identified abuser who is ill. His or her family is frequently part of the problem because of their own tolerance of the misbehavior, a tolerance that masks a tendency to have their own needs met through someone else.

The concept of codependency has been extended to cover a range of pathologies found among people who are deeply enmeshed in relationships with abusive, exploitative, or incompetent Others. The codependent individual hopes to obtain approval from this Other, or from the rest of the family, or from society, as a way of generating a sense of personal worth and identity. People with a codependent personality experience a loss of selfhood from focusing so completely on the needs and behavior of someone else. (Not surprisingly, in a society that encourages men to be assertive and women to be passive, codependents are typically women.)

Codependents have the disconcerting habit of living via someone else. In the lingo of today's teenagers, they need to "get a life."

Codependents such as Cindy are often very good at covering up for the Other, the "dependent": so good, in fact, that they frequently act as "enablers," helping dysfunctional people to remain dysfunctional, especially through heavy use of denial: "Who, Bob? He doesn't really have a problem. He's just under a lot of stress."

Later, we shall consider an extreme example of enemy-awareness, to be called the Ahab syndrome, after the fictional, obsessive sea captain whose life was defined by his obsession with his enemy. The codependent is the mirror image of such people, a kind of anti-Ahab, allowing herself to be eaten alive by the whale—first a foot, then a knee, then the thigh—all the while protesting that deep down inside, the leviathan really is a most fine, admirable, and gentle creature. Codependency is, in a sense, an inability to recognize an enemy. If the Ahabs among us need to be less self-involved, less obsessed with identifying, then avenging any slight to their honor or well-being, the codependent needs, if anything, a hefty dose of enlightened self-interest, a clearer sense of boundaries between Self and Other. Whereas Ahabs wreak havoc by pursuing their whales, often to the point of mutual destruction, the codependent—by enabling and thus unintentionally encouraging the dependent's hurtful behavior—permits the whale to go on destroying its victim, and often the codependent as well.

For both the extreme hater and the codependent, the relationship is everything: negative on the one hand, supportive on the other, but intense, encompassing, and oddly self-effacing either way. And whereas neither hater nor codependent can be healthy so long as he or she is so overinvolved with the Other, both are equally likely to experience separation as very difficult if not traumatic, since for both, to abandon the enemy is also to be abandoned one's self.

Having an enemy may be a lousy excuse for a relationship, but at least it *is* a relationship. E. M. Forster urged, "Only connect!" and this, more than anything else, may be precisely what real-life Ahabs, paranoids, and their codependent counterparts are achieving. Having an enemy may be a way of fending off a bleak, existential loneliness. The expression goes: Better the devil we know than the one we don't. The deeper reality may be: Better anyone—even a devil—than no one at all. In short, better to be enemies than strangers. Say what we will, at least Ahab connected with Moby Dick and Richard Nixon—in a sense—connected with his opponents. To be sure, such connections can be malignant—based on spurious blame, unreasonable rigidity; and often a self-serving blend of egocentrism, paranoia, and delusion—but at least they occur. Cindy's reality came through her codependency with Bob, a pathology that interfered with her ability to identify the real enemy, and that kept her from being her own best friend.

The Infernal Triangle

In geometry, a triangle is a stable structure. Connect four pieces from an erector set to make a square or rectangle, and the whole mess could easily slip into a parallelogram with an infinite number of possible angles and combinations. Try the same thing with a triangle, on the other hand, and only one possibility is available. Triangles don't give. For this reason, triangular bracing is often used to stabilize a bridge or a building. Perhaps there is an analogy in our own behavior as well, because some people also use human triangles to stabilize their interpersonal relationships.

This does not apply so much to the "eternal triangle," in particular, an extramarital affair, which in most cases leads ultimately to destabilization, but rather to what psychologists and psychiatrists refer to as "triangulation," in which a third person (often an "enemy") is used to help stabilize conflict between two others.

Take the situation of Michael and Sarah Kaufman. They had been married for twelve years, with two children, Mark and Brandon.

Mark was ten, a bit shy but a good student and an enthusiastic athlete, basically happy and healthy. Brandon, age seven, was also doing well in his life, except that he wasn't happy at school. His teachers complained that he didn't seem to concentrate very well, although a professional evaluation revealed no organic problems. He often experienced difficulty playing by himself, and would get into trouble after picking fights with his classmates.

It turned out that Michael, Brandon's father, was generally difficult to please, and had very high expectations for his two boys, especially Brandon. Michael would typically go over Brandon's school work with a sharp eye for every mistake, and a seeming blind spot for every accomplishment. Brandon had taken to hiding his work and especially his report cards, sometimes throwing them away before getting home (even though both his work and his grades were generally above average).

The Kaufmans sought counseling for their younger son. It quickly turned out that Michael—Brandon's father—was frustrated and disappointed in his own career (he was a high school science teacher), feeling that he ought to have gone to medical school instead. Michael's mother, in particular, had groomed him to be her "special boy," and although he had difficulty admitting it, the adult Michael knew that he had let her down, and he cringed before that fact almost as much as he resented her unrelenting pressure upon him.

After several weeks of family therapy, it also came out that Sarah, Brandon's mother, harbored immense anger against her father, who had abandoned young Sarah and her mother nearly thirty years before. Sarah began to question her relationships to men; her sexual life with her husband, Michael, became increasingly burdensome. More and more, Sarah found herself "going away" during sexual intercourse, making grocery lists or worrying about the condition of the driveway while looking increasingly askance at Michael's ardor, which seemed foreign and disconnected to her own feelings. As the distance between

Sarah and her husband increased, for reasons that Sarah herself did not identify at the time, she had become ever more involved with Brandon, fussing for hours about his hair, whether he was clean, whether he had eaten enough of the right foods, whether he loved her. The colder, the more distant and formal her relationship with Michael became, the more Sarah lavished praise and attention upon Brandon, who in her eyes could do no wrong and—not surprisingly— was growing downright swell-headed with his mother's smothering indulgence, just as he was becoming ever more fearful and avoidant of his father.

Human relationships are rarely clean and simple. But as it turned out, the case of Michael, Sarah, and Brandon was relatively straight-forward. Unknown to themselves, both Sarah and Michael had been bearing some heavy burdens, and they both had some unfinished emotional work to do: with themselves and with each other—but not directly with Brandon. Sarah needed to revisit her past, clarify what had happened and why, and connect with her own selfhood as well as her feelings about men. (Not boys, mind you, but men.) Michael needed to accept himself for who and what he was, and to ask himself whether in fact he wanted to contemplate a career change and how important it was for him to please others (not whether Brandon would become a disappointment, or a doctor—or both—but whether he, Michael, would). Beyond this, each needed to connect with the other, to confront their shared and separate hurts and disappointments— the realistic ones as well as those that were excessive—and also, not least, to reconnect with their mutual love. Sarah, for example, needed to assure herself on a feeling level, as opposed to a merely rational level, that Michael wasn't her abandoning father, and Michael needed to satisfy himself that Sarah wasn't his disapproving mother. Both of them needed to acknowledge, clearly, that little Brandon Kaufman was a small developing person in his own right and not in any legitimate sense the vehicle of their angers, needs, or fears.

Even when things had been tense and uncomfortable in this family, Brandon had never been anyone's "enemy." But he had provided a third point to their triangle, someone who Michael and Sarah could use—unintentionally, but with effect—as a substitute for dealing with each other. The family now appears poised to live happily ever after, but not without some fireworks and genuine conflict, partly because in their earlier phase, Brandon had provided the temporary stability for which triangles are so justly renowned. As they came to confront their own issues and each other, not through Brandon but through self-awareness and direct communication, old angers erupted and feelings were hurt. The triangle became a straight line, with an adult at each end, a rotating, shifting, volatile structure that was obliged to expand, contract, twist, and turn with the full force of each other's personality and emotions, no longer diverted or diluted by Brandon.

It even looked for a time as though Sarah and Michael might divorce. But the crisis passed and with it a period of discomfort in the lives of all three. (In the case of Brandon's parents, it was a long-standing although unrecognized discomfort borne by each of them, that predated his very existence, and even their marriage.) As to that marriage, it now appears to be solid, deepened, and strengthened by their new-found, growing ability to share with each other. Brandon, no longer the intersecting apex of his parents' triangle, seems to have gained a more stable perception of his own role in a now-healthy family and in the world beyond.

Bulldogs and Red Devils

In the last chapter, we concluded our tour through the biology of enemies by briefly considering a bit of developmental psychology, namely the appearance of stranger anxiety. Now, we segue from psychology into our next topic—the enemy system in society at large

—by considering a notable example of the social psychology of enemies.

Talk about the rigors of field research! More than thirty years ago, M. Sherif and his colleagues journeyed to one of the most mysterious and frightening outposts of the American psychic wilderness, indeed, to its veritable Heart of Darkness: a Boy Scout summer camp. There they conducted a study in the social psychology of enemy-making that has emerged as a modern classic.[14]

The intrepid researchers descended upon a population of unsuspecting, normal, apparently well-adjusted twelve-year-old boys who were randomly assigned to one of two groups, the Bulldogs and the Red Devils. Members of each group were induced to cooperate by giving them shared tasks, such as building a rope bridge, cooking meals together, making a diving board, and so forth. The result, not surprisingly, was a strong feeling of cohesiveness within each group. Bulldogs were proud to be Bulldogs and Red Devils felt similarly about other Red Devils. So far so good. Within each group, the boys seemed, if anything, to be closer friends than before, and there was, as yet, no particular antagonism between the two groups.

Then, the researchers began creating situations of conflict. First, they arranged a series of athletic competitions, including tug-of-war, baseball, and football. All of these were zero-sum games in which prizes went only to the winning team. Red Devils and Bulldogs began to show some hostility toward each other. Then the researchers upped the ante by some diabolical stratagems. For example, they organized a party for all the scouts, at which the food consisted of two very different kinds: some of it was delicious and thoroughly appetizing (better than the usual camp fare), while the rest was ugly, squashed, and altogether unappealing (even worse than normal camp food). In addition, things were arranged so that the Red Devils arrived quite a bit before the Bulldogs.

First come, first served, reasoned the Red Devils, who had eaten or otherwise confiscated virtually all of the desirable food by the time the Bulldogs arrived. The Bulldogs, in turn, were more than a little peeved when they discovered what had happened. First came name-calling, then a food-fight, then in just a matter of minutes, a virtual riot: hungry and embittered Bulldogs versus self-righteous Red Devils.

Somewhat taken aback by the intensity of the hostility they had unleashed (or "created," depending on one's philosophy of human aggression), the investigators then looked into what could be done to reconcile the two warring factions. They increased the amount of peaceful social contact between Red Devils and Bulldogs, providing movies, for example, for all to watch together. Movie-time was even made contingent upon good behavior between the sides. (Remember, this was during the 1950s and thus well before the advent of VCRs, when movie-watching was still a comparatively rare and special treat.) Competitive games were also eliminated altogether. But if anything, hostility continued to escalate. Red Devils and Bulldogs seemed to be warring tribes, or hostile nations, as though they had always been enemies and would remain so forever. It was easy to forget that just a few weeks before the boys had been arbitrarily divided into the two groups, at which time no enmity whatever had separated them.

Eventually, things were turned around, and not because of lectures from disapproving adults or the punishing of troublemakers. What worked, at last, was when the investigators created situations in which Red Devils and Bulldogs became interdependent, in which they were forced to cooperate in order to achieve a common goal. The camp's water-supply system mysteriously failed, and everyone had to pitch in to repair it. Then, when the kids were on a field trip, the bus broke down and had to be pulled up a steep hill; in fact, the only way to get it going again was for all the boys—Bulldogs and Red Devils, regardless of affiliation—to pull together, literally. Pull together they did, and in the process, good humor and friendships were reestablished. Enmity receded. Peace prevailed at last (or at least, for the rest of the summer).

*　　*　　*

From the Charlie Chaplin look-alike contest, through Hoffman's Law, projection, paranoia, codependency, infernal triangles, and the Bulldogs and Red Devils, it seems clear that the psychology of our enemy system is inextricably linked to the bigger picture; that is, to society as a whole, just as the biology of enemies necessarily connects to our psychology. In the next chapter, therefore, we look at enemies in wider context.

Notes

1. Erik H. Erikson, "Ontogeny of Ritualization," in *Psychoanalysis: A General Psychology*, eds. R. M. Lowenstein, L. M. Newman, M. Schur, and A. Solnit (New York: International Universities Press, 1966).

2. Clifford Geertz, *The Interpretation of Cultures* (New York: Basic Books, 1973).

3. Sigmund Freud, *The Taboo of Virginity*, Standard Edition of the *Complete Psychological Works of Sigmund Freud* (London, England: Hogarth Press, 1917).

4. Vamik D. Volkan, *The Need to Have Enemies and Allies* (Northvale, N.J.: Jason Aronson, 1973).

5. Just as previously, for a time, he had pitched for the Cleveland Indians, who, after losing the 1954 World Series in four straight games to my beloved Giants, I viewed as basically a Giants farm team.

6. C. P. Cavafy, *Collected Poems*, ed. George Savidis, trans. E. Keeley and P. Sherrard (Princeton, N.J.: Princeton University Press, 1975).

7. Aleksandr Solzhenitsyn, *The Gulag Archipelago 1918–1956* (New York: Harper & Row, 1973).

8. Aeschylus, *Prometheus Bound*, trans. Rex Warner (New York: New York Heritage Press, 1966).

9. Ernest Becker, *The Denial of Death* (New York: Free Press, 1973).

10. John Dollard, N. E. Miller, O. H. Mowrer, G. H. Sears, and R. R. Sears, *Frustration and Aggression* (New Haven, Conn.: Yale University Press, 1939).

11. Eva Hoffman, *Lost in Translation* (New York: Penguin, 1989).

12. Another interesting coincidence: after World War II, and before the "Department of Defense" was born, the U.S. Army was officially known as the National Military Entity, or NME for short.

13. Certainly, Croats and Serbs killed one another during the Second World War, and on and off before that, but antagonisms of this sort have in fact characterized many people who end up coexisting. Prior to the carnage of the 1990s, the city of Sarajevo was a notable example of multi-ethnic harmony.

14. Muzafer Sherif, O. J. Harvey, B. Jack White, William Hood, and Carolyn Sherif, *Intergroup Conflict and Cooperation: The Robbers Cave Experiment* (Norman, Okla.: University of Oklahoma Institute of Intergroup Relations, 1961).

4

Sociology

How is our social life like an iceberg? Because most of it lies below the surface (and also because sometimes, when we least suspect it, there may be a sudden shift in the center of gravity, turning the whole thing upside down). There is usually much more to our behavior—especially the complex patterns of modern society—than meets the eye. The renowned evolutionary biologist J. B. S. Haldane once commented that life is not only stranger than we imagine, it is probably even stranger than we *can* imagine. Social life is especially like that, consisting of far more than we know, perhaps more than we *want* to know. Maybe more, even, than we *can* know. Take our most lurid fantasies and dreams, our wildest imaginings about our inclinations for love, togetherness, cooperation, aggressiveness, or sex, and we will probably find that the real truth is even stranger, wilder, more secret, and, in some ways, less knowable. Included is our penchant for enemies.

What we say in such cases is not always what we mean, or what is true. Nations like to claim, for example, that their enemies are thrust upon them, Job-like afflictions that arise through no fault of their own, and that force them—against the inclinations and wishes of their deeper, better selves—to gird up their loins and do battle, whether through economic means, political pressure, the mobilization of propaganda, or outright violence. In any event, we tell ourselves, sadly but resignedly, that our enemies demand of us a kind of grim determination, that it may be a messy, unpleasant duty, but that our enemies leave us no alternative.

Whatever discomfort we may experience identifying and confronting our enemies, we may feel as much if not more discomfort admitting that we often derive a substantial "secondary gain" in the process. And this applies to the collective "we" no less than the personal "me." At the level of society, having enemies isn't all bad.

Social Theory and Conflict Theory

Many social theorists, notably Talcott Parsons,[1] have maintained that conflict is fundamentally aberrant, since the primary, defining characteristic of society is the integration of parts into a cohesive whole. Others have not been so sure. Thus, a group of Central European sociologists, doing their most important work around the turn of the century, attributed great importance to conflict. For example, Ludwik Gumplowicz (1838–1909), a Pole living in Austria, maintained that the state was itself born of conflict, when different social and genetic groupings expanded and encountered each other, the victor incorporating the vanquished into the newly emerging whole. As a result, external conflict is transformed into internal conflict, as the constituent ethnic groups continue to oppose each other. At about the same time, fellow Austrian Gustav Ratzenhofer (1842–1904) emphasized that self-interest often resulted in conflict and animosity. He added that personal hostilities are typically overcome by positive bonds, resulting from kin ties and other shared interests.

But of the conflict theorists, it was the German Georg Simmel (1858–1918) who first treated conflict and the importance of enemies in its own right, suggesting, in effect, that conflict can indicate cohesion because only stable relationships are likely to allow hostility to be expressed as conflict. Simmel, along with the American Lewis Coser, went farther yet, emphasizing some of the subsurface benefits of having enemies, and pointing out, for example, that social conflict can actually knit societies together. This paradoxical, unifying effect of enmity derives from the simple luxury of taking sides, as in the universal childhood ritual of choosing teams. Even when the fourth-grader knows that his or her team has only a temporary life span, perhaps only a season or maybe even just an hour or so, there is pleasure in the clarity of union *with* one's team-mates, and, at least as important, *against* the other team.

At the level of adult society, interaction, even hostile interaction, often yields stability, so long as the patterns are crisscrossing and do not tend repeatedly to fracture at the same places. Thus, for example, there may be conflict between employees and management in a local business, but members of both groups might attend the same church, the members of which are joined in theological conflict— not to mention a softball rivalry—with those of a different denomination. The local soccer team may bring together parents who are both Democrats and Republicans, in competition with another soccer team, which also numbers Democrats and Republicans in its cheering section. It may seem paradoxical, but society can thus be "sewn together by its inner conflicts."[2] Enemies and allies are the warp and woof of our social fabric, as the shuttle spins and flashes through the diverse and shifting connections of modern life.

According to Emile Durkheim, one of the founders of modern sociology, even crime can be a unifying factor: "Crime brings together upright consciences and concentrates them."[3] There is nothing like having a robbery or mugging in the neighborhood to make everyone aware of the norms of proper and acceptable conduct. (It is also possible, on the other hand, for illegal behavior to become so common—as with drug-dealing in certain neighborhoods—that it becomes the established norm.) According to Durkheim, even crime is "a factor in public health, an integral part of all healthy societies"[4]— presumably, so long as it is not too integral.

Other, more benign forms of conflict within society can function similarly. Consider regional rivalries, political parties, religious affiliations, or semi-exclusive organizations such as the Elks, the Eagles, or the Shriners. Mild conflict among these groups can reinforce the notion that those on the same side share something important. Common enemies help congeal a common identity. As Lewis Coser puts it, they are made "aware that they belong to the same moral universe."[5]

It matters little whether they really do, whether they are members of what Kurt Vonnegut dubbed a "kavass," a group of people who are meaningfully connected, or a "gran falloon," whose connectedness is artificial and forced. Enemies—be they criminals, or simply law-abiding "others"—provide a kind of safety valve, a socially sanctioned opportunity to let off steam, to do so in the company of others, and with the added emotional lubrication of cheers and mutual approval (combined with Bronx cheers and disapproval directed outward). Just as the details don't much matter, it seems equally irrelevant whether this "steam" is thought of as "action specific energy" à la Konrad Lorenz, unexpressed libidinal drives à la Sigmund Freud, or the "unavoidable antagonism that springs from class consciousness" à la Karl Marx. The result is what really counts.

One of the most important of those results is the unity that comes from having a shared opponent.

In Enmity, Strength?

Social life does not always take place beneath sunny skies, and, ironically, it is precisely this turbulence of the social atmosphere that gives particular value to the additional unruliness that social conflict provides. When people live together—within a household or a nation—it is simply unavoidable that there are occasional sudden squalls and tornadoes, as well as widespread disturbances that might grow into full-fledged hurricanes. At such times of particular tension and animosity, as Shakespeare's King John put it, "So foul a sky clears not without a storm." When social relationships have become grim and confrontational, and especially when the possibility of violence looms on the horizon like a threatening cloud, an enemy can be a much-needed lightning rod; just like a real lightning rod, enemies can drain away energy that might otherwise be destructive.

But a good enemy does even more. It not only provides a convenient outlet for aggression and antagonism, it also draws the members of a group closer together, in the course of making "common cause" and putting up a "common front." In the last chapter, we reviewed the case of the Bulldogs and the Red Devils, focussing on the unpleasantness that arose between these two groups. Less intriguing, perhaps, but no less true, was the relative serenity and good feeling that characterized within-group relationships. Bulldogs got along well with other Bulldogs, and Red Devils felt secure, connected and protected in their bonds with other Red Devils.[6]

In unity is strength, we are told. But there is something else, less often told, but every bit as true: In enmity, there is unity. Hence, in enmity there is strength.

Psychiatrist C. A. Pinderhughes, in a series of technical papers,[7] argued that people experience what he called "differential paired bonding," in which they orient to external events in a surprisingly simple, dichotomous way. Stimuli are perceived to be of one sort or the other, either good or bad, helpful or harmful, friend or enemy, and accordingly, they evoke either affectionate or aggressive responses. Those who share an aggressive aversion to "common renounced targets," according to Pinderhughes, also share the same positive, "affectionate connections." Thus, the presence of an out-group helps provide the social glue that makes for stronger bonding among those who are "in." Just as a fish is unlikely to think of its natural environment as "wet," it would quickly become meaningless for Bulldogs to identify themselves as such if there were no Red Devils—or Dachshunds— nearby. (It is not strictly necessary, incidentally, that the competing groups occur within the same camp: Other rival camps often provide comparable out-groups for each other. What is required is for the groups to interact often enough in zero-sum game situations to stimulate each other's animosity, thereby confirming their own identity.)

In the real world, such opportunities present themselves on a regular basis, and despite the suffering that frequently results, groups typically profit from the encounter. The medieval Catholic Church, for example, was strengthened, doctrinally and organizationally, by its battles with the various medieval heresies—Manichean, Gnostic, Albigensian—as well as by its later struggles with Protestantism. Even before Christianity, God established a covenant with his Chosen People based on the powerful bond of shared enmity: "If thou wilt indeed obey, then I will be an enemy unto thine enemies and an adversary unto thine adversaries" (Exodus 23: 22). A potent offer, this, and one that leaves it unclear which came first: whether the authority of God was enlisted to encourage the development of potent friend/enemy dichotomies among the ancient Israelites, or if God's authority was established in part *because* of his proferred aid in overcoming enemies that already existed. Either way, God is Friend and Other is Enemy, and in the process, the group feels not only protected but also more "together."

Islam, for its part, has also gained substantial coherence by its powerful doctrine of shared enmity. To many people raised in the Judeo-Christian tradition, there is a peculiar ring to the call of modern-day Islamic fundamentalists, beseeching the faithful to rise up and smite the various "enemies of God": Jews (in Israel), Communists (in Afghanistan), secular Arab governments (in Egypt), and so forth. To the non-Muslim, it can sound as though Allah is somehow too weak to stand up for Himself without a helping hand from a wide-eyed, bomb-throwing terrorist.

But in fact, Christianity may actually have originated the notion of "enemies of God," quite possibly seeking the same benefit later discovered by Islam, namely consolidation of its followers. Thus, with Christianity and the concept of God made flesh, there emerged a new realm of possibilities in which human beings could not only displease or disobey God (something found abundantly in the Old Testament), but, in a sense, actually kill him—or at least, his son. "Deicide" may sound oxymoronic to the modern ear, but if God has enemies, then we are merely acting on behalf of a greater good when we claim God's enemies as our own. There is nothing quite like the accusation of deicide to separate the Good from the Bad: the believers, followers, and disciples from the unbelievers, the heathen, and the Christ-killers.

Just as Christianity and Islam have made common cause with God, and in the process, fostered solidarity among their ranks, so has modern-day Israel. From a narrow-minded political perspective, there is a plus side to Israel's ongoing national insecurity. Despite its boisterous and sometimes cantankerous democracy, Israeli hostility from—and toward—the Arab world has produced an extraordinary unity of purpose within that small country. The reluctance of Israeli hard-liners to make peace with the Palestinians and ultimately with all Arabs may thus actually be due less to fear for Israeli military security than to apprehension at the chaos that might ensue if Israel loses its Arab opponents.[8] Peace with the Arabs would not only deprive Israel of much of its cohesion, it would also deprive the hard-line Likud party of much of its *raison d'être*, just as the collapse of Communism now threatens to dissolve the common purpose of the Republican party in the United States.

War as Unifier

Sociologists have long argued that war was fundamental to the rise of the modern centralized state[9] in two ways. First, it enabled groupings of otherwise disarticulated people to defend themselves and even enlarge their domain. And second, by identifying an external enemy, war helped generate the kind of internal solidarity that was needed if disparate groups were somehow to cohere into a larger whole. Max Weber's theory of the development of modern nation-states relies on the significance of replacing feudalism with centrally directed administrative systems, which in turn occurred because the capacity for military violence was concentrated in administrative hands. Power thus became centralized, in Weber's opinion, with war greasing the wheels of bureaucratic aggrandizement.

He was not alone in this assessment. "War does not always give over democratic communities to military government," wrote Alexis de Tocqueville, more than half a century before Weber,

> but it must invariably and immeasurably increase the powers of civil government; it must almost compulsorily concentrate the direction of all men and the management of all things in the hands of central administration.[10]

We are not concerned here simply with dry, theoretical points of technical emphasis or scholarly disputation, or with bureaucratic niceties having implications only for the paper-shufflers. This is the stuff of daily life. Listen to Winston Churchill commenting (not at all critically, incidentally) on the effects of World War I on the British home front:

> The former peace-time structure of society had been . . . superseded and life had been raised to a strange intensity by the war spell.

Under that mysterious influence, men and women had been appreciably exalted above death and pain and toil. Unities and comradeships had become possible between men and classes and nations and had grown stronger while the hostile pressure and the common cause endured.[11]

The crucial factor, however, does not seem to be war itself, but rather the singling out of an enemy, and the unity of purpose that results. One thing about being under siege is that everyone is in it together. (The same applies also to the besiegers, although less intensely.) Of course, outright war is not even required for this purpose: an agreed-upon enemy and an ensuing Cold War will generally do quite nicely, even if actual hostilities do not break out.

Asked why people tend to bond together, forming what social scientists call "positive reference groups," most of us would point to various positive, prosocial forces, such as being similar, sharing values or interests, or just plain liking each other. But a common enemy may be equally effective in causing us to unite. As Freud put it, "Hatred against a particular person or institution might operate in just the same unifying way, and might call up the same kind of emotional ties as positive attachment."[12]

Groups are always threatened by animosities among their members, but when these group members share a common enemy, such threats are lessened. More than four centuries ago, French political theorist Jean Bodin suggested that "the best way of preserving a state, and guaranteeing it against sedition, rebellion, and civil war is to keep the subjects in amity with one another, and to this end, to find an enemy against whom they can make common cause."[13] One and one-half millennia before Bodin, the renowned Greek orator Demosthenes argued that to end their constant wars, the Greek city-states would have to unite against a common enemy. His enemy of choice: Philip of Macedon, and the fiery, enemy-mongering speeches of Demosthenes became known as *The Philippics*.[14] To the present day, Demosthenes has his descendants: Any bitter, denunciatory rhetoric directed against an opponent is known as a Philippic, and it is a good guess that behind such discourse there lurks a desire to unite the listeners in shared hostility.

Shakespeare, too, was familiar with the concept of unity-through-enmity. As Henry IV lay dying, knowing that there would be intrigue and dissension regarding the line of royal succession, he advised his son as follows:

> Therefore, my Harry,
> Be it thy course to busy giddy minds
> With foreign quarrels. (*King Henry IV*, Part 2, Act 4, Scene 5)

Henry V, following this advice, raised an army and attacked France, thereby retaining his father's crown for himself.

But it is not only giddy minds who have been busied with foreign quarrels, in the hopes of quieting the quarrels at home. On the eve of the American Civil War, U.S. Secretary of State William Seward urged that President Lincoln consider declaring war on France and Spain, so as to unify the country and thereby preserve the Union.

And no less an arch-realist than Chancellor Bismarck, that wily and cynical architect of modern Germany, also pursued social unity through shared enmity. Unlike Seward, however, Bismarck was successful: After victoriously pursuing the Franco-Prussian War, Bismarck felt that his newly established nation-state of Germany might still be a bit shaky. After all, for hundreds of years, there had been no "Germany," but rather, the separate principalities of Prussia, Saxony, Westfalia, Hanover, Silesia, and so forth. Thus, fear of centrifugality—in which the various national groups might fly apart from the center—was one reason why Bismarck insisted on taking the French provinces of Alsace and Loraine, precisely because the Iron Chancellor knew that the loss of these regions would guarantee French hostility, thereby assuring that if nothing else, the new German state would at least be France's enemy. In turn, being the recipient of shared hostility would assure German unity.

Writing around this time, Friedrich Nietzsche gave voice to Bismarck's philosophy that war served to unite the populace:

> Our spiritualization of hostility . . . consists in a profound appreciation of having enemies. . . . A new creation—the new Reich, for example, needs enemies more than friends: in opposition alone does it feel itself necessary.[15]

Germany lived up to Bismarck's hopes and Nietzsche's expectations. It really did become France's enemy and, moreover, it remained united. It is very likely, although not strictly provable, that the former contributed to the latter. But even if the entire thing had been made up out of whole cloth, if Germany had not annexed Alsace and Loraine but had simply generated the *appearance* of enmity, the effect on group cohesion would have been the same. There is an important theorem in sociology, which states that "if people define their situations as real, they are real in their consequences." Commenting on the utility of enemies, sociologist Lewis Coser notes:

> If people define a threat as real, although there may be little or nothing in reality to justify this belief, the threat is real in its consequences—and among these consequences is the increase of group cohesion.[16]

The greater the potential for splintering and individuality, the greater the need for a common enemy if unity is to be preserved. French President Charles De Gaulle put it well for his countrymen in a 1951 speech in which he said, "No one can simply bring together a country that has 265 different kinds of cheese." De Gaulle's conclusion: "The French will only be united under the threat of danger."

The threat of danger in general, and of war in particular, exerts great unifying power, in our imaginations no less than our shared history. In George Orwell's *1984*, the world was divided into three mega-states, which constantly made war upon each other, not to win, but to preserve internal cohesion:

> The war, therefore, if we judge it by the standards of previous wars, is merely an imposture. It is like the battles between certain ruminant animals whose horns are set at such an angle that they are incapable of hurting one another. But though it is unreal it is not meaningless. It eats up the surplus of consumable goods, and it helps to preserve the special mental atmosphere that a hierarchical society needs. . . . [T]he war is waged by each ruling group against its own subjects, and the object of the war is not to make or prevent conquests of territory, but to keep the structure of society intact.[17]

The Role of "Basic Consensus"

Comedian Groucho Marx once said that he wouldn't pay good money to become a member of any club that would let him in. Similarly, we might think that any society that requires war in order to keep its internal structure intact hardly deserves to continue. If, as Samuel Johnson maintained, patriotism is the last refuge of a scoundrel, perhaps shared enmity is the last refuge of a tattered and disintegrating society.

Not surprisingly, outer conflict doesn't invariably lead to inner cohesion. Especially if people are to some degree separated and alienated from each other before a conflict begins—that is, if the society is already tattered and disintegrating—they may fail to see the "common enemy" as one that everybody shares. If a group lacks what sociologists call "basic consensus" or "social solidarity," the stress of an external enemy may even fracture rather than unify it, particularly if the conflict erupts into outright war, and if that war is prolonged and/or costly. Enormous Russian casualties during World War I, for example, helped precipitate the Bolshevik Revolution of 1917, and popular resentment over the conduct of the Falklands War led to the downfall of the neofascist Argentine government of General Galtieri in 1982. Similarly, the defeat of Iraq in the Gulf War unleashed revolutionary fervor by anti-Saddam elements among Iraqi Shi'ites in the south as well as Kurds in the north. (On the other hand, the government of Ayatollah Khomeini in Iran was, if anything, strengthened by its earlier war with Iraq. The likelihood is that when the Iran-Iraq War began, Iran enjoyed more "basic consensus" than did Iraq at the onset of the Gulf War.)

Saddam Hussein's Kurdish and Shi'ite opponents failed, however, and not only because the United States and its allies did not follow through on their implied promise to aid the rebels. The Iraqi despot was a successful practitioner of the old policy of divide and conquer, successfully pursued over centuries by, for example, Great Britain in India and the Boers in South Africa. In such cases, power can be maintained (at least temporarily) by stirring up so much hatred and fear that the bubbling cauldron of resulting enmity makes it virtually impossible to mobilize effective, focussed opposition to the oppressor. "Saddam Hussein invents and reinvents his enemies from the entire mass of human materials that is at his disposal," wrote a prominent Arab intellectual, critical of his fellow Arabs' reluctance to acknowledge the cruelty of many current Arab regimes.

> He [Saddam] thrives on the distrust, suspicion, and conspiratorialism which his regime actively inculcates in everyone: he positively expects to breed hate and a thirst for revenge in Sunni and Shi'ite alike. As a consequence civil society, attacked from every direction, has

virtually collapsed in Iraq. . . . The fact that Iraqis are already competing with each other over who has suffered the most is a sign that whether or not Saddam is still around in person, what he represented lives on inside Iraqi hearts.[18]

When "basic consensus" is lacking, brutality—if sufficiently pervasive—can hold sway, sowing just enough disunity to perpetuate the brutalizers.

Stalin had blazed something of a trail for Saddam. But whereas the Iraqi people were given no credible enemy alternative to Saddam Hussein, Soviet citizens had to deal with none other than the original, genuine Hitler. Thus, the German attack on the USSR during World War II ultimately resulted in greater unity within the Soviet Union, when to some extent Hitler replaced Stalin as the object of widespread hatred. Prior to 1941, the "basic consensus" within the USSR had been so poorly established that large numbers of Ukranians, Latvians, Lithuanians, Estonians, and Georgians were initially eager to cooperate with the Nazis against their own Russian overlords. Hitler's national and racial prejudices, however, were so deep that he essentially rebuffed an opening that could have changed the outcome of that war. And so, even such a divided, resentful, and legitimately restive population as the Soviet Union remained largely loyal to Stalin when confronted with an even worse monster who pushed the people of that vast empire together even more than he tore them apart. Americans are not alone in rallying round their flag when it is threatened. Thus, it may also be significant that only by the final decade of the twentieth century, with neither Germany, the United States, nor China filling the role of credible enemy, did the Soviet "Union" cease to exist.

The Gulf War Revisited

Just before the 1990 mid-term elections, George Bush's popularity dropped substantially during prolonged autumn hassling over the federal budget; the president's stock rose, in turn, whenever he switched the subject to the perfidy of Iraq's Saddam Hussein. This led some commentators to wonder aloud whether the Bush administration was going to risk initiating a war in the Persian Gulf several months earlier than it actually did, just in time to rescue—not Kuwait but the Republican party, in advance of the 1990 mid-term election. (It wouldn't have been the first time that electoral pressures contributed to American military aggressiveness: The Kennedy administration, for instance, was all the more determined to face down the Soviets during the Cuban Missile Crisis because Soviet missiles in Cuba had been discovered just before another mid-term U.S. election, this one in 1962, the outcome of which would likely have been disastrous had JFK been humiliated by Khrushchev and Castro.)

Eventually, of course, there was a Gulf War, beginning just after the 1990 election. It is worth reflecting on this war, especially the stubborn U.S. insistence on a direct military confrontation with Saddam Hussein, even when many experts asserted that continued economic sanctions had a substantial chance of success, and with much less bloodshed. To cynics, peace advocates, and more than a few observers from other countries, it appeared that the U.S. leadership actually *wanted* war as a way of inducing Americans to feel better about themselves and about their leadership.

It is troublesome, but true, that the American people have never been so united as when they have been fighting someone else. World War II—the "good war"—brought us together as never before. The Gulf War brought about a similar, although far briefer, glow of unity and common purpose. Before that, the invasions of Grenada and Panama, even the brief bombing of Libya, engendered a transitory feeling of connectedness among our fellow citizens. To some extent, we had real enemies during those times. Certainly, we acted as though we did, fully consistent with the sociological principle of unity-through-enmity. All the while, the American people did very little to disappoint its government, which had done a bang-up job of creating ersatz enemies for our (and their) short-term benefit.

Beyond the sociological motivator of unity-through-enmity, however, there seems to have been another important factor operating behind the scenes at the onset of the Gulf War: the end of the Cold War. For one thing, it seems likely that if the United States and the Soviet Union had been geopolitical enemies when Iraq invaded Kuwait, the U.S. response would have been much less militant. Had the Soviets continued their previous alliance with the Iraqis, this in itself might well have made the United States and its Western allies more cautious. In this sense, however, the end of the Cold War simply *permitted* a strong military response to the Gulf crisis; it did not stimulate it. But a case can also be made that the end of the Cold War did more, that in fact the end of U.S.-Soviet enmity actually provided part of our motivation for war in the Gulf. Without the Soviets to confront and face down, without the Red Menace to justify a huge military budget, without another competing superpower to help ratify our own claim to super-status, there was a potential hollowness and emptiness in America's world posture, and precious few arguments in favor of spending $300 billion per year on the military. In this sense, Iraq's invasion of Kuwait was a godsend, an opportunity not to be squandered.

In making war on Iraq, George Bush did more than beat up an expansionist dictator, try once again to banish his personal wimp factor, liberate an emirate, and help make the world safe for his "new world order." He helped make the Pentagon safe from the much-feared "peace dividend," which had been looming on the horizon. He guaranteed that any subsequent efforts to demilitarize the U.S. economy would encounter warning cries of the potential for "future Iraqs." In short, the Gulf War helped insulate our warriors from the threat that they might lose their enemy.

The states of America were largely united during that brief and highly successful campaign against a shared enemy. Arabs, by contrast, were violently split by that same Gulf War. The governments of Saudi Arabia, the oil emirates, Egypt, Syria, and Morocco opposed Iraq (the latter two, not very vigorously), while Jordan, Yemen, Tunisia, Algeria, and the PLO expressed qualified support (also not very vigorously). It is correctly said that the first casualty in war is the truth. In this case, perhaps the second casualty was "Arab unity,"[19] and not only because some Arab states found themselves lined up in opposition to others. The Gulf War's deepest blow to Arab unity may well have come from Arab ambivalence toward their earlier enemies, the United States, Britain, France, and even Israel. Although not saviors (except in the eyes of Kuwaitis), these countries emerged from the Gulf War as less than full-fledged enemies to many Arabs.

Politics, it is said, creates strange bedfellows. War creates even stranger ones. The Japanese war against China during the 1930s and early 1940s, for example, generated a truce between the bitter rivals Mao Zedong and Chiang Kai-Shek, so that both could wage war against the invaders. After Iran viewed America as "the Great Satan" and America basically reciprocated, the United States tilted toward Iraq during the Iran-Iraq war, hoping to use the Iraqi state as a military counter-balance to Khomeini. But then, with the Iraqi invasion of Kuwait, we demonized Saddam Hussein and began to embrace another former Middle-Eastern "enemy," Syria and its dictatorial, terrorism-exporting, anti-Western leader, Hafez al-Assad.

Most significant for the light it sheds on the meaning of enemies, however, is the diplomatic dance that followed, involving the United States and USSR. Of all the various indications that the Cold War had ended—nuclear weapons treaties, exchange programs, military reductions, the liberation of Eastern Europe, warm smiles and hearty embraces—probably the most dramatic was the USSR joining the United States in condemning Iraqi aggression, and even approving the use of military force in response. Sometimes the most convincing sign of amity is a willingness to join in shared enmity.

Shared enmity, in fact, can even override plain old enmity, making instant friends where just before, antagonism had prevailed. Once again, the Persian Gulf crisis is a perfect example. Analysts worried—correctly, it turned out—that in the event of an attack on Iraq by the United States and its coalition of anti-Iraqi allies, Saddam Hussein would respond by attacking Israel (even though Israel wasn't part of the initial hostilities with Iraq). The method to Saddam's "madness" was as follows: Most of the other Arab states, despite their fear and, indeed, hatred of Saddam Hussein, despise and fear Israel even more. With Iraqis fighting Israelis, it would have been virtually impossible for Arab countries (even the "moderate" ones) to continue making war on Iraq because this would be to align themselves with Israel; the logic of shared enmity could have forced them to make peace with Bagdad, or even to join the Iraqis in a holy war against the hated "Zionist entity."

The Janus Face: Inclusion and Exclusion

Every society, almost by definition, is based on a fundamental inclusion and exclusion. Accordingly, the challenge for all societies—the United States as well—is to include its members but without excluding others to the point of generating hostility and aggression, to achieve the positive aspects of "differential paired bonding" without too great a differential. Early in American history, Protestant theology helped give rise to a society characterized by an unusual degree of equality and democracy. However, as University of California at Berkeley's Robert Bellah describes precolonial America, from the beginning that community was based on exclusion and repression—first, the intrapsychic repression of rejected impulse [Puritan attitudes toward sexuality, for example] and, second, the repression of those members of the society who represented those rejected impulses and had to be controlled and denied full membership. Originally this distinction was put in religious terms: the elect against the reprobates. Later . . . the distinction was between moral, upstanding members of the community and the lazy and recalcitrant. Finally, after the installation of the bitch goddess ["success," according to William James], it was a distinction between the successful and the failures.[20]

For many white Americans, blacks, Jews, and Communists emerged as proxy enemies for working out their deeper fears, as well as their need for making such distinctions.

Political ideologies of both the left and right have sought—often successfully—to profit from such shared exclusion and anger. Socialists and Communists, for example, long rallied their forces around the banner of "class consciousness" and "class struggle," while the right-wing "politics of resentment" have been especially evident as recently as the election campaigns of Richard Nixon, David Duke, and Patrick Buchanan. The greatest upset in modern U.S. political history was engineered by Harry Truman in 1948, when he railed against, and ran against, the Republican-controlled "do-nothing Congress," successfully painting Capitol Hill as the enemy. To some extent, Ronald Reagan also did this in 1980. Not surprisingly, George Bush, who ran effectively against "liberals" as well as African Americans (under the guise of Willie Horton) in 1988, added Congress to his enemies list as the 1992 reelection campaign began. Thus, during November, 1991, Bush's political strategy was described as follows by columnist Leslie Gelb:

"All he's got to do is to create an enemy, and that enemy is Congress," Charles Black, a Republican political consultant told me by way of explaining the strategy launched by Bush two weeks ago in Texas. "Even if the public doesn't like the president, they don't like Congress more," Black said. "He's got to become more confrontational."[21]

As we have seen, there are political benefits to be gained by adopting a confrontational, "us versus them" stance, so long as "they" are external enemies, and if they can readily be defeated—or, at least, if they are unlikely to win. As we have seen, however, such a stance can also be risky, if "they" are powerful, or if basic consensus within one's home society is inadequate. This is especially true for democracies, which rely ultimately on their own internal cohesiveness. In the 1992 presidential election, many Americans decided that George Bush and the Republican party had come to stand for a dangerous degree of exclusivity and divisiveness. Even though social cohesion can be enhanced by conflict, it can also be strained to the breaking point; this becomes especially dangerous if the country faces significant external enemies as well.

States are particularly vulnerable if their internal divisions have become so great that an outside threat is seen as a problem for others within the society—for "them"—rather than for a different, identified group, "us." Under such conditions, the addition of a new external enemy can cause the body politic to fracture rather than unite. As it happens, most countries are surprisingly resilient. During World War II, for example, and despite the racism they suffered at home, African Americans rejected Japanese propaganda attempts to establish a "yellow-black" coalition to oppose the "white" United States. African Americans stayed loyal to the United States even though in many ways the United States had been less than loyal to them.

On the other hand, many colonial people in Asia—Indonesian, Burmese, Vietnamese—feeling less than devoted to their European masters, were more receptive to Tokyo's blandishments about establishing a "greater east-Asia co-prosperity sphere" that would exclude Caucasians. Significant numbers of Indonesians, for example, saw the Japanese as their allies because Japan was making war on their Dutch occupiers. Similarly, many Burmese and Vietnamese were not drawn closer to British and French colonial forces, respectively, just because Japan had become an identified enemy of Britain and France.

During the late 1960s and early 1970s, the American people were bitterly divided by the Vietnam War. Despite the best efforts of both the Johnson and Nixon administrations, the Viet Cong and the North Vietnamese only caught on as deeply felt enemies for a limited segment of the American public. Many Americans instead came to see their own government as the enemy. This alienation led in turn to behavior that expressed their hostility and outrage at the conduct of that war. Such emblems as long hair, beads, drug use, draft card burning, and so forth, generated yet more alienation, especially between young Americans and their government as well as across generations.

Exclusion and inclusion are like hot branding irons. They can make useful long-lasting imprints, but they can also burn the hand that wields them.

Enemies as Enemies

Sigmund Freud was addicted to cigars. Even when he was dying, the founder of psychoanalysis and chief explorer of the unconscious insisted on having his cancer-ridden jaws propped open to accommodate a beloved stogie. When one of his students reproached him with the underlying phallic significance of his stubborn (and lethal) habit, Freud is reputed to have answered, "Sometimes a cigar is just a cigar."

The same thing applies to enemies: Sometimes an enemy is just an enemy. Period.

Many—perhaps most of us—are inclined to see enemies all over the place, even when they aren't there. As we saw in the last chapter, paranoia often figures into our enemy system, helping to create enemies even when they wouldn't otherwise exist. And as we have considered in this chapter, there are also social gains (and some risks) associated with our enemy system. But make no mistake about it: Enemies do exist. They are not simply figments of our fevered imaginations or creations of our social needs. But just as a cigar is never *just* a cigar, enemies are never *just* enemies. Even if their goals are modest and limited, more directed toward serving themselves than toward hurting us, enemies are likely to seem malicious and evil, at least in each other's eyes. Never mind that in most cases, our enemies are less focussed on us than we might assume, or fear, or secretly desire. Like a hungry mosquito, or even a man-eating tiger, our enemies— assuming now that they really *are* our enemies—typically want our blood, not our pain. Nothing personal, you understand. But most of us don't care to understand. We take "it"—the enmity—personally. After all, nature has designed things so that it usually hurts when someone else—by definition, an enemy—takes what we want, or sheds our blood.

Consider this example: To a large extent, Arabs and Israelis really have been enemies, at least insofar as the latter occupy land that some of the former (Palestinians) claim as their own. Even though it has long seemed that mutually acceptable solutions are possible, the posture of mutual Arab-Israeli enmity quickly translated itself into concrete acts of conflict and violence, after which it became increasingly "true." Israeli and Arab didn't have to be enemies, but once they decided that they were, both sides acted in ways that cemented their animosity. We have also considered how the behavior of Bosnian Serbs in particular has become a self-fulfilling prophecy for Muslim-Serb animosity.

Personal or not, real enemies almost always evoke some sort of response, whether fighting back, running away, or—much more rarely—turning the other cheek. These responses can be produced not only by the enemy itself but also by group members, for their own benefit, once a common enemy has been identified. Both Arab and Israeli leaders, for example, have long been able to count on enthusiastic followings when they criticized each other.

Whatever its ultimate origin—resource competition, malignant psychology, sociological syndrome—enmity can also be very real. Ask an Arab or Israeli, a Serb or Muslim. For all his sophisticated brilliance, Sigmund Freud was never more insightful than when he opined about the simplicity of cigars. Even as we consider the complexity of our enemy system, we had best remain aware of this brutal fact: Sometimes enemies exist, and not only in our imagination.

They exist, most especially, in specific personifications, in a Hitler, Stalin, Pol Pot, Fidel Castro, Slobodan Milosevic, the child molester, or the tax collector. The most recognizable enemy looks remarkably like ourselves.

A Human Face

There was a tradition in the ancient world of dealing with specifics and ignoring general rules or principles. In medical tracts from Pharaonic Egypt, for example, we find extensive rules and procedures detailing exactly what to do when a certain disease is present or after different kinds of injuries, but very little concern with underlying processes of health or illness. To the ancient Egyptians, an illness was just an illness—tetanus perhaps or pneumonia or typhus—and not exemplary of any more general phenomenon (such as the role of dietary deficiency or microbes in producing disease). With our supposedly greater sophistication, we look back at these curious omissions with a kind of patronizing bemusement. But on the subject of enemies, we have advanced but little over the pharaoh folk. Like ancient Egyptians missing the forests for the trees, we identify particular enemies—people, countries, ideologies—but we give very little attention to the larger question of what produces enemies, whether they are "just enemies" or something more (or less), and even less attention yet to what happens when they go away and how we are to make do without them.

Most of our enemies take a specific shape: Hitler, Stalin, Khrushchev, Brezhnev, Qaddafi, Khomeini, Castro, Saddam Hussein, Sauron from Tolkien's *Lord of the Rings,* the Wicked Witch from Oz, maybe the real-life jerk who lives down the street, or obnoxious Uncle Herbie. But we err, and grievously—like filling various bottles and jars with water in the hope of determining the shape of the water itself— if we think that by identifying particular enemies in this way we learn anything about enemies in general. Our penchant for enemies is such that they don't need a distinct shape in order to exist.

But having an identifiable shape certainly helps. In 1922 political commentator Walter Lippman introduced the term "stereotype" into modern discourse, by which he meant a rigid and biased perception of others, a kind of mental picture that we hold in our heads that "simplifies complex social reality to manageable, if false, proportions."[22] Often, such stereotypes also help the leader, since he (rarely, she) typically personifies not only the antagonism and enmity of a competing group, but also the shared positive association of the leader's own group. Shared national hostility not only tends to foster increased cohesion within the group, it also amplifies the importance of the group leader. Accordingly, whatever the costs of losing-the-enemy for a group member, these costs are even greater for the leader, because the value and importance of the leader is often intensified in a context of hostility toward others. Thus, Mikhail Gorbachev's decline in popularity within the crumbling Soviet state may ironically have been a partial result of his success in decreasing East-West tensions. For many in the former Soviet Union, communism and Communists became a greater enemy than the United States had ever been.

At the same time as we personify our enemies, we also typically amplify them. Political scientists have identified this process as the "Devil shift," whereby our enemies are characteristically seen as more powerful and more evil than they actually are.[23] This was especially true in our attitudes toward communism and the former Soviet Union. In the 1950s, Billy Graham edified his supporters with the following: "My own theory about communism is that it is masterminded by Satan. I think there is no other explanation for the tremendous gains of communism in which they seem to outwit us at every turn, unless they have supernatural power."[24]

And as the Reagan-era reincarnation of the Cold War was about to begin, Richard Nixon weighed in as follows:

It may seem melodramatic to say that the U.S. and Russia [sic] represent Good and Evil, Light and Darkness, God and the Devil. But if we think of it that way, it helps to clarify our perspective of the world struggle.[25]

We are all stuck in a difficult bind. When we have real enemies, we had better be alert to them. Certainly, it would be maladaptive— biologically, psychologically, sociologically—to ignore or underestimate them. Furthermore, we are most likely to picture our opponents in physical, human form, in part because they often exist in such form, and in part because a personalized enemy is more effective in motivating us. But at the same time, we open ourselves to an array of exaggerations and misperceptions.

Take, for example, this excerpt from *Octavius: A Pagan's View of Christian Practices,* written by one Minucius Felix, around 300 C.E.:

I am told that, moved by some foolish urge, they [Christians] consecrate and worship the head of a donkey, that most abject of all animals. This is a cult[26]] worthy of the customs from which it sprang! Others say that they reverence the genitals of the presiding priest himself, and adore them as though they were their father's. . . . As for the initiation of new members, the details are as disgusting as they are well known. A child, covered in dough to deceive the unwary is set before the would-be novice. The novice stabs the child to death with invisible blows; indeed he himself, deceived by the coating of dough, thinks his stabs harmless. Then—it's horrible!— they hungrily drink the child's blood, and compete with one another as they divide his limbs . . . Precisely the secrecy of this evil religion proves that all these things, or practically all, are true.[27]

Now, skip roughly a thousand years, for historian Edmund Leach's account of Christian attitudes toward the "pagan" Mongols, following a defeat of European forces by Batu Khan in 1241.

As soon as the Europeans had recovered from the shock of their defeat they turned to thoughts of reprisal. Pope Gregory IX preached a crusade against the Mongol terrorists. In order to support the thesis that any form of barbarity would be justifiable in such a holy cause it was proclaimed that "The Mongol princes who had dogs heads ate the bodies of the dead leaving only the bones to the vultures . . . the old and ugly women were divided into daily portions for the common folk while the pretty young women, having been ravished, had their breasts torn open and were then reserved as tidbits for the grandees."[28]

Later, the author points out that "we now know that the dog-headed cannibals against whom Pope Gregory IX preached his crusade were representatives of a far more sophisticated civilization than anything that existed in Europe at that time."

The wild exaggerations of the enemy-mongers aside, it is appropriate that we be sensitive to enemies. We need to be alert to our opponents and to anticipate their actions so as to be able to counter them. As we shall develop further in chapters 5 and 6, however, that alertness and sensitivity can lead to real trouble. But first, let us explore an important principle that governs much of our social perception of enemies, namely, the kinds of impact they have on the games all people play.

Some Games are Sum Games

Earlier, we examined the special kind of "game" known as Prisoner's Dilemma. Let us now consider other games—some playful, some not—in which the common denominator is that the participants receive payoffs, with these payoffs depending on the behavior of each player. First, there are the easy cases, those straightforward situations in which enemies are just enemies: people who, to achieve their goals, must somehow get you out of the way by killing you, injuring you, making you move or relinquish your claim to something that they want. (Or others who, in order for you to achieve your goals, *you* must somehow get out of the way or kill or injure, etc.) The bottom line, in a biological sense, is *competition*, which occurs when someone is trying to get something—money, mates, prestige, food—that is in short supply.[29] If, on the other hand, there is enough to go around, then competition doesn't occur and individuals or groups aren't enemies—unless they find something else to compete about.

Living things don't generally compete, for example, over air, because there is plenty of it to go around. On the other hand, even plants compete over light, or water, or simple living space. As we saw in chapter 2, animals—including human beings—compete in two fundamental ways, known to ecologists as *scramble competition* and *contest competition.*

We also considered that there are other kinds of short-lived, narrowly focussed, and very intense competition and enmity, such as the sort that exists between predator and prey. When a hawk succeeds in catching a rabbit, the rabbit dies; no wonder the rabbit doesn't consider the hawk its friend, even if in the great scheme of natural balance, rabbit-folk are ultimately benefited by hawk-folk. If the rabbit gets away, the hawk or perhaps its hungry offspring may die instead; so, not surprisingly, hawks can be presumed to believe that the only good rabbit is a dead rabbit (that is, dinner). Predator-prey competitions are therefore taken seriously by all concerned, and, to no one's surprise, they are accompanied by strenuous effort, screams, blood, and gore.

What does all this have to do with human society? The likely truth is that we human beings are made of much more primitive stuff than many of us would care to admit. We don't regularly stalk and kill our prey, nor are we often preyed upon (at least not by tooth and claw). But we do have enemies. Again, the most obvious arena is *contest competition,* as in a golf tournament, or a footrace, or when one and only one vice president of a large corporation will be promoted to become Chief Executive Officer (CEO), or when two suitors vie for the hand of a beautiful maiden, or two nations compete for hegemony in a region or in the world. More common yet, however, is *scramble competition,* the cosmic Easter egg hunt, in which we compete for scarce resources, such as money or prestige, in a kind of existential face-off, without a clearly defined foe. In these cases, unlike animals or plants, which pretty much keep their attention on the resource while almost ignoring each other, we have been blessed (or cursed) with foresight. So, we seek to identify—and often mis-identify—many of our scramble contests as direct struggles between rivals in which a loss by our neighbor and fellow competitor means a gain for ourselves, and vice versa. These are what theoreticians of conflict call "zero-sum games," in which the sum of everyone's winning and losing equals zero.

Unless ties are allowed, a football, basketball, or baseball game is zero-sum because there is one winner and one loser, with the winner's +1 balanced by the loser's –1.

The point is that in the game of life, we often interpret encounters as zero-sum contests in which someone must win and someone must lose. Roman philosopher Marcus Aurelius expressed this view when he observed that "the art of living is more like wrestling than dancing." Certainly, Marcus Aurelius spoke for this book in focussing on the importance of enemies, but a major part of this importance is the hurtful and often unnecessary consequence of seeing our enemy system as intrinsic to the "art of living."

To be sure, life involves its share of wrestling matches, but it also consists of more than a little bit of cooperative dancing; that is, positive-sum games, or win-win solutions. The trick is to hear the music, and then simply to perform the right steps without stepping on your partner's feet. Unlike wrestling, dancing is done by partners, not opponents; a duet, not a duel. No one "wins" a dance. (Except in dance competitions, which can be pretty fierce. Even in these cases, however, victory goes to a *team* of dancers: It takes two to tango.)

Famed Harvard negotiator Roger Fisher highlights the tendency to confuse positive-sum games with their zero-sum cousins by telling the following story: In the early 1960s, when the first frisbees were just making their appearance in the United States and were unknown in Europe, Fisher found himself in a park in London, tossing an early model back and forth with his son. It created quite a sensation, and a crowd of people gathered. After a while, a middle-aged man came over and said, in great perplexity, "I've been watching you blokes for almost half an hour. Looks like fun. Can't figure it out, though. Who's winning?"

Unlike a wrestling match, playing frisbee is a "positive-sum game." It is a dance in which there are only winners. In fact, each player needs the other in order to play at all; no enemies involved. But thanks to our oversized and hyperactive brains, we often put a uniquely competitive stamp on our lives, labeling almost everything as a zero-sum game, even if it isn't. Given our tendency—well-documented by sociologists such as Robert Merton—for self-fulfilling prophecies, even the most benign and seemingly noncompetitive interaction can become laden with overtones of strife and enmity.

Sometimes life is a wrestling match, sometimes a dance. It is not always easy, however, to know when it is one and when another, when the other guy is an opponent and when a partner, when it is time to struggle, and when to waltz.

According to poet Gertrude Stein, a rose is a rose is a rose, and ditto, we might add, for cigars. To be sure, sometimes an enemy is just an enemy. But often—probably most of the time—whenever we identify an enemy, we are also fingering a part of ourselves.

Which brings us, finally, to the ultimate enemy.

Enemy Extraordinaire

Meet Satan. The word "Satan," the chief evil spirit of Western religious belief, the very devil himself, is derived from the same root in Hebrew, Greek, Latin, and Old English. Most people do not know that in all these languages, Satan means adversary, opponent, enemy. We like to think of Satan as (D)evil and distinct from ourselves, who of course are on the side of G(o)od. It is therefore interesting that the word derives not from a shared sense of badness, but of enmity. Satan is The Enemy.

Formerly God's right-hand man and chief sidekick, Satan is also a traitor, a once-glorious angel (Lucifer the luminous) who rebelled against God, committed the sin of pride, and fell from grace—very far indeed, all the way to Hell, in fact. Satan is the Enemy not only because he does bad things, but because—even more diabolical—he tries to get *us* to do bad things. Thus, he is often presented as the Great Temptor, seeking to lure us away from obedience to God, trying by his many evil wiles to get us to switch from God's team to his own.

If Satan is The Enemy, he is less incarnate than inchoate. It would therefore be interesting to study Satan from a historical and psychological perspective, since, although reasonable people might debate his bodily existence, no one can discount Satan's metaphysical importance. What, then, are the emotional and social origins of Christian involvement with the Devil? Why was the Devil invented?[30] What needs did he satisfy? What needs does he meet today? The Devil is notably absent from Jewish theology, for example, as is Hell. Why is this, and how have Jews got along without him? Is it because Jews, so often persecuted in this secular world, haven't felt the need to locate additional enemies in the spiritual realm? But if so, why haven't the presence of Jews—historically considered rather devilish themselves—served Christians in the same way? Catholics have had Protestants ever since the Reformation, and of course, Protestants have had Catholics. Why, then, have they also had Satan?

Satan has an unclear role in modern Christianity: Evangelicals and fundamentalists still talk of him, mostly to warn of his blandishments, or to demonize their own worldly opponents while beating their Bibles. Traditional Catholic teaching emphasizes, instead, the role of Satan as chief tormenter of the damned. But most mainline, sophisticated Christian denominations are a bit uncomfortable when the Devil is brought up, rather like an image-conscious family with a cousin who was an axe-murderer. The Devil is an intellectual embarrassment, not to be mentioned in polite company.

Early in the history of Christianity, Satan was a relatively minor unpleasantness, eclipsed by the "barbarians" threatening Rome, which had just converted to Catholicism. Then Islam emerged as the great enemy of Christendom from the eleventh to the thirteenth centuries. Following the Crusades, with Islam no longer serviceable as public enemy number one, Christianity occupied itself with an equally lengthy period of internecine warfare between Protestants and Catholics, the so-called Wars of Religion. Finally, however, it was Satan's time, especially during the late Middle Ages. He surfaced, as every good enemy has, when the other, extramural enemies were no longer convenient. But Satan himself, being rather incorporeal, didn't offer a very good target, even for the sharp-eyed and imaginative guardians of orthodoxy, so the lot fell to witches, both in Europe and America, who—for the most part old, lonely women, frequently mentally ill or deficient—provided ample enemy-fodder.

According to modern Christian theology—chiefly the teachings of Catholicism—human beings aren't sinful because they commit sin; rather, they commit sin because they are sinful. The distinction is important because it means that sinfulness, in the form of "original sin," is inherent in all of us. Badness is therefore part of us, our legacy from Adam—and especially from Eve, who was persuaded by the Serpent to disobey the express orders of God. Now the Serpent, of course, was an emissary of Satan, the Enemy, and insofar as we all carry around a dose of original sin, a bit of Satan resides within each of us. Small wonder then that those who swallow all this stuff are also especially likely to rebel against the idea of being without an enemy, and to insist, to the contrary, that we are surrounded by the embodiments and blandishments of Satan, whether these secular enemies take the form of internal temptations (sex, alcohol, gambling) or external bad guys such as "godless communism," Iran, Iraq, abortion rights advocates, or—heaven help us—liberals.

It is also noteworthy that in Western religious tradition, at least, men in particular have self-righteously blamed women for having wrought the catastrophes of sin and disobedience—and their wages, death—upon us all.[31] It was only after eating the apple that Adam and Eve became ashamed of their nakedness, and presumably, only then did they become sexual creatures. Thereby, man's lust for woman is also blamed, usefully, on woman. Which is almost precisely equivalent to saying "The devil made me do it." Or, as Augustine put it, in genuine anguish, "Oh Lord, give me chastity . . . but not yet." The Devil, in short, can be very useful, especially when the burden of adhering to moral doctrine—whether nonviolence or chastity or even garden variety decency—becomes too heavy.

Here is a final, speculative question: Is there some relationship between monotheism and belief in Satan? If we are all thought to be the children of one great and good God, does this in itself incline us to postulate an opposing side, just to balance the cosmic scales, or—more seriously—to help define our God and thus ourselves by the existence of another, an Enemy and his evil minions? In history class, generations of school children have been taught that one of the great contributions of ancient Egyptian civilization—specifically, of Pharaoh Akhenaton—was the elaboration of monotheism, the belief in a single god. Furthermore, ancient Judaism is to be praised, we learn, for having carried this "advance" yet farther, to the greater glory of the people of Abraham and Moses, and, ultimately, Christ.

But in the spirit of the little boy watching the naked emperor, we might ask: What is so wonderful about monotheism? Is there any basis for thinking of it as an advance, beyond the smug and typically unexamined assumption that—to monotheists at least—it is obviously correct? Thus, what of the possibility that monotheism is actually a step sideways, or even backward, rather than forward? Examined objectively, it is not at all clear that the Jewish, Christian, and Islamic conception of one God is necessarily an advance over, for example, Hindu, Shinto, or Taoist conceptions of many gods (not to mention the supposedly "primitive" animistic and pantheistic religious systems). Moreover, polytheism seems likely to engender a degree of tolerance not found among monotheists: If there are many gods, each with a degree of authority and truth, then clearly, truth itself is relative and authority cannot be absolute.

On the other hand, an absolutist conception of one God, Lord of all Creation, leads rapidly to grandiosity and with it—ironically— to the kind of vulnerability that produces intolerance. "Which side are you on? Which side are you on?" In this chorus from an old labor song of the Depression era, workers were urged to choose between, say, the coal company and the union. They could as well have been committing themselves to the Devil or to God. When the choices are stark and few, there is no margin for error, and little call for tolerance. If my God is the only one, then all others are fakes, pretenders, or errors, while at the same time, any crack in my theological armor threatens to shatter the entire brittle structure of belief. The result: the Crusades; the Inquisition; the extraordinarily brutal persecution of "witches"; the whole sad history of Jewish, Christian, and Islamic intolerance and religious warfare; and our old friend (i.e., enemy) Satan, ever willing to help separate the good from the bad.

*   *   *

Enemies clearly influence and sometimes even determine the relationships within and between societies. It is also clear that societies have certain "emergent properties." They are more than the sum of their parts, the accumulated inclinations and behavior of their component individuals. But each individual, in a personal, idiosyncratic manner, nonetheless makes a private pact with his or her enemies, even if this means nothing more than accepting the prevailing dogma promulgated by the rest of society. Accordingly, in our exploration of the form and function of enemies, we now turn back to this "social atom," the individual, and to an important mechanism of enemy-making, one that has not been identified before now.

Notes

1. Talcott Parsons, *The Social System* (Glencoe, Ill.: Free Press, 1951).
2. Edward Alsworth Ross, *The Principles of Sociology* (New York: The Century Co., 1920).
3. Emile Durkheim, *Division of Labor in Society* (New York: Free Press, 1964).
4. Emile Durkheim, *The Rules of Sociological Method* (Chicago: University of Chicago Press, 1938).
5. Lewis Coser, *Functions of Social Conflict* (Glencoe, Ill.: The Free Press, 1956).
6. The paradox is that if it wasn't for the potentially dangerous hostility that developed between these two groups, there would be no need for any special feeling of protection.
7. C. A. Pinderhughes, "Ego Development and Cultural Differences," *American Journal of Psychiatry* 131 (1974): 171–75; "Differential Bonding: Toward a Psycho-Physiological Theory of Stereotyping," *American Journal of Psychiatry* 136 (1979): 33–37; "Paired Differential Bonding in Biological, Psychological, and Social Systems," *American Journal of Psychiatry* 142 (1982): 5–14.
8. It is significant that the remarkable rapprochment between the Israeli government and the Palestine Liberation Organization (PLO) that began in 1993 was stimulated in large part by the end of the Cold War—as a result of which neither Palestinians nor Israelies could count on the support of patrons who had themselves been enemies—as well as the fact that both Israel and the PLO recognized a powerful, common enemy: violent Islamic fundamentalism.
9. For example, Ludwig Gumplowicz, *Der Rassenkampf Maguerische Universitats-Bechhandlung* (Innsbruck, Austria: Gustav Ratzenhofer, 1883); *Die Socio-logische Erkenntnis* (Leipzig, Germany: F. A. Brockhaus 1998); and Franz Oppenheimer, *The State* (Indianapolis, Ind.; Bobbs-Merril, 1914).
10. Alexis de Tocqueville, *Democracy in America* (Garden City, NY: Doubleday, 1969).
11. Winston Churchill, *The World Crisis. Volume IV: The Aftermath* (London, England: Butterworth, 1928).

12. Sigmund Freud, *Group Psychology and Analysis of the Ego* in *Standard Edition of the Complete Psychological Works of Sigmund Freud* (London, England: Hogarth Press, 1921).

13. Jean Bodin, *The Six Books of Commonweale* (Cambridge, Mass.: Harvard University Press, 1962).

14. It should be pointed out that Philip—father of Alexander the Great—truly was (or became) an enemy of Greece, which he eventually conquered.

15. F. Nietzsche, *The Twilight of the Idols* (New York: Viking, 1954).

16. Lewis Coser, *Functions of Social Conflict* (Glencoe, Ill.: Free Press, 1956).

17. George Orwell, *1984* (San Diego, Calif.: Harcourt, Brace, Jovanovich. 1984).

18. Kanan Makiya, *Cruelty and Silence: War, Tyranny, Uprising, and the Arab World* (New York: Norton, 1993).

19. I place this phrase in quotation marks, because in fact it was never very well developed. The world's Arab states are actually very diverse, and whatever unity they possess seems based less on shared affiliation with Islam than on shared anti-Israeli enmity. The schism between Shi'ite and Sunni, for instance, is every bit as divisive as that between Catholic and Protestant.

20. Robert Bellah, "Evil and the American Ethos," in *Sanctions for Evil*, eds. N. Sanford and C. Comstock (Boston: Beacon Press, 1971).

21. Leslie Gelb, *Seattle Post-Intelligencer*, November 13, 1991.

22. Walter Lippman, *Public Opinion* (New York: Harcourt, Brace, 1922); see also G. W. Allport, "The Historical Background of Modern Social Psychology," in *Handbook of Social Psychology*, ed. G. Lindzey (Cambridge, Mass.: Addison-Wesley, 1954).

23. P. Sabatier, S. Hunter, and S. McLaughlin, "The Devil Shift: Perceptions and Misperceptions of Opponents," *Western Political Quarterly* 40 (1987): 449–76

24. Quoted in Francis FitzGerald, "The Reverend Jerry Falwell," *New Yorker* (May 18, 1981).

25. Richard Nixon, "America Has Slipped to Number Two," *Parade* (October 5, 1980).

26. The author's use of the term "cult," when referring to Christianity, is especially interesting as well as relevant to our discussion of the way modern-day "cults" are received (see chapter 6).

27. Quoted by Norman Cohn, *Europe's Inner Demons* (Brighton, England: Sussex University Press, 1975). This account, incidentally, is remarkably similar to the notorious "Protocol of the Elders of Zion," a fabricated tract purporting to detail Jewish sacrifice of Christian children, and used to whip up anti-Semitic hatred.

28. Edmund Leach. *Custom, Law, and Terrorist Violence* (Edinburgh, Scotland: Edinburgh University Press, 1977).

29. For example, if there had been enough goodies to satisfy both the Bulldogs and the Red Devils (chapter 3), much of the unpleasantness at the Boy Scout camp would never have happened.

30. Assuming, of course, that he was invented and is not real!

31. I believe that a cogent case can be made—perhaps should be made, and soon—that obedience has brought about far more evil and suffering in this world than has disobedience.

5

Passing the Pain Along

We have all seen a bucket brigade: strong, eager hands passing pails of water from one to the other, cooperating to put out a fire; or volunteers standing shoulder to shoulder, tossing sandbags down the line, racing against time to reinforce a wobbly dike against a rising river. Most of us may never participate in such an activity (although we would probably be the better for it if we did). But nearly everyone has taken part in something similar, although far less benevolent: We might call it "passing the pain along." It is remarkably widespread, so much so that it is virtually second nature, even something of an obsession. Yet, most of us are so immersed in the culture of pain-passing that, like a fish that takes its surroundings so much for granted that it would never consider the water it swims in to be "wet," we remain blissfully ignorant of its existence. The passing of pain also helps explain an important part of the enemy system, since much in the identification and creation of enemies takes place when people take part—often unknowingly—in this ritual, one that has virtually the power and automaticity of a reflex.

The Conservation of Pain, and the Golden Rule

In a masterpiece of painfully accurate revelation, the English writer G. K. Chesterton once suggested that Christianity hasn't been tried and found wanting; rather, it has been found difficult and left untried. Never has this been more true than in cases of personal pain and our reaction to it. Christ urged us to love our enemies, and, if slapped, to turn the other cheek. But for millennia—both before Christ and after—we have been far more likely to respond to insults, pain, or injury with a retaliating barrage of insults, pain, and injury.

In the simplest case, this response is directed toward the original transgressor. Benjamin Franklin's recommendation that we choose the North American turkey for our national symbol was overridden, largely because the turkey was seen as insufficiently likely to stand up for its rights or to fight back when provoked. Instead we emblazoned "Don't tread on m," on an early flag of the United States of America, along with the image of a rattlesnake. The message was clear: Step on us and you get bitten, lethally. We settled, ultimately, on a ferocious looking bird of prey. We have enshrined the "intrinsic right" of self-defense into basic Western law. "He deserved what he got," we nod, approvingly, after a fight or argument. "After all, he started it." Or, as one bumper sticker says, "You breaka my car, I breaka your face." Most of us can understand such sentiments, even as we may acknowledge that they don't quite shine as ethical guidelines. We invest such sentiments, albeit ruefully, with the self-justifying bromide that they are among the "facts of life," as when W. H. Auden referred sadly but almost fatalistically to

> What all school children learn:
> Those to whom evil is done
> Do evil in return.[1]

Nonetheless, not all adults—including schoolteachers—learn the same lesson. Thus, although "revenge" is still a bit disreputable, the doing of evil is widely tolerated so long as it is in the interest of getting even, balancing the scales, or obtaining "justice."

On the other hand, most of us are unlikely to approve the following, even though at some level we can understand it: George fails an exam at school and, in return, is mean to his friend Lizzie. Lizzie, feeling hurt, angry at George, and perhaps unhappy with herself as well, takes "it" out on her younger brother, Jason. She passes her pain to him, in an unconscious effort to help heal her own. Of course, Jason then looks around for someone—or something—on which to unload his newly acquired burden. Maybe he finds a playmate or a stray cat or, perhaps, lacking any suitable targets, he does harm to himself, either physically or psychologically. One way or another, the pain marches on, cutting its own swath of destruction, like a miniature Sherman on its way to the sea.

Physicists have given us the laws of conservation of energy and matter, telling us that these things can neither be created nor destroyed, but only transformed in shape and appearance. Maybe psychologists and psychiatrists will someday give us a comparable formulation for pain. After all, we appear to treat pain as though it is a physical quantity, a heavy weight whose crushing burden can be diminished if we pass some of it onto others.

More likely, however, the Law of Conservation of Pain will be closer to the physicists' conception of *entropy*, a measure of randomness or disorder in the universe. Left to its own devices, entropy tends to increase, rather than remain the same; certainly, it does not decrease spontaneously. To diminish entropy requires a positive input of energy, just as it requires a substantial input of human energy tempered with wisdom (sometimes, approaching saintliness) to reduce the amount of pain in the world. Not surprisingly, pain persists. Like entropy, it may even increase.

Look deeply at a child abuser and there is a good chance that you will find someone who was himself (or herself) abused as a child. Inside the domestic tyrant is likely to be someone who was tyrannized at one time. Scratch a victimizer and watch a victim bleed.

Take James Joyce's story "Counterparts," appearing in his collection, *Dubliners*. Here we have the poignant tale of Mr. Farrington, a lowly clerk in a large firm, who had a bad day: He was harassed and embarrassed by his overbearing boss, and in danger of losing his job. "He longed to execrate aloud," writes Joyce, "to bring his fist down on something violently." But he couldn't or he would be fired. Farrington therefore had to bear his pain and humiliation in silence until at last his painful workday was over. Seeking to "let off steam," in typical Irish Joycean fashion, he then goes drinking with his buddies, only to spend most of the money he had obtained that afternoon by pawning his precious watch. While at a tavern, he even loses two arm-wrestling matches to someone much younger (Mr. Farrington, we learn, is a large man and much esteemed—at least in the past—for his strength).

As a result, it was a sullen Farrington who headed home that evening,

> full of smouldering anger and revengefulness. He felt humiliated and discontented; he did not even feel drunk; and he had only two pence in his pocket. He cursed everything. He had done for himself in the office, pawned his watch, spent all his money; and he had not even got drunk. He began to feel thirsty again and he longed to be back again in the hot reeking public-house. He had lost his reputation as a strong man, having been defeated twice by a mere boy. His heart swelled with a . . . fury that nearly choked him.[2]

Farrington's young son comes running down the stairs to meet him, small and vulnerable, pitifully eager to do his father's bidding, altogether innocent of the day's misfortunes, and unaware of the older man's pent-up rage:

> "What's for my dinner?"
> "I'm going . . . to cook it, pa," said the little boy.
> "On that fire? You let the fire out! By God, I'll teach you to do that again!"
> He took a step to the door and seized the walking-stick which was standing behind it. "I'll teach you to let the fire out!" he said, rolling up his sleeve in order to give his arm free play.
> The little boy cried "O, pa!" and ran whimpering round the table, but the man followed him and caught him by the coat. The little boy looked about him wildly but, seeing no way of escape, fell upon his knees.
> "Now, you'll let the fire out the next time!" said the man, striking at him vigorously with the stick. "Take that, you little whelp!"
> The boy uttered a squeal of pain as the stick cut his thigh. He clasped his hands together in the air and his voice shook with fright.
> "O, pa!" he cried, "Don't beat me, pa! And I'll . . . I'll say a *Hail Mary* for you. . . . I'll say a *Hail Mary* for you, pa, if you don't beat me. . . . I'll say a *Hail Mary*. . . ."[3]

Mr. Farrington is not a very likeable character. In some ways, he isn't really a character at all but rather a sluice-way, a conduit for pain. We have all known Farringtons, and to some extent, most of us have probably been Farringtons as well. Furthermore, one needn't be a specialist in developmental psychology or the etiology of psychopathology to predict what sort of father, and victimizer in his own right, Farrington's young son is likely to become when he gets his chance.

Of course, not everyone who is injured responds by injuring, but the pattern is so widespread that the presence of one strongly suggests the other. A searching look at even the worst "bad guys" often reveals that they had been treated badly themselves. Although this doesn't excuse their behavior, at least it helps us understand it.

Not surprisingly, when Erich Fromm undertook to understand *The Anatomy of Human Destructiveness*,[4] he wound up cataloging the public offenses of people who had themselves been offended against in private. Without exonerating the culprits, Fromm's now-classic book documents how the early abuse suffered by Stalin and Hitler, for example, gave rise to their "malignant aggression" in adulthood, with dire consequences for millions. The connection extends to the human imagination no less than to reality, and its powerful hold is almost certainly due to the fact that it accurately reflects a deeper reality. For example, take Iago, arch-villain of literature: Sure enough, he was envenomed because of a painful personal affront. In Shakespeare's play, Othello had passed him over for a coveted promotion. Iago's response then powered Othello's tragedy.

The Golden Rule says "Do unto others as you would have them do unto you." But its goldenness may be due as much to unattainability as to its moral luster. Far more often, we substitute something like "Do unto others as they have done to you." So deeply ingrained is the passing of pain and revenge that this current version seems to require little explanation. We may regret it, but nonetheless we accept it, knowing it as our own. Return for a moment to *Othello*: The tragedy of this renowned play is widely seen to lie in the fact that Othello was tricked by Iago into thinking that his wife, Desdemona, had been adulterous, not simply that he ended up killing her. Thus, Othello's tragedy isn't considered to be his thirst for revenge per se, but the fact that it was misguided. Feeling immense pain at Desdemona's behavior, Othello felt the need to strike at her, to seek expiation of this pain by inflicting some of it on her, to wipe off his sense of dishonor by wiping Desdemona from the face of the earth. This much we understand, even if it makes no logical sense.[5]

Even less logical, although equally widespread, is the following corollary: If you can't get revenge directly, on the one who caused your pain, then unload your suffering on someone else, like the benighted Farrington "taking it out" on his abused son. As with passing the pain itself, we typically take for granted the inclination to satisfy our psychic need for a victim (or an enemy) by redirecting our venom onto substitutes. Once again, pain marches on, cutting its seemingly irresistible swath, devastating innocent victims along the way.

Feuds

Today's innocent victim has a way of becoming tomorrow's vengeful victimizer. Early in this century, a researcher studied a Filipino tribe, the Ifugao, looking at their social rules and means of settling disputes. His findings have since become a classic in legal anthropology. "The Ifugao," wrote author R. F. Barton, "has one general law, which with a few notable exceptions he applies to killings, be they killings in war, murders, or executions. . . . That law is: A life must be paid with a life."[6] Nearly seventy years later, psychologists Martin Daly and Margo Wilson laboriously went through reports for sixty different tribes, distributed throughout the world, to see whether the Ifugao were unusual. Their findings were unequivocal: fifty-seven of the sixty believed that a life must be exacted in precise retribution for any life that has been taken.[7]

Sometimes the principle is "permissive," that is, a relative or tribesman of the victim is *allowed* to retaliate. More often, it is obligatory: retaliation is a duty, a sacred responsibility, required to wipe away the stain of dishonor and often to allow the victim's soul to rest in peace. The only problem, of course, is that such prescriptions generally yield something less than peace for the living.

Here is an account of the South American Jivaro:

> The Jivaro Indian is wholly penetrated by the idea of retaliation; his desire for revenge is an expression of his sense of justice. His great principle is eye for eye, tooth for tooth, life for life. . . . The soul of the murdered Indian requires that his relatives shall avenge his death. The errant spirit, which gets no rest, visits his sons, his brothers, his father, in dreams, and weeping conjures them not to let the slayer escape but to wreak vengeance upon him for the life he has taken. If they omit to fulfill this duty the anger of the vengeful spirit may turn against themselves. To avenge the blood of a murdered father, brother, or son, is therefore looked upon as one of the most sacred duties of a Jivaro Indian. . . . It may happen that a Jivaro keeps the thought of revenge in his mind for years, even for decades, waiting for the opportunity to carry it out, but he never gives it up.[8]

Apparently, the ghost of the murdered King Hamlet—demanding vengeance for wrong-doing, does not only stalk the castles of northern Europe. It is found, in one form or another, throughout the world.

The issue is not only one for dusty ethnographies, or classic literature. It animates some of today's most pressing social tragedies: It keeps the street gangs like Bloods and the Crips at each other's throats, and in various metropolitan morgues. It lies behind seemingly intractable overseas conflicts, from Somalia to Rwanda to what used to be called Yugoslavia. Here is the testimony of Milovan Djilas, who was born into a perpetually feuding Montenegrin clan, and eventually rose to be vice president of Yugoslavia and one of the architects of Titoism. Djilas spanned the interval between tribalism and modernity in his nation, and his insights into vengeance, written nearly forty years ago, ominously foretell the unending enmity that has since devoured his unhappy land:

Vengeance—this is a breath of life one shares from the cradle with one's fellow clansmen, in both good fortune and bad, vengeance from eternity. Vengeance was the debt we paid for the love and sacrifice our forebears and fellow clansmen bore for us. It was the defense of our honor and good name, and the guarantee of our maidens. It was our pride before others; our blood was not water that anyone could spill. It was, moreover, our pastures and springs— more beautiful than anyone else's—our family feasts and births. It was the glow in our eyes, the flame in our cheeks, the pounding in our temples, the word that turned to stone in our throats on our hearing that our blood had been shed. It was the sacred task transmitted in the hour of death to those who had just been conceived in our blood. It was centuries of manly pride and heroism, survival, a mother's milk and a sister's vow, bereaved parents and children in black, joy and songs turned into silence and wailing.[9]

Because of the power of such feuding and the vivid historical memory of its participants, individuals are forced to bear not only their own enmity but also the weight of grudges accumulated by earlier generations. Russian anthropologist Sergei Arutiunov described the situation of many Georgians, Abkhasians, Armenians, and Azeris:

Among the Caucasus highlanders, a man must know the names and some details of the lives and the locations of the tombstones of seven ancestors of his main line. People fight not only for arable land; they fight for the land where the tombstones of their ancestors are located. Revenge is not only for events today, but also for the atrocities from wars eight generations ago.[10]

Consider next another vivid testimony to the power of revenge: the true story of Geronimo, great Apache war chief and bane of both the United States and Mexican armies. One day in 1858, a squadron of Mexican cavalry ambushed a group of Apaches in peace-

time while the men were away; among the slaughtered were
Geronimo's mother, wife, and three young children. The following
year, a large detachment of Apaches, looking for revenge, caught
up with the murderers of Geronimo's family, and the young man
was given command. Here are Geronimo's own words:

> I was no chief and never had been, but because I had been more
> deeply wronged than others, this honor was conferred upon
> me. . . . In all the battle I thought of my murdered mother, wife
> and babies—of my father's grave and my vow of vengeance. . . . Still
> covered with the blood of my enemies, still holding my conquering
> weapon, still hot with the joy of battle, victory, and vengeance,
> I was surrounded by the Apache braves and made war chief of
> all the Apaches. Then I gave orders for scalping the slain. I could
> not call back my loved ones. I could not bring back the dead Apaches,
> but I could rejoice in this revenge.[11]

The entire Mexican force, two companies of infantry and two
of cavalry, was wiped out. Apache losses were also high, but for
Geronimo and his fellows, it seems to have been worth it, just like
the tradition of blood feud among the Djilasi.

Why?

General William T. Sherman, who also proclaimed that, "war is hell,
and all its glory, moonshine," at least had a comprehensible reason
for doing as he did. In cutting a swath of bloodshed and misery
through the South, Sherman was not seeking to debunk the supposed
glory of war, or to confirm its hellacious nature. His goal, and that
of the Union army he led at the close of the Civil War, was to bring
the South to its knees. Not coincidentally, it may also have felt good
for many of Sherman's troops—and for the civilian populace in the

North that followed and cheered his exploits—to bring pain to the rebel South, especially since Confederate forces had earlier wreaked devastation upon the armies of the North. There is room for argument about whether the destruction of Georgia was necessary, or wise. But there was, at least, a strategic (i.e., military) rationale for Sherman's infamous march. It may, as well, have been an exercise in passing the pain along, but it was not *just* this.

But why did Geronimo or the relatives of Milovan Djilas go to such pains (literally) to inflict pain on those who had hurt them? For that matter, what is the rationale for pain-passing in our own lives? Why do we do it?

Here, in the realm of causation—whether the issue is private or public behavior—we are on much less steady ground than when pointing out the phenomenon of passing-the-pain itself. "Bucket brigades" or "transferring weight" may be useful metaphors, but they do not explain very much. It may well be that deeper understanding of the actual mechanism that drives pain-passing will have to wait. Perhaps for now we should be satisfied with simply drawing attention to the phenomenon.

Before elaborating the problem, however, let us take a preliminary stab at explaining it. Once again, a metaphor may be useful. Maybe the reason pain is treated like a hot potato is that like other "hot" topics, pain burns. Maybe personal injury is the driving force in efforts to alleviate one's pain by passing it to others. Furthermore, maybe the primary injury in such cases is to one's self-esteem, which, when linked to other primitive behavioral tendencies, finds expression through the basic system of social competition. Thus, it is easy to imagine that for thousands of generations, people who found themselves "one down," for whatever reason, suffered not only psychologically and possibly physically but also in terms of their social (and hence, biological) success. At the same time, if people finding themselves in this situation were able to respond by dragging down other, potential competitors, they might well have been able to better themselves by doing so. Insofar as life was competitive, getting ahead might have often required climbing over the bodies of one's rivals; and if one was hurt and bleeding one's self, all the more reason to inflict hurt and bloodshed on those otherwise positioned to profit from one's disadvantage. If so, then it would have felt good to our ancestors whenever they responded to situations of personal pain and degradation by inflicting similar pain and degradation on those around them, just as it feels good to eat when you are hungry, or go to sleep when tired.

Not that it always works. These days, we can fool ourselves by eating foods that "feel good"—such as chocolates or fats—but that actually do us harm. We nonetheless find them attractive, perhaps because in our evolutionary past there was an advantage associated with similar behavior, and our deeper selves have not caught up with the fact that times have changed and the advantage has been eliminated. Thus, our primate ancestors almost certainly profitted from eating food that was high in sugar, since they doubtless ate large amounts of fruit, and fruit is most ripe (and accordingly, most nutritious) when it is rich in sugar. In modern times, however, we can fool our taste buds by creating sweet foods of all sorts that are virtually devoid of any nutritional value. In fact, like excessive pain-passing, they can do us harm.

The point is that behavior such as passing along pain may continue to taste "sweet" to us today, even though such apparent "sweetness" may be a poor criterion for judging real desirability. "If it feels good, do it," we have been told, and indeed, in our distant evolutionary past, this may even have been good advice. But these days, some things—such as pain-passing—may feel good but actually be bad for us, and for everyone else, as outmoded as valuing our foods in proportion to their sugar content. Later, in chapter 7, we shall return to this general perspective in evaluating a new hypothesis for the prevalence of enemies in modern life, as well as possible ways of moving beyond our dependence upon them. For now, we rest content with the suggestion that passing-the-pain is an important part of our enemy system, and that it may well represent a persistent but typically misguided attempt to improve the situation of injured and diminished people by injuring and diminishing those around them.

Another, related possibility: Vengeance itself could have been socially and biologically adaptive in the past, since individuals or groups known to insist on "getting even" would be more likely to be left alone in the first place. Consider, by contrast, the sorry state of a lineage which may have lacked the family tradition of demanding an eye for an eye, and a life for a life. Its women, children, and possessions might well have been easy marks, vulnerable to anyone with the will to take advantage of them. But in proportion as a group carried on a tradition of vengeance—of passing not only pain but also death and destruction to anyone who "started it"—that group may have acquired a kind of security. Feuding, then, may simply be an extreme development of the human penchant for passing the pain along, a tendency which may have originated in behavior that was primitively adaptive, functioning as a kind of deterrence: "Don't tread on me, or I will stomp on you." It shows itself, similarly but in more restrained form, whenever an individual—personally pained but not necessarily carrying the bloody weight of a vendetta à la Geronimo or one of the Djilas clan—passes his or her pain onto someone else.

On the other hand, it is clear that a tradition of vengeance can become a deathtrap, as shown by Milovan Djilas:

The men of several generations have died at the hands of Montenegrins, men of the same faith and name. My father's grandfather, my own two grandfathers, my father, and my uncle were killed, as though a dread curse lay upon them. My father and his brother and my brothers were killed even though all of them yearned to die peacefully in their beds beside their wives. Generation after generation, and the blood chain was not broken. The inherited fear and hatred of feuding clans was mightier than fear and hatred of the enemy, the Turks. It seems to me that I was born with blood on my eyes. My first sight was of blood. My first words were blood and bathed in blood.[12]

For all the horror and hurtfulness of so much bloodymindedness, it is at least possible that it provided a brutal kind of protection and security.

Whatever its wellsprings, such behavior is so common (at least in its milder form), and so rarely examined, that to step outside this aspect of our enemy system is almost to become a fish out of water. So let's now shake off the droplets and try to appreciate just how wet we often are.

A Swiss Parable and the Origins of Scapegoating

The story goes like this: In a small, isolated village of Switzerland, not too long ago, a prominent merchant was found dead, the back of his head caved in by a heavy object. The village blacksmith was accused of the murder, and after a fair trial he was found guilty. Justice was demanded: The blacksmith must be hanged. But since this was a farming community, the sentence was easier to pronounce than to carry out. The local economy depended on its horses, and, therefore, on its blacksmith. And in all the village, there was only one blacksmith. He was simply too important to sacrifice, even in the cause of justice. As luck would have it, however, there were seven tailors in the village, so one of them (the least skillful) was hanged instead.

The tale of the guilty blacksmith and the punished tailor is probably apocryphal, but the point is clear enough: When people are outraged and subjected to pain—whether of body or of spirit—something inside them cries out for redress. And often, this is achieved by revenge masquerading as justice. In such cases, the crucial thing is less that the guilty party be punished than that *someone* be punished. We often insist that only the pain of others can allay our own distress. Only someone else's suffering can soak up our blood. (In our story, the Swiss, true to their vaunted practicality, also made sure that this pain was not spread too widely.)

It is an old story, this effort to achieve purification and to lighten the load of human suffering and pain by dumping it on someone—or something—else. Ideally, the guilty party should receive the brunt of the retribution, which explains our discomfort at killing a tailor for the crimes of a blacksmith. But in a pinch, anyone will do. Moreover, even though at a gut level we understand and even sympathize with the need for revenge, we also consider it disreputable. Justice, yes; revenge, no. We tend to equate the degree of civilization with the extent to which retaliation is administered by civil authority rather than by the aggrieved party. One of the reasons for having police, laws, and prisons (as well as executioners) is to prevent wronged and vengeful people from taking the law into their own hands.

The Bible enjoins us to "avenge not yourselves, but rather give place unto wrath: for it is written, Vengeance is mine; I will repay, saith the Lord" (Romans 12:19; King James Version). It is less widely appreciated, however, that this is not only an admonishment but also a promise. Those who share a belief in a Divine Creator should content themselves with something other than revenge, because God promises that He will obtain it for them.

Nothing in the Bible prevents believers, however, from taking a kind of generalized revenge by dumping their badness on something else, especially if that something isn't human. Accordingly, the ancient

Israelites used to hold a ceremony in which the High Priest would lay both his hands over the head of a live goat and

> confess over him all the iniquities of the people of Israel, and all their transgressions and all their sins; and he shall put them upon the head of a goat, and send him away into the wilderness . . . the goat shall bear all their iniquities upon him to a solitary land. (Leviticus 16: 20–23)

Sometimes, after the sins of the community were symbolically placed upon the goat, the animal was ritually slaughtered. Either way, the people were purified and the term "scapegoat" was introduced into the Western vocabulary.

Scapegoating is probably the most clear-cut example of passing the pain along, and doing so in a socially acceptable manner. In some cases, such as the Israelite ceremony, the symbolism is acknowledged and up-front. In others, it is kept in the background, although it generally remains no less real. Jews, who invented scapegoating, have ironically been victimized by it for thousands of years, from the Inquisition to Russian pogroms, to the Nazi holocaust.[13] "I know we are the Chosen People," laments Tevye in *Fiddler on the Roof*. "But next time, couldn't you please choose someone else?"

Of course, Jews have not been alone as scapegoats. In the United States, African Americans have probably been the foremost recipients of this dubious honor. Psychologists Carl Hovland and Robert Sears found, for example, that they could predict the number of southern lynchings taking place during any given year between 1882 and 1930, simply by knowing the price of cotton during that year.[14] When the price of cotton went down, the frequency of black lynchings went up. Not that white southern racists literally blamed African Americans every time cotton prices declined on the northern mercantile exchanges; rather, the onset of hard economic times (low prices for cotton) led to an outpouring of anger, resentment, and frustration, which was then turned against a conspicuous and powerless minority. The economic and social pain of poor whites was passed onto blacks. In the 1990s, we might call it the David Duke Disease.

Most people have a deep belief in cause-and-effect. If something happens (an effect), we assume that something—usually, someone— must be responsible (a cause). Moreover, we would rather not locate that cause within ourselves, particularly if this means holding ourselves responsible for something unpleasant, and most especially if it means that to correct the situation, we must do something that we would rather avoid. Although most of us like to think that we are strong rather than weak, effective rather than helpless, we also find it more pleasant to see ourselves as victims than as victimizers.

In short, it is "natural" to blame others for troubles in the world, especially when these troubles befall us. If there aren't enough goats to go around, or if animal sacrifice has lost some of its panache, other human beings can always be found to shoulder the blame. After all, there are many of us, of many different inclinations and beliefs, languages and customs, along with a great eagerness to pass the blame as well as the pain. And if there is only one blacksmith, you can always find an extra tailor or two.

On the other hand, sometimes there are real abuses and genuine perpetrators; when this is the case, even though it may feel good to spill one's pain on someone—anyone—it generally feels better yet to unload on the real culprit, the genuine source of one's anger rather than a mere substitute. Famed psychiatrist Jerome Frank recounts this bit of behavioral research:

> The experimenter, who was also their teacher, angered some undergraduates by heckling them while they counted backwards from a hundred by twos as fast as they could, making sure that they could not finish in the allotted time. He then told them to

ask a "victim"—either himself or a fellow undergraduate—to guess the number they were thinking of, between one and ten, and to shock him every time he missed over a series of ten trials. The measurement of anger was a rise in blood pressure—readings were taken before and after the heckling, and then after shocking the victim—and the central finding was that the blood pressure rose significantly after the heckling and stayed up after shocking the undergraduate, but fell significantly after shocking the teacher, who had caused all the trouble.[15]

It can also be tempting to inflate the villainy, to milk legitimate grievances for every possible drop of balm, which is acquired by identifying an enemy—the supposed perpetrator of one's pain—and then blaming and if possible punishing him. This was true of JoAnne, whose highly neurotic need to blame others in order to find peace within herself was described in chapter 3. But it isn't limited to the personal level; whole nations can engage in scapegoating. It is true, for example, that the United States inflicted the Shah on the people of Iran, after the CIA engineered the overthrow of his popular, democratically elected predecessor, the socialist Mohammed Mossadegh, in 1953. But there was at least a bit of hyperbole—mixed with psychological potency—in the pamphlet distributed in Iran during the 1980s titled *The True Nature of the U.S. Regime, the Great Satan.* "The world must know," it stated, "that all the miseries of the Iranian nation and other Muslim nations stem from foreigners, from America." Like the college students recounted by Dr. Frank, the Iranians may well have lowered their collective blood pressure by raising ours, by identifying the United States as the Great Satan, who was the cause of "all the miseries," and then by administering a punishing electric shock of sorts: taking the U.S. embassy employees hostage, and generating the economically painful oil boycott of 1979.

As we have seen, it also helps if the identified enemy can be shared. Shared enemies help overcome isolation and private pain. They can also mend an incomplete or damaged sense of self. And they help generate the warmth that comes with shared purpose, as well as the impression—not to mention, occasionally, the reality— of increased strength through unity. Thus, chapter 4 recounted how ethnic bonding increases under conditions of stress, at least partly because such bonding is intimately tied to rejection of others. Just as a coin is defined equally by a head and a tail, ethnic groupings— Irish Catholic, Palestinian, Hungarian, Tutsi—are equally defined by who their members are *not*: Irish Protestant, Israeli, Romanian, Hutu. The most dramatic event in Eastern Europe, after the decommuniza- tion of 1989 and 1990, has been the emergence of nationalist hatreds: Serb versus Croat versus Bosnian Muslim, Czech versus Slovak, Hungarian versus Romanian, Bulgarian versus Turk, and Armenian versus Azerbaijani. This reflects more than the simple fact that rigid Communist control has been lifted, allowing simmering antagonisms to come to the surface. It also results from the complex truth that change is stressful, and so, most especially, is freedom, particularly when it entails wrenching economic and political adjustments. Given these stresses, we can expect in-group identification and out-group antagonism to fill some of the deepest human needs.

Don't look for goats to be sacrificed in post-Communist Eastern Europe; but at the same time, don't be surprised if good-neighborliness and even common decency and peace find themselves on the chopping block.

On a wider scale, the scapegoat also remains useful. It carries the rejected part of ourselves, that part which is so real, so undeniable, that it must be located somewhere, but so nasty that it must be rejected and could not be tolerated within our own skin. As with the shared enemy, which he closely resembles, the scapegoat provides an opportunity for us to join together with other, like-minded good folks, driving out and often destroying the evil while at the same time basking in the warm sense of belonging and good fellowship that comes from unified, cohesive action, directed toward a common end and against a common foe.

Can it be, therefore, that the enemy is really the savior for those in need of a scapegoat? Is this why the peacemaker is often treated as an enemy, because he or she interrupts that cleansing process of finding blame elsewhere, of passing the burden of pain to others? Can it be true, then, that we make enemies because otherwise we would have no friends, and that we make war because otherwise we would have no peace?

At the same time, don't get the impression that scapegoats are found only among those who are different or distant, or that the problem of scapegoating lies only among biblical Israelites, folk-tale Swiss, turn-of-the-century redneck southern bigots, anti-Semitic Nazis, or xenophobic Iranians. Often, it emerges within our own families as well, with someone taking on the role of family bad boy, or problem child. Among so-called dysfunctional families, for example, it is very common for at least one member (typically a child) to emerge as the one who fails at school, "does" drugs, gets in trouble with the law, gets pregnant out of wedlock or gets someone pregnant; in these or a host of other ways, the problem person serves as lightning rod for the family pain. Significantly, therapists often find that if the family scapegoat gets help and stops being the recipient of the family's pain and the most visible indication of its distress, then others in the family may subtly attempt to undercut his or her recovery. Should the scapegoat successfully cast off the onus and really stop being such a goat, other family problems—not uncommonly, the real underlying ones—emerge at last. (We observed several cases of this sort among the true vignettes presented in chapter 3.) We now turn to situations in which the unavoidable pain of life becomes transmuted into pain for others, when victims become victimizers.

Warrior Vulnerability and Psychic House-Cleaning

According to anthropologist Ruth Benedict, there was a

> recommended code of conduct among a tribe of head-hunters: When
> a chief's son died, the chief set out in a canoe. He was received
> in the house of a neighboring chief, and after the formalities he
> addressed his host, saying, "My prince has died today and you go
> with him." Then he killed him. In this, according to interpretation,
> he acted nobly because he had not been downed, but had struck
> back in return.[16]

Chief 1 kills chief 2 even though 2 had nothing to do with the
death of 1's son. It isn't really as strange as it sounds. In fact, similar
"nobility" of action has given us not only a large proportion of the
world's feuds and wars, but also much of the interpersonal and intrapsychic pain that bedevils our planet.

Fortunately, the cultural traditions of most Western societies do
not encourage quite this degree of violent retribution. In fact, this
is one of the primary purposes of legal systems of trial and punishment:
to substitute public "justice" for personal revenge and to replace the
individual's inclination for passing the pain with society's more orderly
mechanisms. We can also rejoice that many people do not live
Farrington-like lives, at least not chronically. Even after experiencing
comparable indignities on occasion, many of us are capable of
behaving with a good deal more restraint. But no matter how loving
and caring and supportive our childhood and our family, none of
us can avoid some sort of scarring and pain. To some degree, it
is fundamental to the human condition, born helpless as we are into
a dangerous world, and destined, ultimately, to die. Andrew
Schmookler puts it accurately:

> We are born more helpless than virtually any other animal. Yet, according to psychologists, we emerge into consciousness with a feeling of omnipotence. We believe the cosmos is ruled by our thoughts and feelings. Tiny, quivering bundles of fears and desires, we enter the world with a boundless egocentrism: we are each the center of our universe. What a painful shock to learn of our true place in the order of things. We are small, and prey to hostile forces we cannot control. Other people, with power over us, may be indifferent to our needs. And the final insult: we learn that we are mortal.[17]

Schmookler goes on to relate the outraged, existential vulnerability of the infant to both the image and the reality of the warrior, who dispenses death to others in an effort that is ultimately futile to affirm his own life.

"I must kill my visible enemy," wrote Eugene Ionesco,

> the one who is determined to take my life, to prevent him from killing me. Killing gives me a feeling of relief, because I am dimly aware that in killing him, I have killed death. My enemy's death cannot be held against me, it is no longer a source of anguish, if I killed him with the approval of society: that is the purpose of war. Killing is a way of relieving one's feelings, of warding off one's own death.[18]

Killing—the ultimate recourse against an enemy—is, in a sense, a kind of personal psychic house-cleaning. Just as societies can occasionally use an enemy to exorcise their demons of doubt, guilt, and pain, individuals have a comparable option. Just as societies seek to achieve internal unity by banding together against a common foe (whether or not the foe really threatens its security), individuals seek psychic unity by identifying an enemy, regardless of whether the enemy has actually done anything to warrant such enmity. The easiest way to deal with household garbage is to throw it out, and similarly with psychic garbage—notably anger mixed often with guilt—except that psychic garbage, by its nature, cannot simply be tossed in the trash bin. It must be passed along, thrown onto someone. Confronted, then, with a choice between tearing ourselves apart by recognizing our complicity in evil, or tearing apart someone else, we opt—not surprisingly—for the latter. As many of the world's religions, notably Buddhism, have long been aware, there is pain, sorrow, and suffering in the world, to which no one is altogether a stranger. Life can be joyous, but it also hurts. Many have argued that such hurt begins even at birth itself, as William Blake suggested in his cynical poem, "Infant Sorrow," and as numerous psychoanalysts have subsequently argued. Listen to Blake:

> My mother groan'd! my father wept.
> Into the dangerous world I leapt:
> Helpless, naked, piping loud:
> Like a fiend hid in a cloud.
>
> Struggling in my father's hands,
> Striving against my swaddling bands,
> Bound and weary I thought best
> To sulk upon my mother's breast.[19]

Significantly, this poem occurs within a group titled *Songs of Experience*. It is not only the experience of birth that inflicts trauma, but often that of living itself. Our ways, the poet laments, are often "filled with thorns" ("Holy Thursday") and the forests of the night are filled with fearful tigers "burning bright" ("The Tyger"). To be sure, life is more than fear and pain, but fear and pain are nonetheless frequent companions, along with disappointment, anger, sorrow, loss, guilt, and humiliation. Who, then, is to blame us if in our search for inner wholeness and peace, we project some of our hurt back onto the world, the ultimate source of so much unpleasant experience? Just as a motion picture is projected onto a screen, we project our psychic pain onto an enemy. And by this process of projection, we seek to cleanse and renew ourselves by throwing our garbage "out there," so that we no longer have to live with it "in here." Unfortunately, however, "out there" is often a real person, someone else's "in here."

In the movie *Dr. Strangelove, or How I Learned to Stop Worrying and Love the Bomb,* we were introduced to General Jack D. Ripper. The noble general—a paradigmatic figure out of deep right-field in American politics—worried constantly about pollution of his "precious bodily fluids," notably by fluoridation, which he denounced as a Communist plot. From the perspective of the Far Right, heterogeneity is suspect, even within the United States, especially if it threatens the internal consistency of our own bodies politic or bodies physical. In turn, the good old USA was long seen as threatened by a homogeneous evil—communism, fluoridation, integration, all joined together in one hideous deviltry—the cause of our own national decline, reflected at the personal level in a certain alarming diminution that the general had detected in his own sexual performance.

Imagine the vanity—to paraphrase Augustine—of thinking that by projecting evil elsewhere, onto enemies, we really and truly expiate ourselves. But also imagine the awfulness of having to live amongst all that psychic garbage, marinating hopelessly in our self-induced fluoridation and ever-diminishing potency, victims of personal slights and unavoidable private pain, as well as the simple, but inexorable process of personal aging and degeneration. All this and more we would have to face if enemies didn't exist, or if we couldn't project our trash—pass our pain—onto them.

Consider Achilles, the ultimate warrior in Western tradition. *The Iliad* recounts how Achilles, sulking because Agamemnon had taken a woman to whom Achilles felt entitled, kept himself from battle.

As a result, the Greeks were in disarray and Achilles' beloved Patrocles was killed. This finally goads Achilles into action; he eventually projects his rage onto Hector, who had killed Patrocles. Then, having killed Hector, Achilles goes further, seeking to reestablish his self-esteem and somehow erase the sting of his lover's death by degrading the corpse of Hector.

We are told that long before the Trojan War, a fellow named Cain killed his brother, Abel. Why? It seems that Cain was enraged because God had rejected his offering in favor of Abel's. In a fit of murderous jealousy, Cain, too, passed his pain along.

The pattern is modern, too. Hitler played with virtuosity on German pain and anger over that nation's defeat in World War I and the national "stab in the back" suffered at Versailles. Daily, Arabs rally around the pain of the Palestinians, and Israelis around the Holocaust. The United States invaded Grenada almost immediately after the truck-bombing of a Marine barracks in Beirut. Then we bombed Libya, in our anger and frustration over the terrorist bombing of a nightclub frequented by American servicemen. Then we invaded Panama largely because George Bush felt a need to banish his own "wimp factor," enhanced by the anger and frustration generated by Manuel Noriega's embarrassing transgressions. Of course, we can't forget the Gulf War, already discussed.

It should be emphasized that the warrior—or modern-day pseudo-warrior—is not alone in reacting to pain and anxiety by dispensing yet more pain and anxiety. There is more than a little Achilles (and Cain) in each of us. Moreover, it is not only death that motivates people to behave in this way. Outrageous fortune, as Shakespeare noted, has more than enough slings and arrows for us all. Each of us, in a starring role as the lead character in the private drama of our own little lives, has more than enough pain to pass along, and plenty of opportunities to do so especially when others are so often aggressive at our expense.

Identification with the Aggressor

One of the weirder examples of pain-passing is known to mental health specialists as "identification with the aggressor." Some of the clearest cases come from the time of World War II. During the 1930s, for example, Jewish parents in central Europe were horrified to witness their children mimicking Nazi storm troopers and giving "Heil Hitler" salutes.

Identification with the aggressor grows out of the traumas of individuals and of larger populations. Modern-day drill sergeants evoke not only subordination on the part of military recruits, but also outright antagonism. The goal is to energize esprit de corps and within-group unity in the face of an "enemy"—the sergeant himself—which will eventually be transferred to an external enemy on the other side of the battlefield. In some cases, identification with the aggressor often involves a kind of unconscious magical thinking whereby the victim associates himself with the victimizer, in this way achieving—at least in his or her mind—the fantasy of protection. By psychologically impersonating the aggressor, a sufferer can magically be transformed from a position of weakness to one of power. According to M. Scott Peck,

> The builders of medieval cathedrals placed upon their buttresses the figures of gargoyles—themselves symbols of evil—in order to ward off the spirits of greater evil. Thus children may become evil in order to defend themselves against the onslaughts of parents who are evil. It is possible, therefore, to think of human evil—or some of it—as a kind of psychological gargoylism.[20]

Those who succumb to psychological gargoylism promote evil and pass along pain in the course of trying to protect themselves from both.

Describing their experiences in a Nazi concentration camp, Rudolf Vrba and Alan Bestic[21] tell about Yankel Meisel, a prisoner who had forgotten to sew some buttons onto his uniform, as he had been instructed, just before an inspection by Heinrich Himmler. As a result, while the entire camp was standing at attention, waiting for Himmler to arrive, Meisel was beaten to death by the guards. As the victim screamed and pleaded for mercy, Vrba and Bestic recount that, "All hated Yankel Meisel, the little old Jew who was spoiling everything, who was causing trouble for us all with his long, lone, futile protest." To the inmates, at least during that gruesome incident, the enemy wasn't Himmler, who, after all, had orchestrated the entire bestial system, or the guards who carried out his orders. Rather, the "enemy" was the old, doomed Jew, like themselves one of the victims!

In her classic book *Patterns of Culture*, Ruth Benedict wrote that culture was "personality writ large." For some people, life itself is a concentration camp writ small. They grow up experiencing iron-fisted discipline, combined, if they are lucky, with rigidity, and if they are not, with outright brutality and abuse. These "guards" are also called "parents."

The Authoritarian Personality

Some people may simply be predisposed toward hatred and prejudice because of their genetic makeup. Thus far, however, no evidence supports this contention. On the other hand, there is little doubt of the crucial role played by early experience, particularly the kind of experience provided by one's parents.

After World War II, social philosopher Theodor Adorno and his associates launched a massive study to uncover the causes of anti-Semitism.[22] They interviewed large numbers of people, inquiring as to their attitudes on a variety of social issues. The researchers soon discovered that anti-Semitic tendencies were closely linked to a number of different attitudes, which could be scored on what became known as the "F-Scale" (F for "fascist").

Ranking on the F-Scale was determined by the extent of agreement or disagreement with such statements as:

> "Most of our social problems would be solved if we could somehow get rid of the immoral, crooked, and feeble-minded people."

> "People can be divided into two classes, the weak and the strong."

> "Obedience and respect for authority are the most important virtues children should learn."

> "What youth needs most is strict discipline, rugged determination and the will to work and fight for family and country."

> "Sex crimes such as rape and attacks on children deserve more than mere imprisonment; such criminals ought to be publicly whipped, or worse."

> "Most people don't realize how much our lives are controlled by plots hatched in secret places."

And so forth. Most readers can anticipate the kind of questions— and answers—that result in a high F-Scale ranking. This is part of the point. In their now famous research, Adorno and his colleagues found that there is a consistent syndrome that linked such people: They showed what became known as an "authoritarian personality."

Intensive interviews with people at each end of the F-Scale— those whose personalities were especially authoritarian and those who were minimally so—revealed that a common denominator for the highly authoritarian types was the kind of parenting they had received in their youth. In particular, parents who were especially harsh and threatening, and who coerced obedience from their children by threatening to withdraw their love as a sign of disapproval, tended to produce children, who, when they grew up, were rigidly authoritarian in their own attitudes.

The mechanism seems to be as follows. The children growing up in such homes tend to be insecure, frightened of their parents, and yet at the same time, highly dependent upon them. The parents inspire fear and lots of repressed hostility. Their children have suffered pain—emotional pain, and sometimes physical pain as well—because of those parents, but owing to their family situations, such children have been inhibited about expressing their anger and resentment. In most cases, they are not even consciously aware that they harbor these feelings, and would likely deny them in any case. These children grow up to be injured and angry adults who—fearful and insecure as well—proceed to redirect their anger toward others: Jews, African Americans, hippies, unwed mothers, welfare cheats, and others. In our terms, they pass their pain along to others, especially those who are relatively powerless, just as the authoritarians, when young, had been powerless against their own parents. At the same time, such people profess great respect—even adoration—for authority.[23]

According to psychiatrist Jerome Frank, correlations of this sort have often been found between personality traits and political attitudes. The usual finding is

> an authoritarian character pattern whose dynamic core lies in repression of strong hostility originally aimed at parents and other severe but close authority figures. Those with this type of character pattern exaggerate the importance in human affairs of power, force, domination, and submission, and displace their own aggression to safer targets than authority figures at home. Greatly valuing conventional morality, they express their bottled-up sexual and aggressive feelings indirectly through condemnatory over concern with "immoral" behavior of foreigners and other out-groups, and they are

similarly prone to externalize their fears, attributing their problems to external enemies rather than inner conflicts.[24]

Other mental health specialists have sought to understand the genesis of authoritarian behavior traits in pre-World War II Germany. Writing at the same time as Adorno and associates, but independently, psychoanalyst Erik Erikson concluded that the political appeal of Nazism to Germans in the 1930s was partly based on the authoritarian style of the typical German family, in which the father was tyrannical and remote, but also seen as crucially weak:

> When the father comes home from work, even the walls seem to pull themselves together. The children hold their breath, for the father does not approve of "nonsense"—that is, neither of the mother's feminine moods nor of the children's playfulness. . . . Later, when the boy comes to observe the father in company, when he notices his father's submission to superiors, and when he observes his excessive sentimentality when he drinks and sings with his equals, the boy acquires . . . a deep doubt of the dignity of man—or at any rate, of the "old man."[25]

It would be a joyless and dispiriting worldview which, after proclaiming the importance and ubiquity of pain-passing, also announced that the process was inevitable. Fortunately, this is not the case, and in chapters 7 and 8 we shall explore ways out of this and other aspects of our enemy system. Before this, however, we pause briefly to acknowledge the disconcerting fact that one "way out" is not really an escape at all, after which we consider the apparent biological commonality of pain-passing in other living things.

Breaking the Cycle?

Hindus speak of the endless cycle of death and rebirth, and of ways to break this cycle and achieve *nirvana*. What about the cycle of pain and anger? What about deciding that this secular cycle, too, can and must be broken, that the pain which has been passed to one's self shall be absorbed or somehow dealt with in other ways, but not passed on? This is the stuff that makes Christs, Buddhas, and Gandhis. It is not, however, for everyone.

Most of the time, the pain-passing cycle is not broken by conscious design on the part of the recipient but rather when the opponent suddenly, unexpectedly—and often, contrary to the other's secret hopes—gives up or changes the terms of the contest (for example, when the USSR ended the Cold War while also disbanding itself, or when a personal enemy dies, gets arrested, or moves to another state). Such events offer a way out of the cycle of passing the pain, but "solutions" of this sort do not develop out of a reasoned decision to transcend the enemy system and break out of the pain cycle; therefore, they typically result merely in a search for opportunities to continue the old ways. But what if Hector had come to Achilles suing for peace? What would Achilles have "done" with his anger and his pain? If Yankel Meisel didn't exist, would the concentration camp inmates have had to invent him? What will the Palestinians do now that they are finally receiving claim to at least part of their homeland? And what will become of Israel when it is truly accepted by the Arabs?

In an experience that is, in one way or another, universally shared, the "enemy" does not go away so much as it remains inaccessible. For example, consider the child in relation to his or her mother, a mother who is loved and is typically caring, nurturing, protective, and so forth, but who, at the same time, is off limits to the feelings of rage, resentment, or jealousy that are also normal since even a "good mother" occasionally has a piece of life to call her own, and cannot in any event provide fully for all of her child's desires. The result: People—even normal, healthy people—usually find themselves laden with at least some contraband emotional luggage, negative feelings that they repress, redirect, or, in the most fortunate cases, sublimate into other, more reputable outlets, such as socially acceptable (indeed, socially rewarded) assertiveness, competitiveness, and plain old-fashioned personal energy.

But for many people, pain that is unresolved, unexpressed, and not passed along reveals itself in pathology of one form or another. This is especially true since many of us trudge through our lives carrying a load of emotional baggage that is far heavier than the normal ambivalences toward one's parents. Often, however, as with the case of our parents, there are powerful inhibitions against acting out these angers. Add to this the sudden removal of the troublesome object— the enemy—and the result can be disorienting indeed. Having gotten up a head of steam, and then suddenly deprived of an object against which to vent it, we find ourselves stuck with an unwieldy dose of momentum. Usually, the best we can do in such circumstances is to dissipate that momentum, rather awkwardly, and then try to regain our balance.

Such cases, however, are far from sainthood. Although the cycle of pain may indeed be ended, experiences of this sort are generally unexpected and disorienting, unanticipated consequences of events thrust upon us. It hardly qualifies as transcendence or overcoming.

There have been several continuing themes in our exploration of the enemy system, including not only its persistence (and thus, our seemingly unquenchable need for enemies) but also the multiple levels that sustain our appointment with enmity, from the biological to the psychological to the level of society. Whenever we identify a pattern that seems both deeply embedded within the human psyche and also widespread, it is reasonable to ask just how deeply this tendency resides—whether, for example, it is found in other living things. It is fitting, therefore, to conclude our examination of pain-passing by showing its parallels (possibly, its origins) among some of our simpler animal cousins.

The Ethology of Pain-Passing

Ethologists have known for some time that animals pass along their aggressive feelings, and that often, when they are—for whatever reason—inhibited from attacking the individual who actually evoked these feelings, the aggressiveness will somehow be redirected toward another individual. Konrad Lorenz described the following courtship interaction among a certain group of freshwater fishes known as *cichlids* (pronounced "sick-lids"):

> At first nervously submissive, the female gradually loses her fear of the male, and with it every inhibition against showing aggressive behavior, so that one day her initial shyness is gone and she stands, fearless and truculent, in the middle of the territory of her mate, her fins outspread in an attitude of self-display, and wearing a dress which, in some species, is scarcely distinguishable from that of the male. As may be expected, the male gets furious, for the stimulus situation presented by the female lacks nothing of the key stimuli which, from experimental stimulus analysis, we know to be strongly fight-releasing. So he also assumes an attitude of broadside display, discharges some tail beats, then rushes at his mate, and for fractions of a second it looks as if he will ram her, and then . . . the male does not waste time replying to the threatening of the female; he is far too excited for that, he actually launches a furious attack which, however, *is not directed at his mate but, passing her by narrowly, finds its goal in another member of his species.* Under natural conditions this is regularly the territorial neighbor.[26] [italics in original]

There is nothing fishy about this behavior. It is relatively straight-forward and very "human." Rather than attack his boss, James Joyce's Mr. Farrington took a strap to his innocent little son. Rather than attack his own mate, and disrupt the happy piscine home he and his ladylove have been busily establishing, the male cichlid fish proceeds—under Konrad Lorenz's watchful eye—to pass his anger and aggression to a neighbor. In so doing, the male cichlid preserves his domestic harmony while reinforcing his status vis-à-vis potential competitors. Mr. Farrington would probably understand, while Far-rington's son might well commiserate with the neighboring cichlid.

Lorenz recounts that when he kept a male and female together in an aquarium tank, without any other fish, domestic violence often developed. However, things typically calmed down between the mated pair when other suitable targets were provided. The best arrangement, he found, was to have an elongated aquarium, with several male-female pairs, each separated from neighboring pairs by glass partitions. Lorenz could tell whenever these partitions were being overgrown with algae because as they became increasingly opaque and the inhabitants found themselves unable to discharge their aggression upon their neighbors, squabbles would break out within each domestic unit.

So, even among fish we have the notion of passing aggression along as a way of preserving domestic harmony. But Lorenz also emphasizes that there is a positive aspect to what ethologists call "redirected aggression." He maintains that it is actually essential to the establishment of the social bond between mated pairs. Among many species, the behavior of attacking someone else—or threatening to do so—has become ritualized into part of the male-female pair bond. Among greylag geese, for example (one of Lorenz's favorite species, which he studied intensively), male and female often share aggression toward outsiders. When successful, this aggression devolves into a mutual sequence known as the "triumph ceremony." Here the mated pair struts about and vocalizes together, the male and female appearing to congratulate each other in their victory, while at the same time reinforcing the bond between them.

Lorenz even goes so far as to say that love itself is derived, at least in part, from successfully shared redirected aggression, ritualized by evolution and pointed benevolently away from the two "lovers" and toward individuals outside the charmed circle of the mated pair.

Lorenz also argues that there is another consequence of shared aggression, directed outward, one that is far more malevolent in its consequences. This he labels "militant enthusiasm," which he sees as a

> specialized form of communal aggression, clearly distinct from and yet functionally related to the more primitive forms of petty individual aggression. Every man of normally strong emotions knows, from his own experience, the subjective phenomena that go hand in hand with the response of militant enthusiasm. A shiver runs down the back and, as more exact observation shows, along the outside of both arms. One soars elated, above all the ties of everyday life, one is ready to abandon all for the call of what, in the moment of this specific emotion, seems to be a sacred duty. All obstacles in its path become unimportant; the instinctive inhibitions against hurting or killing one's fellows lose, unfortunately, much of their power. Rational considerations, criticisms, and all reasonable arguments against the behavior dictated by militant enthusiasm are silenced by an amazing reversal of all values, making them appear not only untenable but base and dishonorable. Men may enjoy the feeling of absolute righteousness even while they commit atrocities. Conceptual thought and moral responsibility are at their lowest ebb. As a Ukrainian proverb says: "When the banner is unfurled, all reason is in the trumpet."[27]

Militant enthusiasm is a kind of redirected aggression writ large, a group-sanctioned passing along of pain and anger, in the guise of patriotic enthusiasm and violence. It is typically directed toward defense of the larger social unit, not simply one's territory or one's mate. It operates either by aggression toward other group members who deviate from accepted norms, or toward members of other groups. For Lorenz, militant enthusiasm is a human instinct, a form of triumph ceremony which differs from the case of the greylag goose in that it serves to enhance solidarity among vast numbers of individuals, embracing an entire nation. Here is Lorenz, a final time:

> Like the sexual urge or any other strong instinct, it engenders a specific feeling of intense satisfaction. The strength of its seductive lure explains why intelligent men may behave as irrationally and immorally in their political as in their sexual influence on the social structure of the species. Humanity is not enthusiastically combative because it is split into political parties, but it is divided into opposing camps because this is the adequate stimulus situation to arouse militant enthusiasm in a satisfying manner.[28]

We recently witnessed militant enthusiasm on a grand scale, activated during the war in the Persian Gulf. Americans, divided and lukewarm about the war before it began, generally rallied round the president, the flag, and the troops once the fighting started. The Iraqis did likewise, even many who opposed the leadership of Saddam Hussein. Significantly, in the Middle East itself, it seemed to be those people who had suffered the most pain—the Palestinians—who were the most eager for war, hoping that Saddam would give the West and the wealthy Arab states a longed-for black eye. When Palestinians danced in the streets, celebrating Iraqi missile attacks on noncombatant civilians in Tel Aviv, the whole world witnessed a spectacle of which the greylag goose offers us only a pale vision: the glee of people in immense pain, revelling as that pain was passed to others. And, of course, the Israelis—not to be outdone in the pain-passing department—schemed how best to pass it back again.

❖   ❖   ❖

Among greylag geese the triumph ceremony is part of a lifetime monogamous pair-bond. Among human beings, by contrast, any triumph that comes from passing the pain is nearly always short-lived, lasting just long enough for the victim to retaliate and, in so doing, revive the cycle of pain yet again. Accordingly, we turn next to those uniquely troubling cases in which pain and anger reverberate and multiply malignantly, creating a truly monstrous situation: the "Ahab syndrome" of enemies in excess.

Notes

1. W. H. Auden, "1939," in *Collected Poems* (New York: Random House, 1940).
2. James Joyce, "Counterparts," in *Dubliners* (New York: Viking, 1958).
3. Ibid.
4. Erich Fromm, *The Anatomy of Human Destructiveness* (New York: Holt, Rinehart & Winston, 1973).
5. Incidentally, to take the other famous Shakespearean story of vengeance, Hamlet's tragedy is that he was not up to the violent revenge—which, after all, is nothing but the passing of pain—that was demanded of him as the son of a murdered father. Once again, for all the profound human insight contained in the play, and all of Hamlet's agonizing about his "duty," nowhere in Hamlet is there a serious examination of why revenge should be called for at all, and whether it is in any way ethical or even useful. Those things we take for granted are often the most revealing about ourselves.
6. R. Barton, *Ifugao Law* (Berkeley, Calif.; University of California Press, 1919).
7. M. Daly and M. Wilson, *Homicide* (New York: Aldine de Gruyter, 1988).
8. Quoted in ibid.
9. M. Djilas, *Land Without Justice* (New York: Harcourt, 1958).
10. Quoted in Center for Foreign Policy Development, Brown University, *Update* 8 (1993): 6.
11. Geronimo, *Geronimo's Story of His Life* (New York: Duffield: 1906). I thank M. Daly and M. Wilson for this reference.

204   BELOVED ENEMIES

12. M. Djilas, *Land Without Justice.*

13. Returning to the story of the blacksmith and the tailor, it may be more than coincidental that tailors in central Europe were often Jewish.

14. Carl Hovland and Robert Sears, "Minor Studies of Aggression: Correlation of Lynchings with Economic Indices," *Journal of Psychology* 9 (1940): 301–10.

15. Jerome D. Frank, *Sanity and Survival in the Nuclear Age* (New York: Random House, 1982).

16. Quoted in Eli Sagan, *Cannibalism: Human Aggression and Cultural Form* (New York Harper & Row, 1974).

17. Andrew Bard Schmookler, *Out of Weakness* (New York: Bantam Books, 1988).

18. Eugene Ionesco, "Journal," *Encounter* 26 (1966): 25–36.

19. William Blake, "Infant Sorrow," *The Portable Blake* (New York: Viking, 1946).

20. M. Scott Peck, *People of the Lie* (New York: Simon & Schuster, 1983).

21. Rudolf Vrba and Alan Bestic, *I Cannot Forgive* (Bellingham, Wash.: Star & Cross).

22. Theodor Adorno, Else Frenkel-Brunswik, Daniel Levinson, and R. Nevitt Sanford, *The Authoritarian Personality* (New York: Harper & Bros., 1950).

23. It is interesting to note the apparent irony, for example, that in Adorno et al.'s original study, those professing to be most strongly anti-communist also proved to be the *least* committed to democracy, a correlation that seems to have been carried on by the most virulent right-wingers of today.

24. Jerome Frank, *Sanity and Survival in the Nuclear Age* (New York: Random House, 1982).

25. Erik Erikson, *Chidlhood and Society* (New York: W. W. Norton, 1950).

26. Konrad Z. Lorenz, *On Aggression* (New York: Harcourt, Brace, Jovanovich, 1966).

27. Ibid.

28. Ibid.

6

Enemies in Excess

It is "natural" to have enemies: in the world of animals and even plants (why else do roses have thorns?), between groups of people, among individuals, between differing ideologies, and even, perhaps, within individuals themselves. But at some point, legitimate concern with one's enemies can become obsessional, that is, inappropriate or excessive. It is difficult to imagine a cauliflower, or even a chimpanzee, whose focus on its enemies is "unnatural." It is all too easy, on the other hand, to identify a "paranoid" or "neurotic" style among our fellow human beings.

The Heart of the Hater

Take, for example, the paradigmatic case of someone harboring enmity in excess: Captain Ahab. What is Ahab without his nemesis, Moby Dick? Just an old man, unusually bitter we might assume, but—and here is the crucial point—utterly empty as well. Ahab was *filled* with his hatred of Moby Dick. This is not simply to say that he was well-stocked with hatred. Rather, he was filled with it, inflated by his animosity and nothing else, like a pillow by its feathers, or a balloon by air. Remove the stuffing, and the pillow or the balloon or the man shrinks and shrivels. In such cases, the one does not exist without the other.

Some things are defined by their opposites—*in a sense, their natural enemies.* Try to define "up" and it is hard not to mention "down." Similarly, what is "left" without "right," "east" without "west," or "in" without "out"? A moment's reflection shows, similarly, that left and right aren't really enemies (even if leftists and rightists sometimes are). Rather, each relies on the other for its meaning, like the head and tail of a coin.

Can we imagine Ahab healthy and whole—aside from the fact that he lost a leg to the white whale—having let go of his obsession with his enemy? To some extent, of course, this question is a strawman, since Ahab never really existed; he is a fictional device, a creation of author Herman Melville, designed to depict just such an enemy-obsessed character. But that is also the point: Ahab succeeds brilliantly precisely because he is so effectively defined by his enemy.

The biblical Israelites also were no strangers to anger or to vengeance. Consider their exultation at the drowning of the pharaoh and his armies in the Red Sea, or the enthusiasm with which they carried out Yahweh's many Old Testament injunctions to kill their (i.e., His) enemies, often sparing neither women nor children. Yet, they were also called upon to show compassion. "Ye know the heart of the stranger," the Israelites repeatedly admonished themselves, "for ye were strangers in the land of Egypt" (Exod. 23:9). Do we not similarly know the heart of those who hate, because there is hatred within our own hearts?

In some cases, that hatred is in dreadful excess. Such people are—often simultaneously—buoyed up as well as dragged down by their antagonism. They surf on their anger, riding the waves of its energy, propelled by its heady surge of momentum and power. These are the Ahabs among us, the people for whom an enemy becomes a consuming passion, a blessing no less than a curse, a reason for living as much as for dying. Although hatred and the search for revenge are as old as human history and well documented in our most ancient writings from the Homeric epics to the Old Testament or the sacred Hindu text, the Mahabharata, polite society recoils from the raw emotion, as well as from the haters and the seekers after vengeance themselves, who are expected to couch their quest in softer, more acceptable terms such as "recompense," "fairness," or "justice."

Yes indeed, we know the heart of the hater, and we shun it. Maybe we simply fear the intensity of the hate-obsessed, for the same reason that we don't like bad tidings or its bearers. As Terrence Des Pres, chronicler of concentration camp survivors, puts it,

> Refusal to acknowledge extremity is built into the structure of existence as we, the lucky ones, know it. More perhaps than we care to admit, spiritual well-being has depended on systems of mediation which transcend or otherwise deflect the sources of dread. . . . Too close a knowledge of vulnerability, of evil, of human insufficiency is felt to be ruinous. And therefore we assert that death is *not* the end, the body is *not* the self. The world is *not* a film upon the void, and virtue is *not* without Godhead on its side. So too with the survivor.[1]

Substitute for "survivor" the hater, the enemy-obsessed, the modern-day Ahab, and you have a good account of our own discomfort and resistance. Such rejection is not altogether misplaced. After all, Captain Ahab and his ilk have an intensity and monomania that is not only eerily familiar but that—as the ancient Greeks well knew—often forebodes disaster and tragedy. Frequently, in fact, it causes that disaster.

Almost by definition, obsessive clinging to enemies can only result in trouble. In part, this is because excess in anything is widely recognized to be unhealthy. (As former Republican senator and failed presidential candidate Barry Goldwater learned to his sorrow, even "extremism in the defense of liberty" is not widely perceived to be virtuous.) But in a deeper sense, the almost certain tragedy of excessive enmity seems to come from the simple fact that such a posture— whether directed toward a white whale, an ideology, another person, or a larger group—is bound to deform any human being. Whatever the magnitude of our animosity, we are only human, after all.

But what leads to such extremes of enmity? One clue lies in the phenomenon of passing the pain along, which was explored in the previous chapter.

Anatomy of the Ahab Syndrome

Virtually whenever it appears, excessive enmity can be traced to pain, injury, loss, and rage. In Ahab's case, the loss is straightforward and physical: the amputation of his leg. When we meet him in *Moby Dick*, Captain Ahab had already been "dismasted" by the great whale. It was this mutilation, we are told, that evoked Ahab's vindictive fury. Indeed, just as it is impossible to imagine Ahab without his great enemy, it is also impossible to imagine Ahab behaving as he does if he had not been dismembered by the whale. Maybe the young Ahab was already inclined to harbor grudges, to be rigid in his goals, and bitter when crossed,[2] but it is significant that his behavior only became remarkable after he had been severely injured. Then his pain— mental no less than physical—gradually filled his being as Ahab came to connect Moby Dick with all his hurts, frustrations, and disappointments:

> Ever since that almost fatal encounter, Ahab had cherished a wild vindictiveness against the whale, all the more fell for that in his

frantic morbidness he at last came to identify with him, not only all his bodily woes, but all his intellectual and spiritual exasperations. The White Whale swam before him as the monomaniac incarnation of all those malicious agencies which some deep men feel eating in them, till they are left living on with half a heart and half a lung. . . . He pitted himself, all mutilated, against it. All that most maddens and torments; all that stirs up the lees of things, all truth with malice in it; all that cracks the sinews and cakes the brain; all the subtle demonisms of life and thought; all evil, to crazy Ahab, were visibly personified, and made practically assailable in Moby Dick. He piled upon the whale's white hump the sum of all the general rage and hate felt by his whole race from Adam down; and then, as if his chest had been a mortar, he burst his hot heart's shell upon it.[3]

In a curious sense, Ahab's fury became his sole nourishment, feeding malignantly upon itself:

As the grizzly bear burying himself in the hollow of a tree, lived out the winter there, sucking his own paws, so, in his inclement, howling old age, Ahab's soul, shut up in the caved trunk of his body, there fed upon the sullen paws of its gloom.[4]

"Malignancy" is in fact the appropriate term, since Ahab's quest for revenge almost literally devoured him, just as a malignant cancer might have done. To be sure, he had been partly eaten by the whale, but in a deeper sense, Ahab was consumed from within. "Beware thyself, old man" warns the prescient mate, Starbuck. And later, he warns again, "Moby Dick seeks thee not. It is thou, thou, that madly seekest him!"[5]

Pioneering psychoanalyst Karen Horney puts it this way:

> In simplest terms the vindictive person does not only inflict suffering on others but even more so on himself. His vindictiveness makes him isolated, egocentric, absorbs his energies, makes him psychically sterile, and, above all, closes the gate to his further growth.[6]

Ahab has no capacity for growth. There is simply no additional room in the human personality structure once it is occupied by so fulsome a determination to destroy an enemy. As Ahab himself recognizes, his enmity has destroyed his own freedom of action:

> The path to my fixed purpose is laid with iron rails, whereon my soul is grooved to run. Over unsounded gorges, through the rifled hearts of mountains, under torrents' beds, unerringly I rush! Naught's an obstacle, naught's an angle to the iron way![7]

There we have it: the iron way of vengeance, of unending enmity. It is not surprising that we shrink from it with true fear and loathing: There is something inhuman about it. And yet, there is also something about this "iron way" that human beings, in their hearts, know all too well.

Inspector Javert

Captain Ahab is one of two great enemy-obsessed characters in Western literature. The other is Inspector Javert of Victor Hugo's *Les Misérables*. Just as Ahab exudes a superhuman determination, so does Javert: "He was one of those people who, even glimpsed, make an immediate impression; there was an intensity about him that was almost a threat. His name was Javert and he belonged to the police."[8]

Just as Ahab hunts Moby Dick, Javert spends literally decades hunting escaped convict Jean Valjean, who had committed the crime of stealing a loaf of bread to feed his starving sister and her family. Although Valjean has long since reformed and has been leading a more-than-exemplary life, Javert is obsessed with his task. As with Ahab, Javert's life is given meaning by his enmity, by his commitment to pursue and destroy his foe.

And when it comes to rigidity, Javert yields nothing to Ahab:

> His mental attitude was compounded of two very simple principles, admirable in themselves but which, by carrying them to extremes, he made almost evil—respect for authority and hatred of revolt against it. Theft, murder and every other crime were to him all forms of revolt. Everybody who played any part in the running of the State . . . was invested in his eyes with a kind of mystical sanctity, and he felt nothing but contempt, aversion and disgust for those who, even if only once, transgressed beyond the bounds of law. His judgements were absolute, admitting no exceptions. . . . He was stoical, earnest and austere, given to gloomy pondering, and like all fanatics, both humble and arrogant. His eyes were cold and piercing as a gimlet. His whole life was contained in two words, wakefulness and watchfulness. He drew a straight line through all that is most tortuous in this world. . . . He would have arrested his own father escaping from prison and denounced his mother for breaking parole, and he would have done it with a glow of conscious rectitude. His life was one of rigorous austerity, isolation, self-denial and chastity without distractions; a life of unswerving duty, with the police service playing the role that Sparta played for the Spartans.[9]

Inspector Javert, about to make an arrest, is as arrogantly self-assured and self-righteous, as utterly bereft of any doubt or introspection as Ahab poised to destroy a whale. Javert's prey—in the case described below, a poor woman named Fantine—is as undeserving of his violence as any freeliving, innocent leviathan is of Ahab's lance. But nonetheless, closing in on the guiltless Fantine,

> Javert was in heaven. Without being fully conscious of the fact, but still with a sense of his importance and achievement, he was at that moment the personification of justice, light, and truth in their sublime task of stamping out evil. Behind him and around him, extending into infinite space, were authority and reason, the conscience of the law, the sentence passed, the public condemnation and all the stars in the firmament. He was the guardian of order, the lightning of justice, the vengeance of society, the mailed fist of the absolute, and he was bathed in glory. There was in his victory a vestige of defiance and conflict. Upright, arrogant and resplendent, he stood like the embodiment in a clear sky of the superhuman ferocity of the destroying angel, and the deed he was performing seemed to invest his clenched fist with the gleam of a fiery sword. He was setting his foot in righteous indignation upon crime, vice and rebellion, damnation, and hell, and was smiling with satisfaction as he did.[10]

Ahab had been physically injured, and his commitment to destroying Moby Dick grew from the anguish of his injury. Javert had also been maimed by life, not physically but emotionally:

> He had been born in prison, the son of a fortune teller whose husband was in the galleys. As he grew older he came to believe that he was outside society with no prospect of ever entering it. But he noted that there were two classes of men whom society keeps inexorably at arm's length—those who prey upon it, and those who protect it. The only choice open to him was between those two. At the same time, he was a man with a profound instinct for correctitude, regularity, and probity, and with a consuming hatred for the vagabond order to which he himself belonged. He joined the police.[11]

Great writers such as Melville and Hugo, just like Shakespeare before and James Joyce after, have long recognized the human tendency to pass the pain along, and how, in extreme cases, the results can be deforming and tragic.[12]

But whereas Melville's great whale can respond only with dumb rage to Ahab's persecutions, Hugo's Jean Valjean responds with an almost saintly compassion and forgiveness: Granted the opportunity to kill Javert, Valjean frees him instead. Thus, near the end of *Les Misérables,* when Javert has finally succeeded, when he has finally gotten his nemesis, Jean Valjean, in his grasp, Javert finds himself utterly undone by his own triumph. Ahab gets his vengeance, and is killed in the process. Javert gets the opportunity to achieve his vengeance, but cannot bring himself to do it; tormented by the prospect of having to arrest the man who saved his life, he drowns himself in the River Seine.

Both Ahab and Javert are tragic figures, but Javert is by far the more sympathetic character. He refrained from destroying his enemy, after which, unable to contain his own torment at the impossible bind in which his conscience and his "duty" had entrapped him, he had no choice but to destroy himself:

> The man of action had lost his way. He was forced to admit that infallibility is not always infallible, that there may be error in dogma, that society is not perfect, that a flaw in the unalterable is possible, that judges are men and even the law may do wrong. What was happening to Javert resembled the derailing of a train—the straight line of the soul broken by . . . the inwardness of man . . .[13]

For our purposes, however, the similarities between *Moby Dick* and *Les Misérables* are more important than the differences. Both are fiction, to be sure, but both are psychologically compelling portraits of people being destroyed by their enmity, or rather, by their personal surrender to the demon of enemies in excess.

The Burdens of Ahab

As limiting and distorting as it is, the Ahab syndrome is also not
without a kind of grandeur. We may pity or despise and often avoid
the Ahabs of this world, but we are nonetheless inclined to view
them with a degree of wonder, if only because most of us are not
guided by so potent a will, nor do we bear such immense burdens:

> Captain Ahab stood erect, looking straight out beyond the ship's ever-
> pitching prow. There was an infinity of firmest fortitude, a determinate,
> insurrenderable willfulness, in the fixed and fearless, forward dedication
> of that glance. Not a word he spoke; nor did his officers say aught
> to him; though by all their minutest gestures and expressions, they
> plainly showed the uneasy, if not painful, consciousness of being under
> a troubled master-eye. And not only that, but moody stricken Ahab
> stood before them with a crucifixion in his face; in all the nameless
> regal overbearing dignity of some mighty woe.[14]

But despite their power and the awe they often evoke, the fact
remains that Ahabs are miserably unhappy. Toward the end of *Moby
Dick*, Ahab encounters the ship's blacksmith, who is repairing a steel
implement that had become "seamed and dented" from hard use:

> "And can'st thou make it all smooth again, blacksmith, after
> such hard usage as it had?"
> "I think so, Sir."
> "And I suppose thou can'st smoothe almost any seams and dents;
> never mind how hard the metal, blacksmith?"
> "Aye, Sir, I think I can; all seams and dents but one."
> "Look ye here, then," cried Ahab, passionately advancing, and
> leaning with both hands on Perth's shoulders; "look ye here—*here*—
> can ye smoothe out a seam like this, blacksmith," sweeping one
> hand across his ribbed brows, "if you could'st, blacksmith, glad

enough I lay my head upon thy anvil, and feel thy heaviest hammer between my eyes. Answer! Can'st thou smoothe this seam?"

"Oh! that is the one, Sir! Said I not all seams and dents but one?"

"Aye, blacksmith, it is the one; aye, man, it is unsmoothable; for though thou only see'st it here in my flesh, it has worked down into the bone of my skull—that is all wrinkles!"[15]

Such people are dangerous, and not only to themselves. Generations have been riveted by the story of Ahab's obsession with his own personal revenge. In so doing, they often lose sight of the fact that Ahab brings ruin and tragedy not only upon himself, but upon his ship and the entire crew. He does so because his own personality is so powerful and overwhelming that he is able to enlist the crew's emotions and commitment on behalf of his own needs. Only Starbuck, the grim and pessimistic first mate, remains critical of Ahab's undertaking, but even he is unable to change the old man's mind, and unwilling to disobey his orders.

When in positions of command and authority—a situation which, as we shall see, happens often—the Ahabs of the world are mortal threats, both to themselves and to others.

Is Revenge Sweet?

Erich Fromm relates the following story, a telling one for our purposes. A fascist Spanish general, Millan Astray, had been maimed and crippled in battle. His ironic motto was *Viva la muerte* ("long live death"). When Astray gave a speech at the University of Salamanca in 1936, shortly before the horrific bloodletting of the Spanish civil war was to begin, one of his supporters shouted, "Viva la muerte." In response, the great writer and philosopher Jugo Miguel de

Unamuno, then rector of the university and in the last year of his own long and productive life, rose and announced:

> This outlandish paradox is repellent to me. General Millan Astray is a cripple. Let it be said without any slighting undertone. He is a war invalid. So was Cervantes. Unfortunately there are too many cripples in Spain just now. And soon there will be even more of them if God does not come to our aid.[16]

There can be no doubt that the enemy-obsessed need help, whether from blacksmiths, psychotherapists, or the deity of their choice. And so do the rest of us, lest we wind up caught in the carnage of future Spanish civil wars, or in the same boat as the *Pequod's* crew.

Near the climax of *Moby Dick*, once the epic battle between man and whale has been joined, Ahab allows himself to fantasize—if only briefly—about victory. He imagines Moby Dick's carcass lashed to the side of his ship. But the thought is only fleeting, and to no one's surprise. Just as it is virtually impossible for us to imagine Captain Ahab without his nemesis, Moby Dick, it is equally difficult to picture a victorious Ahab, calm and peaceful in his triumph, made whole by his revenge. The point is not simply that killing his enemy can never literally restore Ahab's leg, it is—as we often say but rarely believe—that two wrongs really do not make a right. Not only is enemy-obsession likely to be dangerous if not tragic, it often is deeply unsatisfying as well.

Let us rewrite the ending of *Moby Dick*: After a lengthy struggle (or, worse yet for the captain, perhaps one that is all too easy), Moby Dick spouts his last. He lies there, literally dead in the water, huge rivers of blood making an estuary where it joins the salty foam, his great bulk utterly insensate, no longer lashing his mighty tail, incapable of even the slightest twitch. Ahab gives a great shout of triumph.

Balancing uneasily with his ivory leg upon the sloping, slippery back of his vanquished foe, he thrusts his harpoon again and again, while his crew cheer and then, after a time—embarrassed, perhaps, by their captain's excess—avert their eyes. Then begins the time-consuming process of butchering the whale, and eventually sailing home to Nantucket. But what of Ahab all this time? Does he dance a jig in Moby Dick's intestines? Drink his blood? Bathe triumphantly in his rendered blubber? Make a hundred artificial legs out of the creature's jaw-bone? Is he happy at last? Is he finally at ease? Or, having achieved his announced and all-consuming goal, does he feel just a wee bit empty and devoid of purpose, still mangled in body and no more peaceful in soul?

There is an oft-cited observation that "revenge is sweet." But let us set the record straight, for this is a blatant misquote. The original, in Milton's *Paradise Lost*, actually reads:

> Revenge, at first though sweet
> Bitter ere long back on itself recoils.

The initial sweetness of revenge leaves a bitter aftertaste.

It also leaves some unanswered questions. For example, U.S. Senator Robert Kerrey is an interesting foil to Melville's doomed, fanatical whale-hunter. What makes for an Ahab, on the one hand, and for a Robert Kerrey, on the other? Kerrey is a former governor of Nebraska and a Vietnam War hero who—like Ahab—lost part of his leg, not to Moby Dick but while serving as a Navy SEAL in Vietnam. He also earned a Congressional Medal of Honor in the process. Robert Kerrey would seem to have all the necessary qualifications to have become a full-fledged Ahab, hating the white whale that dismembered him, taking out his rage at post-war Vietnam or communism or revolutionary nationalism more generally. Yet Senator Kerrey has emerged as one of the more thoughtful, compassionate spokespeople for liberal causes and a nonmilitary approach to world events. He is not a hater. He does not crave vengeance. He even seems to oppose violence rather than promote it. He does not fantasize great shoals of monstrous leviathan enemies circling ever nearer, hungrily eyeing himself or his country, or floating menacingly in the oceans of geopolitics.

It is a good bet that Senator Kerrey had a better childhood than either Captain Ahab or Inspector Javert. Maybe we can derive some comfort from the fact that whereas Ahab and Javert are both fictional characters, the Robert Kerreys of this world are real.

Unfortunately, however, the Ahab syndrome recurs with depressing frequency in real life. In fact, the miserably obsessed, demon-driven souls of fiction pale in comparison with those that reality sometimes vomits forth.

Cults

The word "cult" is hardly value neutral. Most people would not object, for example, if they were described as belonging to a particular religious "sect," whereas they would likely feel quite differently about being labelled a "cult" member. Perhaps the fairest definition of a cult is any group that does not include one's self, and that one does not like. More objectively, cults are closed communities, the members of which share a rigidly defined ideology. Membership generally also involves substantial renunciation of one's prior life, including family, friends, and often, material possessions. Especially important is the leader, who is virtually deified, likely considered infallible or otherwise possessing supernatural insights, often because he (she) is thought to be a direct descendant or reincarnation of a god. The leader usually agrees.

The recent American experience with cults has included the

followers of the Rev. Jim Jones, MOVE in Philadelphia, and the Branch Davidians who followed David Koresh near Waco, Texas. These three cases were especially dramatic because of the violent and tragic end in each instance: More than nine hundred people took poison (Kool-Aid laced with cyanide) at Jonestown, Guyana, in 1978; an incendiary attack by the police against MOVE in 1985 resulted in several deaths and a massive conflagration; and the Branch Davidians' shootout with federal agents led to a fifty-one day standoff, which then culminated in a fiery mass suicide in which nearly ninety people—including many children—died in 1993.

Of course, many other cults can also be identified, including the snake handlers of Georgia and West Virginia, the Divine Light Mission (former followers of the teenaged guru Maharaj Ji), the Unification Church (devotees of the Rev. Sung Myung Moon), and the hare krishnas. The definition of a cult becomes uncertain at the boundaries of social respectability: for example, what about Alcoholics Anonymous and other "twelve-step" programs, or devotees of EST, Transcendental Meditation, chiropractic, fly fishermen, or square dancers? An influential fundamentalist church leader in Kirkland, Washington, recently derided members of the Unitarian Universalist Association as cultists. Certain mainline church leaders undoubtedly consider many charismatic, evangelic "born again" Christian groups to be cults as well. Cultism, to some degree, is in the eye of the beholder. Nonetheless, most of us can probably substitute cults for the noted jurist's definition of pornography: I may not be able to define it, but I know it when I see it.

In their paranoid qualities and their penchant for violence, some of the more readily acknowledged cults also represent some of the most extreme aspects of enemies in excess. This seems to be produced by a combination of the extreme isolation of cult members, a rigid and critical us-versus-them attitude by cultists toward the outside world, as well as the frequently antagonstic response of that outside world, which further confirms the cultists' sense of embattled isolation. Also, as we shall see, the leader is crucial.

Cult members are often recruited from people who are seeking to achieve a new identity (because of their prior pain?). In any event, cult membership gives recruits the opportunity to bury their past while also relieving themselves of the need to make their own choices in the present and future. The cult member does not simply adopt a life style, but rather a complete belief system that specifies clear limits to what is acceptable and what is not. He (she) typically experiences the warm glow of belonging and acceptance—often, for the first time. Not coincidentally, the recruit also undergoes massive "deselfing," since under the extreme circumstances of cult membership, belonging and acceptance are contingent upon the recruit suspending virtually all capacity for critical thinking or dissent. Recruits eagerly shed their prior selves like snakes or crabs molting an ill-fitting skin. Continuing the metaphor: Like a freshly molted animal, the new member finds himself (herself) uniquely vulnerable as well as relatively shapeless. The cult's belief system provides a psychological exoskeleton of a sort, one that becomes crucially important—indeed, a prerequisite for survival. Like the carapace of a recently molted crab, the cult's ideology quickly hardens around the new member, providing form and structure, and at least the illusion of security, an intensely protective and all-embracing family.

In this respect, the cult leader looms large. From Jim Jones of the People's Temple, to John Africa of MOVE, to David Koresh of the Branch Davidians, most cults with a penchant for violence have been led by people who are themselves both charismatic and at least semi-psychotic. They are typically filled with delusions of grandeur, seeing themselves as saviors of their own group and often of humanity at large. At the same time as they feast on the adulation of their followers, these leaders also tend to be highly vulnerable to rejection.

Not surprisingly, rejection is precisely what they and their faithful are likely to experience, since the outside world does not take kindly to groups that march to a distinctly different drummer. As that rejection begins to bite—and especially if there are overtones of physical threat and potential violence—it is only a very small step before the cult leader defines the outside world as not only different and dangerous, but also the Enemy.

Given the extraordinary and unquestioned power of the leader over his followers, his vision of enmity is readily accepted by the group as a whole, which then becomes a kind of *Pequod*'s crew, responding to the leader's perception of the outside society as a white whale. Observers of Jim Jones, John Africa, and David Koresh have all been struck by the unshakable certainty of these cult "captains." And there can be little doubt that such fixed determination (what Ahab called "the iron way"), in turn, contributed to the blind adherence of their followers, so many of whom persevered in loyalty even to their deaths.

Writing in the early years of World War II, psychoanalyst Fritz Redl explored those factors that make for successful group leadership. He concluded that above all, leaders who inspire unquestioning obedience are those who adhere to their beliefs with unwavering certainty. As Redl saw it, there is something especially magnetic and universal about the "infectiousness of the unconflicted person."[17]

The "unconflicted" leader is especially well positioned to motivate followers. Human beings do not march enthusiastically to an uncertain trumpet, but they rally round a voice that is commanding and un-conflicted. Unfortunately, such a leader may also be dangerously un-conflicted about the consequences of his (or her) behavior. Thus, for example, at the outbreak of World War I, the German kaiser remarked "Even if we are bled to death, England will at least lose India," and the Japanese war minister rationalized the decision to bomb Pearl Harbor in 1941 by declaring, "Once in a while it is necessary for one to close one's eyes and jump from the stage of the Kiyomizu Temple" (a popular suicide spot). Similarly, Hitler remarked privately, "We may be destroyed," in anticipation of the war he was about to provoke. "But if we are," he added, as though in reassurance, "we shall drag a world with us—a world in flames."[18]

The passion, charisma, and often paranoid conviction of such leaders dwarfs the more human-sized, questioning, and conflicted emotions that might otherwise prevail among their followers. It is easy to mistake unconflicted determination for wisdom or special knowledge, or to prefer an inhuman certitude over an all-too-human ambivalence. Much of the disdain, in fact, that was heaped upon former President Jimmy Carter may well have derived from the fact that he appeared to be so conflicted—in a sense, so ordinary. He agonized, he debated, he committed the sin of noting a "malaise" among the American public (leaders are supposed to be free of any malaise, and to assume the same, apparently, from their followers). Carter even spoke openly and sympathetically with his nine-year-old daughter, thereby, it seems, demonstrating that he was unfit to lead the United States.

By contrast, the American people were entranced by Ronald Reagan, even though he was poorly informed, hidebound, careless of his facts, and generally unmindful of reality, because Reagan's ignorance was superceded by a breezy, unconflicted certainty that he was right and the other side (notably the Communists, liberals, and "welfare queens") were wrong. It was widely said of Reagan that he made America stand tall largely because he stood tall himself.

In fact, charismatic leaders are often deeply troubled, and far more conflicted and complex than they appear to their followers. Listen to historian Hugh Trevor-Roper's description of the mind of Adolf Hitler:

A terrible phenomenon, imposing indeed in its granite harshness and yet infinitely squalid in its miscellaneous cumber—like some huge barbarian monolith, the expression of giant strength and savage genius, surrounded by a festering heap of refuse—old tins and dead vermin, ashes and eggshells and ordure—the intellectual detritus of centuries.[19]

If he had had fewer followers, Hitler might have been remembered as a mere cult leader. For his part, Reagan was not a cult leader, and was probably too well adjusted to become one. Others, however, such as David Koresh, John Africa, or Jim Jones combined charisma with paranoia, and recruited followers ready to believe their leader's pronouncements on matters ranging from daily life and theology to group enmity and personal death. Thus, since most cult members had forgone much of their selfhood and had withdrawn their critical faculties in the face of the unconflicted certainty of their leaders, they were highly susceptible to a profound sense of shared, embattled enmity once those leaders went afoul of the law. And of course, the violent behavior of the authorities—in the case of MOVE as well as the Branch Davidians—confirmed the paranoid certainty of the cult leaders, while also solidifying their hold on their followers.

To some extent, "outsiders" have often been as intolerant and quick to establish and confirm enmity as have cultists. This was true of the supposedly sophisticated San Franciscans, most of whom disdained and rejected the Divine Light Mission and its teenage guru, Maharaj Ji, no less than the rural inhabitants of Antelope, Oregon, who feared and detested the Baghwan Sree Rajneesh and his followers. Fortunately, societal intolerance does not push all cults to violence or, perhaps, not all cults are equally prone to such recourse.

In any event, the potential for extremes of enmity exists whenever vulnerable followers, eager to be deselfed, meet up with charismatic, unconflicted leaders, especially if those leaders are suffering from more than their share of the Ahab syndrome. Add a dash of paranoia, a pinch of societal intolerance, stir vigorously with an arsenal of lethal weaponry, and you have a guaranteed recipe for tragedy.

Lest we become self-righteous, however, it is worth noting, first, that the attitude of society at large toward cults is often only marginally less prone to excesses of enmity than are the cults themselves. Second, full-blown certifiable cults are not unique in manifesting a paranoid tradition within the United States. Historically, Americans have had more than their share of experience as members of Ahab's crew.

"The Paranoid Style in American Politics"

It was November 1963. The American political historian Richard Hofstadter delivered a lecture at Oxford University. Subsequently published in *Harper's* a year later and titled "The Paranoid Style in American Politics," it is unsurpassed as a description of the Ahab tradition in the political history of the United States.

Clearly, the United States does not have a monopoly on political paranoia. The politics of Italy or Greece, for example, are especially rife with Byzantine plots, counterplots, and—even more—rumors of such plots. But it may come as a surprise to many Americans, who cherish an image of the USA as fresh, young, optimistic, and straightforward in its political dealings, that we have a paranoid streak with a substantial pedigree. In part, this regular stirring of paranoia may be due to our early (and for many, our continuing) sense of specialness: the knowledge that we are the preferred people of God, chosen to be a light to the benighted nations of the world—a New Jerusalem, a shining City on the Hill. Possessed of total goodness as we are, any excess in our defense or aggrandizement is naturally justified. Furthermore, given that the United States of America is so indubitably good, any individual, group, or ideology setting itself in opposition to us must necessarily be evil. We have a particularly acute, demanding sense of mission that can make us insufferable in our own self-congratulated purity, rather like Sir Lancelot in the musical *Camelot*. But, also like Lancelot, we may be especially vulnerable to sin, particularly insofar as a heightened conviction of our own goodness makes us especially likely to demonize others who threaten our cherished self-image.

Also involved, perhaps, is a deeply rooted awareness that we have some dirty little secrets in our own closets, a hazy recognition that we may be secret sinners. Consider, for example, our early treatment of Native Americans and Mexicans, as well as our own black slaves. "I tremble for my country," wrote Thomas Jefferson, "when I consider that God is just." Those who most loudly proclaim their virtue are likely to be the most insecure, and for good reason considering such holier-than-thou televangelists as Jim Bakker or Jimmy Swaggart.

In any event, since America's founding, an explosive mix of certainty as to its blessedness, combined with its transoceanic isolation from the Old World, (to which we could possibly add a guilty conscience), has led to a recurrent paranoid streak in the United States. Until the middle of the twentieth century, America was determinedly isolationist in world affairs. However, we were also expansionist, and—at least in our own minds—under siege, from within more than from without. We have regularly provided ourselves with enemies, and have persistently endowed those enemies with remarkable powers. As Hofstadter puts it,

> This enemy is clearly delineated: he is a perfect model of malice, a kind of amoral superman: sinister, ubiquitous, powerful, cruel, sensual, luxury-loving. Unlike the rest of us, the enemy is not caught in the toils of the vast mechanism of history, himself a victim of

his past, his desires, his limitations. He is a free, active, demonic agent. He wills, indeed he manufactures, the mechanism of history himself, or deflects the normal course of history in an evil way. He makes crises, starts runs on banks, causes depressions, manufactures disasters, and then enjoys and profits from the misery he has produced. The paranoid's interpretation of history is in this sense distinctly personal: decisive events are not taken as part of the stream of history, but as the consequences of someone's will. Very often the enemy is held to possess some especially effective source of power: he controls the press; he directs the public mind through "managed news"; he has unlimited funds; he has a new secret for influencing the mind (brainwashing); he has a special technique for seduction (the Catholic confessional); he is gaining a stranglehold on the educational system.[20]

This enemy has been immensely useful. As with Ahab and Javert, the political paranoid has been able to employ the enemy as an explanation for why he has been hurt, and as a plausible cause for whatever mutilation (physical or emotional, real or imagined, personal or social) the victim must confront. As we have seen, this enemy not only provides an explanation, an understandable cause for otherwise confusing and confounding effects, he also locates that cause outside one's self: over There, in Them. Just as Hitler found it immensely useful, for example, to place the blame for German dissatisfaction during the 1930s on that country's Jews, the late Wisconsin senator Joseph McCarthy made an "ism" out of blaming Communists and "Communist sympathizers" for what he and many others saw as America's parlous state during the late 1940s and early 1950s. In 1951, for example, McCarthy made the following statement to the U.S. Senate:

How can we account for our present situation unless we believe that men high in this government are concerting to deliver us to disaster? This must be the product of a great conspiracy, a conspiracy on a scale so immense as to dwarf any previous such venture in the history of man. A conspiracy of infamy so black that, when it is finally exposed, its principals shall be forever deserving of the maledictions of all honest men. . . . What can be made of this unbroken series of decisions and acts contributing to the strategy of defeat? They cannot be attributed to incompetence.[21]

No indeed, it could not possibly be incompetence. Nor could it be the result of simple error, miscalculation, or the ebb and flow of events. If the Soviets "got" the atomic bomb, or Mao and his followers "got" China, these and other disconcerting post-World War II "getting" can only mean that They have been out to "get" us, that we have been under attack by malign powers, a "conspiracy of infamy" directed at Us—the Godly—by Them, the vile.

Don't get the impression, by the way, that we are dealing here with a disorder limited to the political right-wing (although historically, American conservatism has been especially susceptible to such delusions). Following is part of a manifesto issued by leaders of the left-leaning Populist party of the United States in 1895:

As early as 1865–66 a conspiracy was entered into between the gold gamblers of Europe and America. . . . For nearly thirty years these conspirators have kept the people quarreling over less important matters, while they have pursued with unrelenting zeal their one central purpose. . . . Every device of treachery, every resource of statecraft, and every artifice known to the secret cabals of the international gold ring are being made use of to deal a blow to the prosperity of the people and the financial and commercial independence of the country.[22]

As William Jennings Bryan claimed in one of the most famous speeches in American political history, the people of the United States

were being crucified on a "cross of gold," with the federal government
as Pontius Pilate and the international gold conspirators playing the
part of Roman soldiers wielding the mallets of corrupt European
finance.

Even before the Communist menace and its predecessors, the
international gold traffickers, American political paranoia had been
notably fastened on another insidious and dangerous enemy, the
Catholic Church and the threat it was thought to embody. In 1855,
for example, this article appeared in a Texas newspaper. Its frothing,
wild-eyed anti-Catholicism made it about average for its time:

> It is a notorious fact that the monarchs of Europe and the pope
> of Rome are at this very moment plotting our destruction and
> threatening the extinction of our political, civil, and religious in-
> stitutions. We have the best reasons for believing that corruption
> has found its way into our executive chamber, and that our executive
> head is tainted with the infectious venom of Catholicism. . . . The
> pope has recently sent his ambassador of state to this country on
> a secret commission, the effect of which is an extraordinary boldness
> of the Catholic Church throughout the United States. . . . These
> minions of the pope are boldly insulting our senators; reprimanding
> our statesmen; propagating the adulterous union of church and state;
> abusing with foul calumny all governments but Catholic; and spewing
> out the bitterest execrations on all Protestantism.[23]

For each of the three enemies—Communists, gold financiers, and
Catholics—the paranoid imagination was whetted at the time of its
greatest fervor by the villains' mysterious ideology, and further
enhanced by the nefarious fact that they emanated from foreign lands:
in the case of communism, the Kremlin; for the gold financiers, London
and Zurich; and for the Catholics, the Vatican.

Even the vicious anti-Catholicism of the mid-nineteenth century
was not the earliest sign of U.S. political paranoia. Several decades

earlier, there had been yet another period of comparable fear and hatred, aimed this time at Freemasons. For example, in "Light on Masonry," a renowned anti-Masonic tract published in 1829, Masonry—a nonsectarian, fraternal organization devoted to religious tolerance and "good works"—is described as "an engine of Satan . . . dark, unfruitful, selfish, demoralizing, blasphemous, murderous, anti-republican and anti-Christian." In the first few decades of the nineteenth century, Masons were held to practice secret, unspeakably evil rites and to threaten the very cornerstones of American civilization, accusations almost identical to those later to be raised, in turn, against Catholics, gold financiers, and Communists.

Even before the Masons, American paranoia around the end of the eighteenth century fastened on yet an earlier enemy, this time a secular, scientific, and humanistic creed known as Illuminism. For a sense of the tone and content of anti-Illuminism, listen to the following sermon, preached in Massachusets in 1798:

> Secret and systematic means have been adopted and pursued, with zeal and activity, by wicked and artful men, in foreign countries, to undermine the foundations of this Religion [Christianity] and to overthrow its Altars, and thus to deprive the world of its benign influence on society. . . . These impious conspirators and philosophists have completely effected their purposes in a large portion of Europe, and boast of their means of accomplishing their plans in all parts of Christendom.[24]

Journeying through the annals of political paranoia, we find that the danger was always immediate and the peril, mortal. And so, the American patriotic paranoid, a reincarnated Paul Revere, rode forever through the night, roaring at the top of his lungs to alert his somnolent countrymen to the arrival of the enemy. But unlike the more fortunate Revere, the paranoid generally evoked no more than a modest response, which spurred him on to ever more florid heights of agitated hyperbole. Consider this, from an anti-Catholic diatribe of 1835:

> The serpent has already commenced his coil about our limbs, and the lethargy of his poison is creeping over us. . . . Is not the enemy already organized in the land? Can we not perceive all around us the evidence of his presence? . . . We must awake, or we are lost.[25]

The enemy provides the overheated, paranoid hater with someone who can be wholly condemned, but also—ironically—imitated, especially when such imitation is thought necessary in order to defeat him. The secrecy and violence of the anti-Masons, for example, rivalled the excesses of which the Masons themselves were accused. Nothing in recent U.S. history has come as close as McCarthyism to the deviltry ascribed by Joseph McCarthy to communism. Ironically, those in the Reagan administration who hungered for such abominations as "limited" nuclear war, counterforce strategies, and civil defense (which has never been either) justified their grisly enterprise by pointing with alarm to the specter of precisely these policies on the part of the Soviet Union. The way to beat 'em, apparently, is to join 'em (at least in techniques)—and when possible, exceed 'em.

In the process, reality becomes irrelevant; truth, an inconvenience. But don't think that the paranoid hater is happy, even when he succeeds in destroying or defeating his enemy.[26] No, the enemy always exists, and is always ready to be rediscovered or reinvented. Woe betide us all if, perchance, the enemy cannot be found for a time, since this not only "proves" how clever and secretive he can be, it also actually enhances the danger posed, since, of course, the *unseen* enemy is the greatest threat of all. As Richard Hofstadter has put it, we are all "sufferers from history," but the paranoid suffers doubly, afflicted not only by the world as it is, but also by his most energetic fantasies.

Paranoia and the Prisoner's Dilemma Revisited

Pity the poor paranoid, for sometimes he really does have enemies. James Forrestal, investment banker and U.S. Secretary of Defense from 1947 to 1949, became psychotically paranoid while in office; he eventually killed himself by jumping from a window of the Walter Reed Army Hospital, where he had been admitted for psychiatric treatment. Among other things, Forrestal claimed that he was being trailed constantly by the Israeli Secret Service. After his death, it was revealed that he really had, in fact, been trailed by the Israelis. James Forrestal suffered from delusions of persecution, but he wasn't always deluded. The case of Secretary Forrestal carries a lesson for us: The paranoid is sometimes correct. But it obscures another, more important, lesson: Often, paranoids create precisely the enemies they so dread and of whose existence they are so sure.

Consider the Prisoner's Dilemma once again. Remember, in the Prisoner's Dilemma each player is faced with a simple but difficult decision: to cooperate and be "nice" or to defect and be "nasty." Under the terms of the Prisoner's Dilemma, there is a double pull toward nastiness, first because of the temptation of catching the other fellow being nice, and thus getting a very high pay-off, and second because of the fear of being nice at the same time the other guy is nasty, thus winding up a sucker, with the lowest pay-off of all. The result is a tendency for both players to be nasty and uncooperative, which causes them both to do relatively poorly (when compared to the outcome of being nice and cooperating).

But as political scientist Robert Axelrod has demonstrated,[27] there is a way out of the Prisoner's Dilemma, especially if the "game" is played not once but many times. In such cases, the ultimate pay-off gained by interacting regularly with a cooperating partner can be so high that individuals—even the most selfish—will do best if they are nice to each other. Axelrod's analysis is based on the strategy of "tit for tat," in which the players seek to be nice (that is, cooperative, altruistic, etc.), but reserve the right to retaliate with comparable nastiness if the other fellow is nasty.

Axelrod's discovery has occasioned great enthusiasm on the part of biologists and social scientists because it promises a way out of the longstanding dilemma of destructive but seemingly unavoidable selfishness. It suggests that living things, including human beings, can achieve mutual cooperation with all the benefits that cooperative activity entails. Less often appreciated, however, is the fact that "tit for tat" also has a dark, retaliatory side, the face, perhaps, of the paranoid. Paranoids think the worst of others. They assume that virtually anyone and everyone is their enemy, plotting against them behind their backs, laughing at them, trying desperately to bring them to grief. In short, to the paranoid, everyone is a defector, a cheater, a low-down rotten snake in the grass, a representative of some malign power directing its energies toward his downfall. Not surprisingly, the paranoid plays "nasty." Convinced that the world is against him, the paranoid conducts his own version of "tit for tat." In the process, his behavior becomes a self-fulfilling prophecy, as others—ranging from neutral, indifferent bystanders to even friends and relatives who might otherwise be positively disposed—respond eventually with their own version of tit for tat. They often turn against the paranoid, disliking him, shunning him, or arresting him. (Which, of course, merely proves to the paranoid that his assessment was correct in the first place!)

What, then, causes such paranoia? To some extent, there seems to be a genetic predisposition, related presumably to an imbalance of neurotransmitter chemicals in the sufferer's brain.[28] Also, there can be genuine enemies, real people "out there" who are not interested in maximizing your welfare and who may even actively conspire against you: recall James Forrestal, not to mention Freud's cigar. In addition, the paranoid may find himself stuck in a straightforward but malignant game of Prisoner's Dilemma, in which the player's sense of the Other's enmity becomes a self-fulfilling prophecy.

As the Prisoner's Dilemma shows us, there is an unbroken line that unites our inner conflicts, our behavior, and our "external" enemies. But as Ahab shows us, it is a line that can break, and that can break us. Moreover, enmity can also do us harm indirectly, insofar as it creates and orients oppositional attitudes toward the nonhuman world as well.

Nature as Enemy

"We have lived for a long time," writes sociologist Robert Bellah, "with a model of man as one charged by a stern God to carry out His commands, a man who must be up and doing, a man in quest of mastery and success."[29] It hasn't been all bad. True to our self-image, we have been masterful and successful, but at a price: distancing ourselves from the natural world and from our fellow human beings. We have often made nature something to be avoided, overcome, destroyed, changed, tamed, or bent to our will. In short, we made enemies. It was the price of our success.

In a sort of Faustian exchange, we gained much, but in return, like Dr. Faust, we forfeited much as well. Even, perhaps, part of ourselves, because if we take seriously the wisdom of the East, the deep truth of connectedness between all things, then it is clear that we can no more call another person or a forest or an animal our enemy, than we can declare war on our lungs or on our large intestine.

Sometimes our own internal organs do become, in a sense, opposed to our own well-being, but such cases are actually quite revealing. Our lungs may develop emphysema and our intestines become inflamed or blocked, but the problem in such cases is not that part of our body has turned against us, but, rather, that it has become sick and in need of help, often because of our own abuse.

Cancer is a notorious example of the body becoming an enemy to itself, and, interestingly, it is often associated with severe "insults"— chemical or structural irritants—or with actual genetic changes in which the cancer cells no longer carry the same DNA fingerprint that characterizes the surrounding tissue cells. With this loss of genetic identity, the cancer cells no longer treat the remaining cells as friends; by becoming different, they become enemies. In medical jargon as well as common sense, they become malignant.

Although we claim to recognize ourselves as part of nature, the truth is often otherwise. Although the Earth is no longer thought to be the center of the universe, in our heart of hearts we presume that the third planet from the Sun is especially blessed and deserving. Although most people acknowledge the truth of evolution by natural selection, we continue to resist the implications of that fact, pressing for a Brahean solution whereby the tight-lipped acknowledgment of our connectedness with the rest of organic nature is kept divorced from the deeper implications of that reality.

Listen to the wife of the Bishop of Worcester when she had been told about Charles Darwin's disquieting ideas: "Descended from monkeys? My dear, let us hope that it isn't true! But if it is true, let us hope that it doesn't become widely known!"

Of course it is true, and by now it is also widely known, but, Brahe-like, we have tended to shy away from its implications, and to persevere in a worldview that not only separates man from nature, but also sets up the two as opponents, as enemies in a cosmic struggle ordained by no less an authority than God himself.

Western religion is unique in the degree of its anthropocentrism, the extent to which it places human beings at the center of the natural order. But rather than ensconcing ourselves comfortably and securely within a nurturing web of ecological connections, our predominant spiritual tradition *separates* us from the rest of nature: on the one hand, mushrooms and redwood trees, snails and elephants, and on the other, human beings. We may speak, in one breath, of cabbages and kings, but to most followers of Judeo-Christian (and, it appears, Islamic) tradition, the two are literally worlds apart. After all, in an extraordinary assertion of hubris, believers have proclaimed ourselves uniquely made in the image of God. Made out of clay, to be sure, but we and we alone are also—by our own account, at least—possessed of a supernatural spark as well as some unspecified transcendence of the merely material, a specialness based on nothing less than commonality with the divine. We, and we alone, are chips off the Old Block. Neither monkeys nor mastodons make the grade.

This distinction is pernicious enough, with its literally holier-than-thou attitude setting the stage for alienation, separateness, and a kind of species snobbery. But regrettably, such an anti-nature ethic does more than this; it enthrones *Homo sapiens* as lord and master, tyrant over nature. First we separate ourselves from nature, then elevate ourselves above the rest of life, then, in a *coup de grâce*, we declare outright war on it. Few statements, echoing down the centuries, have been more damaging to ecological harmony and more influential in establishing an enduring antagonism between humanity and nature than God's supposed commands to Adam and Eve: "Be fruitful and multiply, and fill the earth and subdue it; and have dominion over the fish of the sea and over the birds of the air and over every living thing that moves upon the earth" (Genesis 1:28 RSV).

This Old Testament directive went far to establish a mind-set of opposition and enmity in which human beings and the natural world were fixed as adversaries. Our job was to subdue the earth, to exercise dominion over its living creatures, to do battle with God's creation as with an implacable foe. Those were our marching orders, conveyed to us—we have long assumed—by the Chief General. As an assumption, it undermines the fundamental principle of environmentalism and conservation, which is to live in harmony and co-operation with the world ecosystem. It provides much of the intellectual underpinnings for the environmental abuse that has characterized Western technological civilization. Although we sing of our love for and devotion to the land of the free and the home of the brave, we must ask, with pioneer conservationist Aldo Leopold,

> just what and whom do we love? Certainly not the soil, which we are sending helter-skelter downriver. Certainly not the waters, which we assume have no function except to turn turbines, float barges, and carry off sewage. Certainly not the plants, of which we exterminate whole communities without batting an eye. Certainly not the animals, of which we have already extirpated many of the largest and most beautiful species.[30]

Often, our "love" is that of the generous conqueror, willing to modulate our antagonism only after the battle is over, and won. In our case, however, we can only lose by winning.

We have "defeated" most of the ancient forests that originally clothed the North American continent, and in the Pacific Northwest many people are now scrambling to cut down the remaining stands, while some, at least, seek desperately to halt the carnage. If the cutters succeed, then these "victors" will shortly be defeated in any event, as they literally cut themselves out of jobs, not to mention the consequences of denuded land for soil erosion, declining ecological diversity, enhanced greenhouse warming, and so forth. Perhaps we must therefore ask, with Rachel Carson, "whether any civilization can wage a relentless war on life without destroying itself, and without losing the right to be called civilized."[31]

It must be pointed out, as well, that the Judeo-Christian religious tradition is not unique in being afflicted with anti-nature enmity. The former Soviet Union, to take a notable case, was anti-religious in its ideology, and yet if anything the Soviet environment was more abused than that of the capitalist West. Production goals were enshrined with religious enthusiasm, while the natural world was treated with indifference at best, and most often with outright contempt. "We cannot expect charity from nature," Stalin once said. "We must tear it from her."[32] Under capitalism, it was said, people exploit other people, whereas under communism it is the other way around! Either way, nature took it on the chin.

To be sure, nonindustrial societies are also capable of disregarding and destroying nature. If, in some cases, they have been less vigorous about it than their industrial counterparts, it is typically not because they are more sensitive, but rather, less equipped to wreak havoc. In the Himalayas, centuries of overcutting the forests have led to catastrophic killer floods, unknown in earlier times. This is because forested slopes absorb rainwater, releasing it slowly and evenly, whereas denuded land provides virtually no such reservoir. African wildlife is destroyed by impoverished people who look at elephants and see ivory, or at crocodiles and see shoes. There is also some justification, of course, in farmers seeing elephants as potential tramplers of crops, or crocodiles as predators of children.

The scene repeats itself on a grand scale and in microcosm, from the suburban homeowner who resents an adjacent marsh while also profiting from its role in filtering ground-water contamination, to the widespread dislike of dirt combined with our utter dependence upon soil. For most Americans, wilderness has long been something to conquer, not to savor.

There are two different views, then, of nature: as enemy and as friend. Many of us, especially in the West, subscribe to the former. We see ourselves and society in general—if not the entire species *Homo sapiens*—locked in a profound battle, one for which Judeo-Christian hubris has done much of the intellectual heavy-lifting, but which has also been buttressed by parts of our own experience. Thus, as Robert Bellah pointed out, we cherish an image of ourselves as masterful, as doers, as creatures that have accomplished much. Furthermore, much of our success has in fact taken place at the expense of others, especially the natural world which has only grudgingly (and sometimes only after the application of considerable effort, skill, and frequently, violence) yielded up its bounty.

There is probably more to it, however.

The Universe as Enemy?

Our identification of nature-as-enemy may well come from something even deeper than our religious tradition. Indeed, perhaps religion itself derives in part from a subconscious recognition that there is a more fundamental enemy out there: not this tree or that boulder, not wolves at night or floods in the spring, or anything else so readily identified and opposed, but a much more formidable opponent, namely, death, and—lurking behind it—a bleak and uncaring universe. After all, the universe is very large and we are very small, each of us a tiny flame in an endless void, an insignificant flicker of self-awareness that can be snuffed out at any time, and eventually, will be. While we struggle and worry, triumph or fail, feel ecstasy or despair, around us stretches a vast eternity of time and space that existed long before we took shape and will continue to exist long after we are no more.

We personify one enemy or another, but whatever we call it, and whatever we do, much of our struggle and opposition is merely part of a greater and more general battle against our own mortality— one that we are doomed to lose.[33] "We who are about to die demand a miracle," wrote W. H. Auden (and who also died, it should be noted), giving a curiously modern ring to the ancient salute of the Roman gladiators. We shall never overcome death, but by our Sisyphean struggle—as Camus pointed out—we define ourselves as fully human. Not that this struggle must specifically be against mortality, although much time and effort is expended in just this battle, notably by medicine. In fact, there is something unpleasantly self-serving and crassly limited about obsessing over ways to prolong one's own life. No, the life-affirming, human-defining struggle is more diffuse than merely trying to avoid our personal appointment in Samarra. Rather, we seek to affirm and define ourselves by a whole slew of comings and goings and doings. Many of us hesitate to give up the struggle with our enemies because to do so would be to concede defeat in that greater struggle, our ultimately hopeless tug-of-war with our own looming dissolution.

"Life is trouble," said Zorba the Greek in Nikos Kazantzakis's immortal novel. "To be alive is to undo your belt and look for trouble." For others, to be alive is to look for enemies, to wrestle, like the biblical Jacob, but with devils instead of with angels, with enemies, both real and imagined. There are people—not just Ahabs, but normal, everyday people—whose lives are filled with such struggles, who turn with equal vigor from trying to subdue their personal enemies, to trying to achieve success at work, to struggling—with great intensity and frequently little success—to achieve a happy relationship (with a child, a spouse, a friend, even a pet) or a really dynamite orgasm, or just an adequate night's sleep. The more they struggle, it seems, the more unsuccessful they are.

Back, then, to the two contrasting ways of relating to our surroundings. On the one hand, many people see life as conflict: if not the existential battle against death and meaninglessness, then a competitive fray in which, as the Duchess suggested in *Alice in Wonderland,* "The more there is of yours, the less there is of mine." Under such a view, enemies are unavoidable and, in fact, essential. Like Albert Camus's view of Sisyphus, we define ourselves—we actually *create* ourselves—by struggle, which requires something to fight against: a rock, perhaps, or a mountain, a disease, a competing economic or political system, or, better yet, a person or group of people—an enemy.

But there is also another way. The transcendentalist Dorothy

Thompson once announced, "I accept the universe." (To which a wag is said to have responded, "She had darned well better.") We too can accept the universe. We can see ourselves as part of a process, lovingly enfolded in a web of life. Rather than setting ourselves, Ahab-like, against others, we can see our own lives as part of a supportive, cooperative endeavor, or, better yet, less an endeavor than a float down the river of existence. The perception of "enemies," in this view, is mostly a result of our own self-delusion, a misapprehension of the way the world really is, of the marvelous forces that buoy us up and help us on our way.

Which is correct?

Even the insistence that one side or another is correct—and the other, wrong—implies a mindset that assumes enemies; that is, it assumes that the world is built around mutually incompatible alternatives, such that each one is the enemy of its competing opposite: right/wrong, either/or, black/white, good/bad, and so forth.

This brings up a favorite baseball story. Once there were three umpires who were asked to explain their way of determining balls from strikes. The first (a rookie) responded, "I call 'em how they are." The second (more experienced) answered, "I call 'em how I see 'em." And the third (a veteran) chimed in with, "They ain't nothing 'till I call 'em."

❖   ❖   ❖

By now, it should be obvious that enemies and the enemy experience are, at least to some extent, ours to call. They are also part of life itself. Whether in geo-political maneuvers, societal encounters, bio-ecological events, theological stances, or our own private and personal lives, we meet and struggle with our enemies. Sometimes we avoid them; occasionally, we even embrace them. But like our shadows, our enemies are always there, just as—again, like our shadows—they are sometimes magnified and distorted. By the simple fact of living, we create them in our minds no less than in reality. In the final analysis, as we shall see, overcoming them is nothing less than overcoming a part of ourselves. We therefore turn to a hypothesis of the modern origins of our enemy system, part of a broad, inclusive theory of the nature and dilemma of human beings.

Notes

1. Terrence Des Pres, *The Survivor* (New York: Pocket Books, 1977).
2. I.e., to be an "authoritarian personality," as described in chapter 5.
3. Herman Melville, *Moby Dick* (New York: Airmont Publishing Co., 1964), p. 161
4. Ibid., p. 138.
5. Ibid., 441.
6. Karen Horney, "The Value of Vindictiveness," *American Journal of Psychoanalysis* 7 (1948): 3–12.
7. Melville, *Moby Dick*, p. 149.
8. Victor Hugo, *Les Misérables* (New York: Penguin, 1976), p. 64.
9. Ibid., p. 166.
10. Ibid., p. 267.
11. Ibid., p. 165.
12. There are many examples of the Ahab syndrome in literature; significantly, in virtually all cases, the pursuer has already been injured, and in seeking to pass the pain along, causes yet more injury. The other book—besides *Moby Dick*—often cited as the greatest American novel is Nathaniel Hawthorne's *The Scarlet Letter*, in which we are given the relentless pursuit of Rev. Dimmesdale (Hester Prynne's lover) by the remorseless, outraged husband, Roger Chillingworth. It is also noteworthy that in Hawthorne's tale, Chillingworth dies shortly after Dimmesdale, largely because having been deprived of his enemy, he had nothing left to live for.
13. Hugo, *Les Misérables*, p. 1207.
14. Melville, *Moby Dick*, p. 116.
15. Ibid., p. 384.
16. Erich Fromm, *The Heart of Man* (New York: Harper & Row, 1980).
17. Fritz Redl, "Group Emotion and Leadership," *Psychiatry* 5 (1942): 573–96.

18. Quoted in Gordon Wright, *The Ordeal of Total War* (New York: Harper & Row, 1968). Particularly in the case of the Kaiser and Hitler, we also see evidence of the potency of passing the pain along.

19. Hugh Trevor-Roper, "Introduction," in *Hitler's Secret Conversations, 1914–1944* (New York: Farrar, Straus & Young, 1953).)

20. Richard Hofstadter, *The Paranoid Style in American Politics and Other Essays* (New York: Alfred A. Knopf, 1965).

21. Ibid.

22. Ibid.

23. Ibid.

24. Ibid.

25. Ibid.

26. Of course, the paranoid isn't always successful, either. Often—probably most of the time—he fails, but usually after first causing great mischief in the process. One recent notable failure appears to have been at the Republican National Convention in 1992, where hate-mongers and purveyors of rigid, paranoid intolerance such as Pat Robertson and Patrick Buchanan, failed to ignite the country to join in their version of a "cultural war" against homosexuals and other deviants from the prescribed norm.

27. Robert Axelrod, *The Evolution of Cooperation* (New York: Basic Books, 1984).

28. H. Kaplan and B. Sadock, *Comprehensive Textbook of Psychiatry* (Baltimore, Md.: Williams and Wilkins, 1989).

29. Robert Bellah, "Evil and the American Ethos," in *Sanctions for Evil*, eds. N. Sanford and C. Comstock (Boston: Beacon Press, 1971).

30. Aldo Leopold, *A Sand County Almanac* (New York: Oxford Unviversity Press, 1949).

31. Rachel Carson, *Silent Spring* (Boston: Houghton Mifflin, 1962).

32. Quoted in Murray Feshbach and Alfred Friendly, Jr., *Ecocide in the USSR: Health and Nature Under Siege* (New York: Basic Books, 1992).

33. According to some critics, Moby Dick was also a sign of death, an indication of Ahab's—and our—shared mortality.

7

The Neanderthal Mentality

The late Loren Eiseley had a gift for ideas as well as words. A paleontologist with an interest in human origins combined with a deep sensitivity to biology, Eiseley scoured the past as well as the present in a productive search for the nature of human nature. In a few sentences, he once captured the essence of part of that great dilemma, with special reference to our own search for the origin of the enemy system. "The need is now," wrote Eiseley,

> for a gentler, a more tolerant people than those who won for us against the ice, the tiger and the bear. The hand that hefted the ax, out of some old blind allegiance to the past, fondles the machine gun as lovingly. It is a habit we will have to break to survive, but the roots go very deep.[1]

This chapter shall explore the consequences for our enemy system of what Eiseley called that "old blind allegiance to the past." It shall argue that we have difficulty dealing creatively with enemies—and with their absence—because of this persistence of old habits in new times, a stubbornness that is symptomatic of a deeper problem: the discordance between biological and cultural evolution in human affairs.

243

Let's start with a modern animal, which is also a metaphor for ourselves.

Of Musk Ox and Men

On the tundra of northern Canada and Greenland, you can find them: great, shaggy bison of the arctic, with long, silky hair that droops almost to the frozen ground. But musk ox are not so easy to find now as they were in centuries past; their predators have diminished the once great musk ox herds almost to extinction. At first glance, it might appear that musk ox are almost immune to predators. Superbly adapted to their arctic lifestyle, and with a thousand pounds of muscle backing up a pair of formidably sharp horns, it is hard to imagine a musk ox falling prey to anything.

This perception is reinforced by the very efficient behavior of musk ox when threatened: Like American pioneers circling their wagons, they respond to predators by forming a living ring, with the adults arrayed like the spokes of a wheel—armored heads pointing out—and the comparatively vulnerable juveniles safely in the center. For millennia, wolves have been the only serious predators of musk ox, and no wolf (not even an entire wolf pack) can hope for much success against such a fearsome defensive phalanx.

The musk ox, nonetheless, are in deep trouble and ironically, it is precisely their very efficient and effective defensive behaviors that are responsible. (Or rather, they share part of the blame.) As you may have guessed, the predators that are so troublesome for modern-day musk ox are no longer wolves, but human beings riding snowmobiles and brandishing high-powered rifles. The problem—from the musk ox's point of view—is not that their defensive maneuvers are inadequate but rather that they have been all too adequate in the past. As a result, they don't lend themselves to being upgraded.

When approached by twentieth-century hunters, musk ox do what they have always done. They form their trusty circle, just as their great-great-great grandparents had always done. You can almost hear their genes commanding: "Do it. Go ahead. It has always worked—against wolves." The advice, however, is bad. The musk ox's doughty circle maneuver is the worst possible tactic when the primary foe are no longer wolves but human hunters. But the musk ox is an obedient and unimaginative creature; it listens to the outmoded advice of its genes. The entire herd stands its ground, and every animal is easily killed because it does the right thing, but at the wrong time.

At the one-year anniversary of the atomic bombing of Hiroshima, Albert Einstein sent a telegram to the world's physicists recruiting them for a new effort to control the Frankenstein's monster that their combined genius had created. In that telegram Einstein noted that, "The unleashed power of the atom has changed everything but our ways of thinking, and thus we drift toward unparalleled catastrophe." We, in turn, might note that the invention of the snowmobile and the high-powered hunting rifle has changed everything but the musk ox's way of thinking, and thus, it, too, drifts toward unparalleled catastrophe.

The issue is similar in both cases, and therein lies the relevance of the musk ox as metaphor for ourselves. The musk ox—both in its anatomy and its behavior—is a product of its biological evolution. Confronted with something altogether new, it simply cannot adapt. If musk ox are to survive, it will be because human beings choose to protect them, not because the animals will evolve new and adaptive responses to rifle-toting hunters. It is possible, of course, for Darwinian evolution to equip musk ox with such responses—after all, natural selection managed to outfit them with an excellent armamentarium for use against wolves. But the process of adaptation was undoubtedly very slow, while the leisurely pace was not an overwhelming problem because generations of musk ox had lots of time: After all, their "enemy," the wolf, was also evolving with comparable Darwinian slowness.

By contrast, the "evolution" of rifles and snowmobiles has taken place according to rules that are quite different from those first elaborated by Charles Darwin. These modern implements are the product of a new kind of evolution, one that is cultural rather than biological. In high school biology classes, we learn that Jean Lamarck (1744-1829), with his theory of the inheritance of acquired characteristics, was mistaken. We learn that evolutionary change takes place very slowly, when genetic mutations are rearranged through sexual recombination until eventually—after many generations—certain patterns of DNA tend to predominate: those that confer even a slight biological advantage to their possessors. Almost by definition, biological evolution is a relatively gradual affair. Even occasional episodes of "explosive" evolutionary change require thousands of years, hundreds at the very least.

But when it comes to *cultural evolution*, Lamarck was precisely correct. Gunpowder, for example, was invented not by a random reorganization of the molecules making up DNA, and it was not passed along only to the direct genetic descendants of its inventor. Rather, it was a cultural creation, picked up, passed along, modified, and perfected by a process that was almost entirely cultural, not biological. Whereas a useful biological innovation can never even begin to spread more rapidly than the time required for an entire reproducing generation, a useful cultural innovation—such as gunpowder, machine guns, transistor radios, internal combustion engines, literacy, TV dinners, computers, fire, nuclear weapons, the wheel, legal codes, teenage mutant ninja turtles, corn flakes, medicine, poetry, yo-yos, science, or rap music—can arise and be modified within a single lifetime. Moreover, it can spread to thousands, millions, even billions of individuals.

In the case of the musk ox, the disparity is between its biological evolution and our cultural evolution. The former simply cannot keep up with the latter. In the case of human beings more generally, the disparity is of the same sort, but entirely within ourselves: between cultural evolution (which produced, among other things, snowmobiles and hunting rifles) and our own biological evolution (which produced us). The tragedy of the musk ox is that its biological evolution has been too slow for our cultural evolution. The tragedy for ourselves is the impossible race between the biological tortoise and the cultural hare. The impossibility lies in the fact that both creatures are ourselves. Therein lies much of our glory as well as our despair, our orientation toward enemies as well as our difficulty in transcending them.

The Neanderthal Mentality

Try the following thought experiment. Imagine that you were able to switch a Cro-Magnon infant from the mid-Stone Age—say, 50,000 years ago—with a modern, upper-middle-class infant, say, from Greenwich, Connecticut. The chances are very good that in each case, so long as the transfer was completed while the children were very young, the switched babies would grow up to be perfectly normal members of their cultures. The child of a Connecticut stockbroker would grow up carrying a club, perhaps, and chipping flint tools for use in skinning mastodons. The Cro-Magnon youngster would become computer literate about the same time he or she graduated from preschool, and would probably join the Little League or Campfire Girls, en route to Wellesley, perhaps, and a seemingly normal life in the late twentieth century.

Now, try the same imaginary switch once again, but this time between *adult* Cro-Magnon and *adult* Connecticut stockbroker. The results would undoubtedly be catastrophic. Neither grown-up could possibly function effectively in the other's environment. The Cro-

Magnon would be confused, terrified, and/or enraged by telephones, automobiles, television, and electricity, not to mention chairs, spoons, toilets, running water, written language, laws, and so forth. Similarly, the stockbroker would be lucky to survive a day or so, deprived of the cultural accomplishments that we in the late twentieth century take for granted. The point is that in our imaginary experiment, the infants were able to adopt each other's lives because they are made of essentially the same biological stuff. One size fits all. But whereas the adults, too, are biologically equivalent, their cultures most assuredly are not. Our biology has scarcely budged in the last fifty thousand years, while our culture has travelled light-years. As a result, our species finds itself in an extraordinary position, with one foot rooted in its biological past and the other thrust into the cultural/social/techno-logical present and rocketing toward the future. It is an uncomfortable posture.

So, here we are, unique among living things in the complexity and grandeur of our social and technological creations, and yet also unique in another respect, one that is far less enviable: We are the only living things which are, in a sense, out of joint with ourselves. No other animal can point to comparable accomplishments, and, at the same time, none can be considered comparably "unnatural." We are undoubtedly part of nature, yet oddly outside of it as well. We have transcended the realm of the purely organic, imagining and doing things that no other animal has ever accomplished, and yet deep inside we also remain perfectly good mammals, creatures of mud and bone and hair and hormones, slurpers of the primordial organic soup.

The Romans named the first month of the year January, after Janus, the two-faced god who looked back toward the old year and also forward to the new. We, too, are not only Janus-faced but also Janus-souled, riven with a deep-seated dualism that is both our glory and our curse.

As a result of this discordance, this curious discrepancy between the slow-moving tortoise of biological evolution and the sprinting hare of cultural advance, our (culturally constructed) reality has tended to outpace our (biologically constructed) modes of thinking. Little wonder that in his *Essay on Man* Alexander Pope lamented that

> He hangs between, in doubt to act, or rest,
> In doubt to deem himself a God or beast;
> In doubt his mind or body to prefer;
> Born but to die and reasoning but to err.[2]

Writing more than a hundred years before Darwin, it is no surprise that Pope did not quite perceive the fundamental unity behind the apparent duality he decried. Now we know what the poet did not: We are both God *and* beast. We do not so much "hang between" the two as we are stuck in both, simultaneously and irretrievably, creatures of permament paradox.

> Created half to rise and half to fall;
> Great lord of all things, yet a prey to all;
> Sole judge of truth, in endless error hurled:
> The glory, jest, and riddle of the world.[3]

If we have been preeminently a riddle, there is at least a possibility that we now have some insight into the root of that riddle: the clash between our biology and our culture. It explains much. It explains why, as Albert Camus observed, "consciousness is always lagging behind reality: History rushes onward while thought reflects. But this inevitable backwardness becomes more pronounced the faster history speeds up."[4]

It has been argued that many of our problems—perhaps most of them—can be attributed to this discrepancy between our biology and our culture, and the "inevitable backwardness" of our thinking that has resulted.[5] This backwardness might usefully be called our Neanderthal mentality, by, in a sense, demoting our Cro-Magnon to the status of his beetle-browed relative.[6] For our purposes, we shall concentrate on the implications of Neanderthal thinking (and often not thinking) for our troublesome enemy system.

The Neanderthal at War

In the simplest case, it is a matter of aggressiveness. Animals don't always fight, but in some way or other, and at some times or other, they generally do, even creatures as diverse as the seemingly immobile and stoically indifferent sea anemones, or the reputedly peaceful doves. Of course, animals don't fight all the time, and neither do human beings. By and large, they restrict themselves to situations that are to their benefit (for example, cases of competition, as was explored in chapter 2). The same appears to be true of ourselves. Moreover, it seems that we do not *need* to fight, in the same way that we need to eat or to sleep. At the same time, it is virtually certain that throughout our long evolutionary history as biological beings, we did fight on some occasions, notably over living space, mates, or food. Primitive "warfare" remained common into modern times, and has been documented in people as diverse as the Tsembaga Maring of New Guinea or the Yanomamo of the upper Amazon. In such cases, success in battle typically brought success in life: status, animal protein, *lebensraum* ("living space"), and, often, women.

It seems likely that the identification—even, the creation—of enemies was crowned with social and biological success. Moreover, adherence to such an enemy system was rewarded during a stretch of literally thousands of human generations. (One might argue that since many aggressive interactions are zero-sum games, there were failures too: In most cases, a positive pay-off for one side was balanced by negative returns for the other. But then, we are the descendants of those who succeeded, who in some sense profited by their enemy systems.)

No one would argue that we have no enemies today. But just as we have not outgrown the literal having of enemies, it may be even more portentous that we also have not outgrown that part of our Neanderthal mentality that insists on having those enemies, or that interprets a wide range of (potentially benign) circumstances as indicating that our enemies are all around us and closing in.

There was a time when our enemies were concrete and immediate: other Neanderthalers out to usurp our caves, our food, our mates, or perhaps nonhuman enemies such as a nearby volcano, advancing ice sheets, or the disease epidemics. Ironically, as our evolving culture has rendered us in many ways insulated from such nonhuman enemies, our circle of human enemies has, if anything, widened during historical times. We have, for instance, "evolved" weapons that kill at increasing distances and that can devastate ever larger areas: consider the progression from club to bow and arrow, to rifle, to machine gun, to howitzer, to nuclear warhead.

At the same time as our technology has grown more deadly, we have become less discriminating as to targets. In his book *Sentimental Journey Through France and Italy*, English author Laurence Sterne recounted how, in the eighteenth century, he traveled through France, entirely forgetting that at the time England and France were fighting the Seven Years' War.[7] There was a time, in short, when war and the identification of national enemies was not especially an issue for the general populace. In 1808, for example, with the Napoleonic Wars raging, the French Institute conferred its gold medal on Sir Humphrey Davy, an Englishman, who blithely crossed the Channel to accept his award to the enthusiastic cheers of the great scientists of France. However, this separation of enmity at the state level and enmity at the civilian level was not to last.

As the nineteenth century proceeded, we moved increasingly toward the era of "total war," in which the entire citizenry of a state was seen as contributing to the war effort, and thus, as "legitimate" enemies. From Napoleon's *levée en masse*, which essentially initiated the universal draft, to Sherman's notorious march through Georgia, which destroyed civilian morale and the means of production as a direct strategy of war, the boundaries of enmity came to include ever larger numbers of our fellow human beings. Total war was institutionalized during World War I, with the first use of the term "home front," and the military targeting of those industrial and agricultural workers who maintained that front. Early in that war, George Bernard Shaw wrote to the *London Times*, suggesting that the British government design emergency evacuation plans in case Germany began dropping bombs (by hand) on the innocent British populace from zeppelins or biplanes. He was reproved editorially by the *Times* for being so cynical as to suggest that "highly civilized people" such as the Germans would stoop so low, even during war. From Guernica to Hiroshima to My Lai, Shaw's cynicism now seems quaintly romantic, and the *Times'* editorial, absurd.

Our biologically mediated Neanderthal penchant for enemies has, if anything, been reinforced by our culturally mediated capacity and inclination to widen the circle of those we can injure, and who can injure us.

The Neanderthal as Groupie

We are social creatures. Although we lack the obligatory sociality of ants or honeybees, for example, which cannot even reproduce as individuals and which require the cooperative existence that only a colony can offer, human beings are nonetheless strongly drawn to social groups. As was explored particularly in chapter 4, these social groups are also fundamental to our enemy system, since on the one hand, people go to extraordinary lengths to define in-groups versus out-groups, while on the other hand, groups themselves can be strengthened by the existence of enemies, both internal and external.

Group orientation is basic to human social life and to survival. Indeed, it is almost certainly because our survival depends on our orientation toward others that we are so deeply drawn to social life in the first place. At birth, the human infant is utterly dependent on a fundamental relationship, typically with its mother. Like every other mammal, we require milk for our sustenance, and—at least before the invention of artificial infant formula—we obtained that milk exclusively from the secretions of the body of another individual. We also depend on adults (typically our parents) for care and nurturing in thousands of ways, including physical protection, teaching, and emotional support. Without others, our future would be bleak indeed; there is no doubt that selection would weed out any human beings who were not at least in a basic sense, "pro-social."

As the young person grows, his or her circle of involvement grows as well, encompassing siblings; other, more distant family members; and also friends and acquaintances. Peer groups become especially important, as the playpen is replaced by the playground, and the developing child learns many of the basic social rules, including how to establish and maintain one's place in these mini-societies. Protection and sustenance, by and large, still flows most reliably from the family network, although to a lesser—but nonetheless crucial—extent, contributions start coming from the youngster's association with non-kin. As we have seen, adolescents become especially prone to intense group identifications, from clubs and teams to gangs. Once more, none of this is surprising, given that even the adult Neanderthal relied crucially upon group association in order to survive and ward off outside threats. This is true whether the primary danger emanated from the need to obtain food, shelter, mates, or defense against other, potentially hostile groups. A solitary Neanderthal would have been in more danger than a lone wolf, and almost as unthinkable as a solitary ant.

In the inevitable competition between groups, it is very likely that smarter, luckier groups—including those that were well co-ordinated and thus, cooperative—were more apt to prosper. But of all the factors that correlated with success (of the groups, and hence, of the individuals comprising them), it is almost certain that size was a winning ticket.

On the wild and rocky coast of the Pacific Northwest, there lives a small, black-and-white shorebird, not much larger overall than a robin, with a distinctive red bill. This animal, the American oyster-catcher, lays mottled, camouflaged eggs about the size that you might expect: somewhat smaller than those of an undersized chicken. Un-like most chickens, however, which have been bred for laying eggs rather than tending them, oystercatchers in nature proceed to incu-bate their eggs just like other birds. But when given the opportunity, a female American oystercatcher will unhesitatingly abandon her own clutch and perch, preferentially, on an artificial egg, so long as it is painted with the appropriate color pattern—even if this artificial egg is grossly oversized. In fact, it will do so *especially if* that egg is much too big.

And so, researchers in animal behavior have treated themselves to the amusing spectacle of oystercatchers ignoring their own eggs and instead, perching with absurd contentment and apparent delight on a painted watermelon, which outweighs the animal by at least ten to one. If oystercatchers could talk, they would probably proclaim that such watermelons are irresistibly cute, perhaps even viscerally compelling. Ethologists refer to such cases as "supernormal releasers," in which animals with a biological penchant for certain stimuli (e.g., eggs of the right shape and color pattern) can be victimized by artificially created stimuli which exceed the normal, and which release a comparably excessive response. Exaggerate the stimulus and you exaggerate the response.

It seems maladaptive and inexplicable, until we realize that under natural circumstances, oystercatchers are never exposed to such grotesque egg mimics. Their biology has equipped them with an altogether adaptive preference, especially since among their own eggs, the larger ones are more likely to hatch and to produce large, healthy offspring. Only when troublemaking scientists substitute oversized "eggs" does the oystercatcher's behavior seem foolish.

There is no direct connection between the Neanderthal mentality and the oystercatcher's preference for huge artificial eggs, except for this: It is quite possible that just as evolution equipped the female oystercatcher with a curious fondness for the stimuli associated with large eggs, human beings may have been equipped with a fondness for the stimuli associated with large groups. As far as the Neanderthal within us is concerned, the larger the better. This may help explain the peculiar tendency of *Homo sapiens* to choose ever-larger social units, to perch contentedly atop a biologically meaningless cultural artifact known as a nation, or nation-state, often ignoring other considerations that are far more relevant to our actual health and survival. Much of the powerful tug of ethnicity and nationalism may thus be due to the deceptively simple fact that large groups comprise a sort of supernormal releaser for our own kind.

Unlike the oystercatcher, of course, we possess the ability to examine our behavior and to reject our inclinations if they seem ill-advised. When it comes to the seductive allure of nationalism, however, most latter-day Neanderthals hardly do so. In the era of ancient Greece, the size of the fundamental political unit was essentially set by the number of people who could hear the sound of a human voice; in modern times, cultural evolution has made it possible for millions to listen, see, and thus feel connected to their leaders and to their huge, shared social group. Adhering themselves to these biologically (and even socially) meaningless political units—like moths to a flame or oystercatchers to their watermelons—they extend their age-old propensity for identifying in-group and out-group, friends and enemies, to the immense nation-states that modern communication and transportation can cobble together and present as reality.

From here, the next steps are easy. They include, as we have seen, the process of dehumanizing members of other groups, at the same time latching onto various mechanisms whereby the individual confirms membership in the chosen group. As George Orwell put it, the nationalism that results is:

> first of all the habit of assuming that human beings can be classified like insects and that whole blocks of millions or tens of millions of people can be confidently labelled "good" or "bad." But secondly—and this is much more important—it is the habit of identifying oneself with a single nation or other unit, placing it beyond good or evil and recognizing no other duty than that of advancing its own interests.[8]

Thus is the Neanderthal satisfied: part of one group (if at all possible, a large one) and opposed to another, comfortably equipped with both friends and enemies. But what of that small and very special group, composed of man and woman?

Sex and the Neanderthal

Sex, paradoxically, is an antisocial force in animal evolution.[9] Thus, even though sexual reproduction requires a degree of coordination and sometimes even physical union between male and female, it also sets the stage for vigorous contests between individuals, centering especially around reproductive competition among individuals of the same sex—usually males—for access to members of the opposite sex, usually females.

Groups, therefore, are not the only units that experience and express competition and enmity. To be sure, such disruptive processes must be suppressed, to some extent, within any group if that group is to cohere (and also, to stand a chance of prevailing against other, similar groups). Nonetheless, there is considerable reason for enmity *within* groups as well. By and large, the reasons for within-group enmity are similar to those making for between-group antagonisms: notably, competition for relatively scarce resources. And among these resources, there is one category that warrants special attention; namely, potential mates.

When biologists consider the bees, wasps, and ants that live in large colonies, they employ the term *eusocial*. It derives from the Greek prefix *eu*, meaning "perfect," and is intended to emphasize a special characteristic of these creatures: the odd fact that the individuals within eusocial insect societies cooperate with each other to such an extreme that they do not even seek to reproduce. Instead of the usual push and pull of reproductive competition, these "perfectly social" animals all work together for the successful breeding of someone else, namely the queen. The eusocial insects have largely avoided the sexual competition that characterizes most other species, apparently because the shared genetic interests of workers is so great that individuals do more to further their own evolutionary success by staying home and reproducing than by seeking to raise a family of their own.[10]

But the eusocial insects are highly unusual, their remarkable restraint due to a genetic peculiarity found in their taxonomic group, the order Hymenoptera. For most other living things, including the mammals to which *Homo sapiens* belongs, social life is less than perfect, and individuals joust with each other to project copies of their genes—not someone else's—into the future. As was considered in chapter 2, this is especially a phenomenon of males, since males are sperm-makers, and sperm, being small and cheap, are produced in great abundance, thereby making each male capable of fertilizing relatively large numbers of females. This, in turn, sets up a pattern of potentially vigorous male-male competition, in which males are often selected to be relatively large, showy, and aggressive.

In the animal world, there are some interesting exceptions to these generalizations, but human beings are not among them. Men are, on average, somewhat taller, heavier, faster, and more muscular than women. They also reach sexual maturity somewhat later, and are more prone to aggressiveness and even violence. All these traits are consistent with predictions based on the evolutionary differences between maleness and femaleness (that is, between sperm-making and egg-making). Based on the above, we might also expect that the human species—like other mammals with this same constellation of traits—would be inclined toward *polygyny,* the reproductive pattern in which one male is often mated to more than one female.

In fact, this is the case. Surveying most families, at least in the Western world, we first discover that monogamy is the overwhelming winner. However, it must be remembered that this depressingly homogeneous pattern is largely a consequence of the cultural and technological imperialism of Western (mostly, Judeo-Christian) doctrine. The cross-cultural samples of anthropologists consistently show that before the advent of missionaries and other representatives of "modernity," around 80 percent of indigenous human societies were polygynous. This does not mean that 80 percent of all men were polygynously married; typically, the number of successful polygynists was small in even the most pro-polygyny social group. Rather, polygyny was striven for—by men—and was achieved by a small, successful subgroup, in most cases those who were unusually lucky, smart, strong, aggressive, wily, or wealthy. The others settled for monogamy, or, in the worst case, bachelorhood.

The above relates directly to our contention that men are especially prone to perceiving enemies, particularly in other men. Since the number of marriageable women is limited, notably so in many small tribal bands, reproductive success by men tended to be a zero-sum game: Success by one male was achieved at the cost of success by another. Little wonder, therefore, that men are particularly likely to see other men as potential competitors and enemies: Often, they *are* competitors and, thus, evolutionary enemies, even though they might nonetheless be inclined to unite with these same other men in opposition to shared enemies from outside the group.

The evolutionary biology of male-male competitiveness also relates importantly to our conception of the Neanderthal mentality, and the degree to which we may well be burdened with biological baggage, rendered inappropriate by our own cultural processes. In this case, we must note that the world-wide prevalence of monogamy—which, just a few paragraphs ago, we disparaged as a mere cultural artifact— is the overwhelming norm, at least for the English-speaking readers of this book. So, it is not irrelevant. In fact, it stands as powerful testimony to the way cultural and biological patterns may conflict: Biologically inclined toward polygyny, men are required to accept monogamy. More importantly for our purposes, the culture of monogamy serves as a kind of biological equalizer. Given that a small number of unusually successful men can no longer monopolize a large number of women, the current reality is that the great majority of men will be able to find a mate (as well as most women, although that is likely to be true under either monogamy or polygyny). Even though an individual may still perceive another man as a romantic/biological/ social competitor for the hand of a woman sought by both, in theory the degree of competition and thus of enmity, should be greatly reduced. Whether it really is, however, is another question. The competitive, aggressive, and violent inclinations of many men suggest that in this respect, our biology has not caught up with our culture.

The argument goes beyond the unique competitiveness and enemy-proneness of men. Modern culture serves as a Great Equalizer in many ways, not just with respect to monogamy. It is the Colt .45 of the twentieth and twenty-first centuries. The threatened spread of nuclear weapons to other countries, for example, diminishes the pay-off otherwise associated with military/technological advancement (analogous, if only vaguely, to the pay-off enjoyed in an earlier era by successful polygynous men). Certainly, it remains true that wealthy countries, like wealthy individuals, receive a disproportionate share of the world's benefits while remaining at least somewhat insulated from the pains of our planet. Nonetheless, our inter-connectedness is if anything more true today than when John Donne wrote that "no man is an island." World-wide problems of terrorism, over-population, resource shortages, and environmental degradation are shared by all. In addition, a large part of the problem is our Neanderthal penchant for personalized competitiveness and enmity in a world which has rendered such behavior maladaptive.

Let us turn next to Africa's Lake Tanganyika, for a cautionary tale with an optimistic moral.

The Strange Case of the Snaggle-Mouthed Cichlids of Lake Tanganyika

The so-called Rift Valley lakes of Africa are home to hundreds of species of fishes known as *cichlids* (relatives of those animals encountered in chapter 3 when discussing the research of Konrad Lorenz). Among them is a group known as *Perissodus*. We may call them snaggle-mouthed cichlids because each individual has his or her mouth twisted to one side or the other, either left or right. These bizarre twists of fortune are caused by a cold-blooded evolutionary logic: *Perissodus* fishes make their living by sneaking up on other fish and snatching a few scales out of their sides. The best way to approach undetected is to sneak up directly from behind, but a *Perissodus* that approaches in this way has a difficult time taking a quick bite out of the base of the victim's tail so long as the attacker is oriented straight ahead. (Although it would be easier to approach from the side at right angles, this would alert the potential victims, whose eyes, after all, are located on either side of their bodies.) So, the evolutionary solution has been for the attacking, scale-stealing *Perissodus* to have their jaws twisted in one direction or the other. After sneaking up on their victim's tail, those *Perissodus* that are twisted to the right, not surprisingly, attack the left side of their victims, and those twisted to the left attack on the right side.

So far, so good—at least for the snaggle-mouthed cichlids. The victims, on the other hand, can be expected to see things differently; in fact, they strain to see their attackers, to detect an approaching *Perissodus* before getting nipped. Once bitten, they become especially shy, looking behind and over their shoulders[11] from whence the snaggle-mouthed cichlids appear. Now, the plot thickens. When the left-twisted form of *Perissodus* becomes abundant, their victims—having been attacked primarily on their right flanks—become especially vigilant about additional attacks from that side. As the victims get particularly leery about being approached on their right flanks, left-twisted *Perissodus* are less successful in their hunting, and their numbers begin to decline. As a result, right-twisted *Perissodus* gain an advantage. They increase in abundance until, eventually, their victims "wise up" and stop looking over their right shoulders, turning their attention instead to their left. The system reaches equilibrium at some point, with equal numbers of right- and left-twisted *Perissodus*, and with victims scarred equally on both sides of their bodies.

What is the message for modern-day Neanderthals? Unlike the victims of the snaggle-mouthed cichlids, stuck with a kind of fishy futility (defend yourself against left-snagglers and the right-snagglers become more abundant, and *vice versa*), we can control our fate. We aren't doomed to being gnawed by our enemies, capable only of influencing whether they rip scales out of our left side or our right. To a much greater extent, we are masters of our fate. When Mephistoles, in Goethe's *Faust*, comments that, "In the end, we are all dependent on monsters of our own creation," he is actually affirming a level of creative independence that may be uniquely characteristic of human beings. This is why it is crucially important that so often we create our own monsters: not in the sense of the snaggle-mouths' victims, which are caught in a structural trap wherein the neutralization of one enemy automatically generates more trouble from another, like an eternal teeter-totter. By contrast, in escaping from the Neanderthal mentality, we can escape from the cycle of unending enmity.

For example, many Americans keep guns—especially handguns—out of fear of prospective enemies. As a result, more than a hundred of our own citizens are killed *every day* by firearms. If we chose, as a society, to end this carnage by severely restricting access to such weapons, it is always possible that we would find new ways of killing each other, perhaps by beating our "enemies" over the head with VCRs or toaster ovens. But it is unlikely. In contrast to the experience of *Perissodus*'s finny victims, if we were to eliminate one type of enemy, we would not automatically be stimulating their replacement by another type. They are *our* monsters. Having created them, we can uncreate them. (After all—to continue the example—Japan and Great Britain, with about one-third the U.S. population each but also with far more restrictive gun-control laws, each experience about the same number of gun-related homicides in a *year* that the United States endures in a *day*.)

Let us grant, if only for the sake of argument, that human beings have at least the potential for insight and for acting in their own self-interest. What about those difficult and personal cases of sexually generated enmity?

War Between the Sexes?

As we have seen in the natural world, enemies are the result of competition in which many of the contestants are in fact playing zero-sum games. A pair of bull elk treat each other as enemies so long as one or the other—but not both—will succeed in fertilizing a herd of cows. Success by one is failure by another. The bulls prance, strut, bugle at each other, and lock antlers in titanic combat, while occasionally another bull—enemy of the other two—sneaks in among the cows. By contrast, each cow elk is pretty much guaranteed her small, regular share of reproductive success (her calf, with one born pretty much every year, regardless of who is the father, and regardless of what the other cows in the herd are doing). Not surprisingly, therefore, cow elk get along relatively well with each other; in most cases, they are not enemies. To some degree, however, even the cows compete, notably by proxy, over the relative success of their offspring.

Just as there is no way for the victims of the snaggle-mouthed cichlid fishes to diminish the toll of enmity visited upon them, there also is no way for elk, whether bulls or cows, to overcome their enmity. It will take many millennia for a new world order to dawn for them. Competition and a world of zero-sum games is their bequeathal from natural selection and they are stuck with it, just as the musk ox is stuck with its defensive circle. To some extent, we *Homo sapiens* may bear a similar evolutionary burden: It may well be that we are stuck with a degree of interpersonal competitiveness, especially sexual competitiveness among men. (It is also at least possible that the Great Equalizers of modern times will pressure our Neanderthal inclinations for an easing up of inappropriate animosities, just as monogamy has outmoded the trappings of polygynous male strivings.)

When it comes to male-female differences, on the other hand, an honest assessment must also deal with one of the oldest, and perhaps least tractable patterns of conflict in our species, or any other: the special kind of competitiveness—bordering on enmity—that often characterizes interactions between male and female.

In Boccaccio's rollicking *Tales of the Decamaron*, written more than six hundred years ago, there is the comic story of an old man who brings his young wife to trial for adultery. She does not deny her many extramarital liaisons, but argues instead that her husband has no real claim against her, because she has always been a dutiful (if not faithful) wife. The old man acknowledges that in fact the attractive young woman never denied any of his sexual advances: Since he is old, there were very few of them. It is just that she *also* had sexual dalliances with other men. In her case, the sexual supply exceeded the demand (at least, at home), and so, she argued, her elderly husband was not actually deprived by the arrangement. He had nothing to complain about—or so claimed the wife—and the court agreed.

Real life is rather different, however. It appears that sexual jealousy—especially male sexual jealousy—is fundamentally driven not by sexual satisfaction but by deep-seated concerns about the avoidance of cuckoldry, which, in turn, is likely linked to the male/female, sperm/egg dichotomy that we have already explored. The enraged husband (or wife) is not angered because the spouse's dalliance with someone else has deprived him (or her) of sexual opportunities during the actual times of their rendezvous. Rather, the trespass is psychological—a deep, outraged sense of betrayal and dishonesty—and beneath this, in all probability, is a biologically driven worry about losing one's mate to another, losing his or her resources, or being tricked into raising a child that isn't one's own.

Maybe some day the lion and the lamb will indeed lie down together, but don't hold your breath. Not only would this require both of them to transcend their immediate behavioral inclinations, there are also long-term problems, not the least being nourishment for the lion and survival for the lamb. Maybe *Perissodus* and its victims will all switch to munching on aquatic tofu in perfect piscine harmony. More likely, however, animosity and enmity will continue, at least in many cases. The chances are, moreover, that we shall never treat adultery (by either husband or wife) with equanimity. Even without marriage or adultery, and regardless, perhaps, of monogamy or polygyny, triangulation or codependency, maybe the proverbial "war" between the sexes will be everlasting. It is likely that whenever competition is intense, whenever individuals differ in their interests,[12] enmity won't be far behind.

But fortunately, human beings need not buck their deepest biological/structural natures in order to coexist peacefully and with a minimum of enmity. In fact, the same differences that create the potential for enmity also generate the conditions that make life interesting, even worth living. Between man and woman, for example, much would be sacrificed if we were somehow to lose sexual tension, energy, excitement, all of which comes with differences and healthy differentiation. And there can still be closeness, sharing, understanding, and above all, love. Despite their occasionally conflicting biological equipment, men and women do in fact have a common evolutionary interest: the rearing of successful children and other descendents. It is entirely possible, in fact, that love flourishes in part when we recognize the biological, psychological, and societal unity that underlies our differences, promising to transform and transcend our enmity. As *The Three Marias* suggested more than two decades ago, where the body is concerned "no battleflag should be hoisted on the flagpole gently planted high between our thighs."[13]

The "battle of the sexes" may well rage so long as there are men and women (or male elk and female elk, etc.). But not all battles are bound to produce casualties or even losers. Transcend our Neanderthal selves and all can be winners.

The Toilet-Trained Neanderthal

But can we realistically hope for transcendence? After all, if deep down inside we are nothing but Neanderthals at heart, blindly acting out the demands of our evolutionary heritage, supremely indifferent to the fact that cultural evolution has changed the terms of our social/ technological contract, then no change is possible. The truth, fortunately, is much more encouraging. We are Neanderthals, but we are not merely Neanderthals. We are also the most adaptable, intellectually flexible, and creative creatures the world has ever known. If any living things are capable of breaking the bonds of biology, we are.

For a homey and rather homely example, consider toilet training. It is a strange irony, rarely noticed even by biologists, that primates such as monkeys or chimpanzees, for all their vaunted intelligence, cannot be toilet-trained, whereas comparatively simple-minded creatures such as dogs and cats can be house-broken quickly and easily. A moment's reflection suggests the reason: Dogs and cats live on the ground, in dens or lairs, so that it has long been adaptive for them to learn where they may urinate and defecate, and where they ought not. Primates, by contrast, evolved in the trees; when it comes to toilet habits, fastidiousness is simply not a concern for such creatures and their ancestors (although it can be a problem for those unfortunates who happen to live below them).

We, too, are primates. We, too, evolved in trees. And, true to our primate heritage, we, too, have a difficult time being toilet-trained. Indeed, it is striking that it takes the average child—large brain and all—about three years to acquire the same training that the average puppy or kitten picks up in a day or so. Does that mean that the situation is hopeless? Look around. The chances are that everyone you know (infants excepted) is toilet-trained. Millions of years of biological evolution have outfitted us with a deep-seated indifference to toilet training, and yet we are quite capable of transcending this fundamental aspect of our natures. Is it any less realistic to expect that sometime soon, those of us who are unable to control other aspects of our Neanderthal mentalities will be considered every bit as inappropriate as people who are unable to control their bowels?

❋   ❋   ❋

In the last chapter, we examine possible routes toward overcoming not only our Neanderthal tendencies, but our enemy system generally.

Notes

1. Loren Eiseley, *The Star Thrower* (London, England: Wildwood House, 1978).
2. Alexander Pope, *The Works of Alexander Pope* (London, England: J. Murray, 1889).
3. Ibid.
4. Albert Camus. *Neither Victims Nor Executioners* (New York: Continuum, 1980).
5. David P. Barash and Judith Eve Lipton, *The Caveman and the Bomb* (New York, McGraw-Hill, 1985); David P. Barash, *The Hare and the Tortoise: Culture, Biology and Human Nature* (New York: Penguin, 1987).
6. No implication here of strict anthropological accuracy. There is debate, for example, over whether Neanderthals were in any sense ancestral to *Homo sapiens*. It is also increasingly clear that Neanderthals may have been reputable fellows, burying their dead with flowers and otherwise experiencing a rich social life. The term "Neanderthal mentality" is nontheles useful, emphasizing the primitive, and often unpleasant, aspects of our primitive biological heritage.
7. Laurence Sterne, *Sentimental Journey Through France and Italy* (New York: Oxford University Press, 1968).
8. George Orwell, *Such, Such Were the Joys* (New York: Harcourt, Brace, 1953).
9. This was first pointed out, I believe, by biologist E. O. Wilson.
10. See, for more detail, any basic textbook of sociobiology, such as Edward O. Wilson's *Sociobiology* (Cambridge, Mass.: Harvard University Press, 1975).

11. Or whatever passes for shoulders among fish. In any event, the whole fascinating system was described by Japanese ecologist Michio Hori, "Frequency-dependent Natural Selection in the Handedness of Scale-eating Cichlid Fish," *Science* 260 (1993): 216–19.

12. Evolutionary biology teaches us that whenever genetic differences exist between individuals, self-interest also differs.

13. Maria Isabel Barreno, Maria Teresa Horta, and Maria Velho Da Costa, *The Three Marias* (New York: Doubleday: 1971).

8

Shall We Overcome?

What now? We have explored some of the many dimensions of enemies: their causes and effects, their simplicity and complications, their stubborn persistence, and—when and if they go away—the additional, often unexpected problem of doing without them. A colleague, hearing that this was to be a book about enemies, wondered if it would be a "how-to" book, filled with advice about how to overcome one's enemies. An interesting idea, perhaps, but what, precisely, would it mean? Simply put, to overcome one's enemies would be to emerge victorious, just as capitalism overcame communism, we overcame Iraq in 1991, Panama in 1989, and before that we overcame Grenada in 1983. Four decades earlier, we emerged victorious from World War II, having overcome Germany and Japan. Vietnam, on the other hand, overcame us: not in the sense of leaving us vanquished, but, rather, depriving us of our goal (maintaining a separate noncommunist South Vietnam), and succeeding in its own (unification of the North and South under a communist government).

But there are also other ways of overcoming, ways that are less clear, and, therefore, more interesting, and, perhaps, more important.

Dimensions of Overcoming

There is, for example, a broader, deeper, more general sense of over-coming, as in surmounting something onerous such as a handicap, an addiction, or a tendency to write bad checks or to overeat. Consider, for example, that revered anthem of social protest and achievement, "We Shall Overcome," almost universally applicable because it speaks to a wider effort: the attempt to defeat injustice, poverty, war, racism, and the like. Nonetheless, it still implies *winning*, although there is nothing wrong with that, especially when the opponents are nasty.

On the other hand, there is a different kind of overcoming, as reflected for example in what is probably the greatest speech in American history. Abraham Lincoln's second inaugural address was written and delivered in 1865, when the end of the Civil War was clearly in sight, and Lincoln was seeking to guide the victorious Union toward forgiveness and a renunciation of enmity. That address—a mere eight minutes long—is best read not simply as a call for healing after a bloody and divisive war, but as a sermon on behalf of over-coming our own animosity. It ends as follows:

> With malice toward none, with charity for all, with firmness in the right as God gives us to see the right, let us strive on to finish the work we are in, to bind up the nation's wounds, to care for him who shall have borne the battle and for his widow and his orphan—to do all which may achieve and cherish a just and lasting peace among ourselves and with all nations.[1]

Lincoln could have engaged in an orgy of triumphalism, like George Bush's address to the United States Congress at the conclusion of the Persian Gulf War. In a narrow sense, he would have been justified in doing so. It might even have been politically popular. After all, the Union had been unambiguously victorious in the Civil

War. The cost in lives and treasure was greater than in any war in our history. No one would have blamed Lincoln if the beleaguered president—triumphant at last—had preened and puffed and sought to cover himself in reflected glory. But Lincoln's sense was not narrow, and his concerns evidently went beyond self-glorification and the merely "political."

A similar greatness of vision has been seen in our own times, when Nelson Mandela, elected president of South Africa after having been imprisoned for twenty-seven years, reached out to his former oppressors and opponents—black and whie—in a search for healing and reconcilization. "We place our vision of a new constitutional order for South Africa on the table not as conquerors, prescribing to the conquered," he declared at his inauguration in May 1994. "We speak as fellow citizens to heal the wounds of the past with the intent of constructing a new order based on justice for all." For Lincoln, achieving a true end to the bloody and destructive experience of the Civil War required far more than simply vanquishing the other side, just as in our day the notion of truly overcoming our enemies requires more than simply vanquishing Grenada, Panama, Iraq, the Soviet Union, or even "drugs," "crime," and "terrorism." It implies not so much the defeat of our opponents or the overcoming of something bad or even the saintly quality of forgiveness, but rather the vanquishing of our underlying reliance upon enemies in the first place. It is something that Nelson Mandela has glimpsed, and striven for. It is a tall order, and not necessarily one that can ever be completely filled, at least not by most of us.

These two kinds of "overcoming" resemble a distinction made by radical feminists, one that deserves wider dissemination, between "power over" and "power to." "Power *over*" implies the ability to dominate or manipulate another. It is associated with systems of oppression and coercion. "Power *to*," by contrast, is what is commonly meant by "empowerment," the ability to take control of one's life in a positive, affirming way. In this sense, to overcome one's enemies by defeating them is to achieve power *over* them. To overcome the having of enemies is to become empowered, in a sense, to achieve power over the most challenging opponent: one's self.

One possibility, and in some ways the simplest means of overcoming the having of enemies, is to diminish competition itself. South of Worcester, Massachusetts, near the Connecticut border, there is a small lake with the wonderful Mohican name of Chaubunagungamaug. In English, it means "You fish your side, I fish my side, nobody fishes the middle: no trouble." We may assume that the early lakeshore residents of this mellifluously named body of water were not enemies. They also knew something about managing human affairs. By diminishing competition—thereby, in a sense, overcoming it—they overcame enmity. It is not usually so easy, however, to eliminate "trouble."

Rephrasing Lincoln, can we ever achieve and cherish a just and lasting peace, among ourselves, with all nations, and also within ourselves, while we remain enemy-ridden? No less than political or societal peace, peace of mind may well require that we go beyond the *having* of enemies. Maybe it requires the kind of renunciation that Westerners, at least, can almost never attain. To be sure, Western thought has long yearned for a life free of enemies; e.g., Marx's paradise of a classless society, fundamentalist dreams of a world in which everyone is "saved," or the right-winger's ideal world of prosperous entrepreneurs without labor agitators or other untidy, disgruntled troublemakers. Typically, heaven itself is envisioned almost by definition as an enemy-free environment, a place of infinite bliss at least in part because all miscreants and opponents (of one's self, as well as of God's righteousness) reside elsewhere: in hell, under the sway of the great Enemy himself.

Certain religious traditions of the East, by contrast, revolve around the paradoxical goal of going beyond the having of goals, and thus, we must presume, beyond the having of enemies as well. In the *Bhagavad-Gita,* perhaps the most sacred of all Hindu scripts, the warrior Arjuna is urged by the god Krishna to achieve a mental state of "selflessness" in which he functions without striving. Although Arjuna indeed kills his enemies (many of them!), he does so in a peculiarly selfless state that, in the twentieth century, inspired Gandhi and his followers to humankind's greatest heights of nonviolent accomplishment. Gandhi often said that whereas British colonial occupation of India was his enemy, individual Britons were not, just as poverty was his enemy, but not individual wealthy industrialists. Violence, in particular, was his enemy, as were stupidity, intolerance, and cowardice. I do not know if the having of enemies was also his enemy. I am not even sure if it deserves to be ours. But there seems little doubt that insofar as we are capable of rising above our enemies and the having of enemies, we will have truly "elevated" ourselves.

Gandhi's Way

If anyone shows us the way, perhaps it is that small, nearly naked Mahatma out of India. Picture the scene: The neophyte barrister Mohandas Gandhi, barely out of law school, had been granted a brief audience with the legendary general Jan Smuts of South Africa, and—much to the General's amusement—the impertinent young Indian was laying down a gentle but firm challenge. This account of David meeting Goliath comes from one of Gandhi's most respected biographers:

> "I have come to tell you that I am going to fight against your government."
> Smuts must have thought he was hearing things.
> "You mean you have come here to tell me that?" he laughs. "Is there anything more you want to say?"

"Yes," says Gandhi. "I am going to win."

Smuts is astonished. "Well," he says at last, "and how are you going to do that?"

Gandhi smiles. "With your help."[2]

Recollecting this meeting years later, Smuts added that Gandhi turned out to have been entirely correct.

There are many facets to nonviolence, as Gandhi developed and refined it. The key is *satyagraha*, literally translated from Hindi as "soul-force" or "soul-truth." Unfortunately, however, *satyagraha* has often been misunderstood to be "passive resistance." But defining *satyagraha* as merely passive resistance is akin to treating *light* as merely "non-darkness," or *good* as "non-evil." Something crucial is missing, namely, its positive, creative aspect. Gandhian *satyagraha* is passive only insofar as it refrains from doing violence to others; in all other respects, it is active and assertive, requiring great energy and courage. It requires, in Gandhi's words, "the pitting of one's whole soul against the will of the tyrant," and, in the process, "a willingness to suffer."[3] It is not for the weak-kneed or the passive.

As Gandhi saw it, his discipline did not involve a purging of anger so much as a transforming of it:

> I have learnt through bitter experience the one supreme lesson, to conserve my anger and as heat conserved is transmuted into energy, even so our anger controlled can be transmuted into a power which can move the world.[4]

For practitioners of Gandhi's particularly assertive brand of nonviolence, overcoming one's enemies requires the moral courage to be immune, not only to the threat of violence directed toward them, but also to the inclination to employ violence themselves. This, in turn, comes from having sufficient clarity of purpose (echoing Arjuna, Gandhi would call it "selflessness").

Without such clarity, the struggle to defeat one's enemy leads to the pernicious doctrine that the end justifies the means. Gandhi believed, instead, that means and ends were inseparable, and that noble ends can only be achieved by techniques that were equally laudable. He maintained that there was "the same inviolable connection between the means and the end as there is between the seed and the tree."[5] Most political figures have thought differently. Thus, V. I. Lenin proclaimed that "to achieve our ends, we will unite even with the Devil," and two decades later, Winston Churchill used a strikingly similar metaphor in describing his willingness to ally with Stalin (whom he detested) in order to defeat Hitler: If Nazi Germany should invade hell, the prime minister told the British parliament, Churchill would cheerfully make common cause with the devil.

In its pursuit of the white whale of "international communism," seen—erroneously but persistently—as a unitary enemy, the United States has acted as Churchill recommended, sometimes becoming as monomaniacal as Ahab himself, and even less scrupulous. We united with no end of "devils," embracing (and often, creating) such unsavory characters as Batista in Cuba, Somoza in Nicaragua, Marcos in the Philippines, Pinochet in Chile, Duvalier in Haiti, the Shah in Iran, Mobutu in Zaire, and Suharto in Indonesia. Seeking to overcome our enemies, we even blurred the distinction between them and ourselves, especially during the 1980s and early 1990s. Worried that the Soviet Union was planning to win a nuclear war, we did the same. Convinced that the USSR was approaching a first-strike nuclear capacity, we tried to beat them to it. Proclaiming that "they only understand force," we threw our weight around in Grenada, Libya, Panama, and Iraq. Perhaps the defining example, however, was the Iran-contra affair, when the Reagan administration illegally subverted the U.S. Constitution while secretly selling arms to Iran and using the proceeds to finance an illegal and brutal war against the government and people of Nicaragua—all in the name of freedom and democracy.

The far left, for its part, has been no more sensitive than the far right to Gandhi's awareness of the connection between means and ends. In the ostensible pursuit of a workers' paradise, workers in "socialist" countries were often muzzled and oppressed, denied even the right to organize and strike. The various "Peoples' Republics" offered precious little to the people. In his poem "To Posterity," Bertolt Brecht, playwright and conscience-struck Marxist, anguished over how violence and oppression have frequently corrupted and perverted the noblest intentions:

> Even anger against injustice
> Makes the voice grow harsh. Alas, we
> Who wished to lay the foundations of kindness
> Could not ourselves be kind.[6]

Gandhi's approach was radically different, rooted in the notion that the only way to overcome one's enemies was to convert them into allies. If Joe hits Tom, after which Tom hits back, this nearly always encourages Joe to strike yet again. Violence escalates as, in a revealing phrase, push comes to shove. Gandhi was not fond of the biblical injunction "an eye for an eye, a tooth for a tooth," pointing out that aside from the regrettable means, the outcome would inevitably be a population both blind and toothless![7] He emphasized that if Tom were to respond with nonviolence, this could not only break the chain of anger and hatred (analogous to the Hindu chain of birth, death, and rebirth), it would also put the initial attacker in an unexpected position.

"I seek entirely to blunt the edge of the tyrant's sword," wrote Gandhi, "not by putting up against it a sharper-edged weapon, but by disappointing his expectation that I would be offering physical resistance."[8] Accustomed to counterviolence—and even, perhaps, hoping for it—the violent person becomes a "victim" of a kind of moral judo when he encounters a nonviolent opponent who is courageous and respectful, even loving, willing to suffer but also firm and unyielding. The attacker is typically unbalanced when his own energy is unexpectedly redirected.

Even the Old Testament, typically more inclined toward blood-thirstiness than compassion, recognized how baffling and disconcerting it can be when enmity evokes compassion rather than violence. Listen to the Book of Proverbs (25:21-22): "If thine enemy be hungry, give him bread to eat; and if he be thirsty, give him water to drink. For thou shalt thus heap coals of fire upon his head, and the Lord shall reward thee." The "coals of fire" thereby heaped upon the head of one's enemy are the confusion and disorientation experienced when a foe, anticipating tit for tat, unexpectedly encounters nonviolence, or—more troublesome yet—love.

Admittedly, Mikhail Gorbachev was no Gandhi, and whatever it was that he offered the West, it was something less than Christ-like *agape*. But he certainly disoriented us, nearly as much as he confused his own people, when he jettisoned the long-standing Leninist-Stalinist assumption of permanent Western hostility, concluding that the West did not constitute a military threat to his countrymen, whereas a stagnant, repressive social and economic system did.

For his part, Gandhi was less interested in heaping coals or in gaining heavenly reward, and more concerned with practical consequences, although he clearly intended that nonviolence would enoble the "enemy" no less than the *satyagrahi*. "It would at first dazzle him and at last compel recognition from him," wrote Gandhi, "which recognition would not humiliate him but would uplift him."[9] Those who experienced Gandhian nonviolence might dispute whether they were in fact uplifted, but government authorities, South African as well as British, undeniably found Gandhi's tactics extremely baffling and exasperating. They also found them irresistible, to the extent that the world's greatest empire (and one that had been none too gentle or kind itself), eventually granted independence to a country of five hundred million people, after a lengthy campaign in which remarkably few people lost their lives.

Of those who "only understand force," it is widely presumed that they cannot be moved by anything other than force or the threat of it, wielded firmly by their enemies. The truth, however, may be precisely the opposite, since those who understand and expect violent force can generally deal with it effectively. What gives them fits is Gandhi's forceful use of nonviolence, of stubborn, persistent, highly assertive yet loving disagreement without enmity. One sympathetic scholar of nonviolence used the following analogy: If an iceberg floats into warm water, it begins to melt below the waterline, invisibly but inexorably, until eventually its weight shifts and it may flip over unexpectedly.[10] In just this way, the consciousness of the oppressor can be changed suddenly and dramatically, just as enemies themselves are transformed.

"If my soldiers began to think," wrote Frederick the Great, "not one would remain in the ranks."[11] Part of the power of nonviolence and *satyagraha* is that it induces not only feeling but also thought. And it is precisely thought—good, hard, productive thought—that we all could use right now, enabling us perhaps to terminate the various cold wars in our personal lives, as well as to take advantage of the opportunity offered by the end of the U.S.-Soviet confrontation.

Moreover, as proposed in the last chapter, much in our enemy system seems to derive from primitive inclinations and behavior patterns, once adaptive but now inappropriate and even downright dangerous. Furthermore, we are unlikely to solve this problem by simply waiting for our Neanderthal biology to catch up with modern times because, by definition, evolutionary processes are slow and cultural events move quickly. We must do the work ourselves, and hard work it will be, employing most of the intellectual and creative resources for which our species likes to compliment itself.

Just as we will not evolve quickly enough—in biological terms—to overcome our Neanderthal penchant for enemies, most of us probably will never evolve high or deep enough—in moral terms—to become modern day Gandhis. Nonetheless, the good news is that there are other way stations in our shared pilgrimage toward overcoming enmity. Two key concepts are, first, empathy (broadly defined), and second, replacing the negative focus on enemies, who we are against, with a positive affirmation of what we are for, and thus, who we are.

Empathy

Empathy is defined by the *Random House Dictionary* as "the intellectual identification with or vicarious experiencing of the feelings, thoughts, or attitudes of another." It often involves projecting one's own personality onto another, so as to understand the other more clearly. It derives from the Greek *path* (from *paschein,* "to suffer"); empathy therefore has the same root as the theological term "passion," as in the suffering of Christ.[12] At its root, empathy implies sharing the feelings of another, if need be to the extent of suffering along with that other.

Empathy is similar to sympathy, but the two are not quite the same. Thus, sympathy implies pity or compassion—feeling sorry for another—but not necessarily feeling *the same* as the other. We might sympathize, for example, with an automobile accident victim, and offer to help, but without feeling empathic. This is especially true if the victim was drunk or driving recklessly, behaving perhaps in a manner of which we might disapprove, or to which we cannot "relate."

It is unlikely, on the other hand, that two bitter enemies engaged in a violent conflict will ever sympathize with each other, at least not while tempers are hot. By contrast, empathy is possible. It can also be argued that anyone who can empathize with an opponent has an advantage, if nothing else, in anticipating the opponent's next move. Consider, also, the experienced hunter or fisherman who is able to "think like a partridge," or like a trout.

Sympathy is good. Certainly, it is better than antagonism, or even indifference. It leads to a degree of tolerance, and often, to assistance. But empathy is far more powerful, and also more valuable. There is a wise story that if we give a starving man a fish, we feed him for a day, whereas if we teach him to fish, we feed him for a lifetime (assuming, of course that there are enough fish!). Sympathy leads us to donate a fish; empathy, to fishing lessons.

Empathy also evokes a uniquely powerful response from the person with whom we empathized. If there is a single, multi-purpose, guaranteed-to-work sentence that can be used by just about any psychotherapist at any time, it is: "I can really feel your pain." (It is possible—although as yet untested—that a would-be therapist who speaks nothing but, say, medieval Estonian, could get by perfectly well in the United States if he or she knew only this crucial bit of English.) The need for empathy is so deep that people will pay large sums of money to be told that a virtual stranger understands and shares their feelings, and feels their pain. This need for empathy is so deep, moreover, that these same people will actually believe it. In fact, many of them even get better as a result!

There is nothing, absolutely nothing, so evocative and yet re-assuring as being told that someone empathizes with our own personal situation. No one knows why. But it is probably not going too far to suggest that the powerful hold that empathy exercises on the human psyche derives from the simple yet profound fact of our existential loneliness, a loneliness that is particularly intense when people are suffering. "Laugh and the world laughs with you; cry and you cry alone." But in fact, most of us are alone, nearly all the time, although we feel our aloneness most acutely when we also feel like crying.

When novelist Milan Kundera writes that "love is a constant interrogation," he is referring to this same fact: Because of our loneliness, we have a deeply shared need to feel known, understood, empathized with.

Indeed, this need is so deep that the most seductive thing one person can do toward another is to ask genuine questions, show real interest, endeavoring to break down the barriers that separate people, thereby making both less isolated and more connected. By the same token, the self-centered jerk is perhaps the greatest of all turn-offs. Consider the ego-inflated movie star who finally said to his date: "We've talked enough about me. Let's talk about you, instead. What did *you* think of my latest movie?" He probably spends a lot of time sleeping alone.

Not unlike what is said of God, empathy works in strange ways its wonders to perform. Its magic works not only on the person empathized with, but also on the empathizer. To perceive someone else as not just another person (literally, an Other person), but as a reflection of one's self, even, perhaps, a part of one's self, is to undergo a profound reorientation indeed. Whatever else may result from the experience, it is unlikely that the subject of one's empathy will long be perceived as an enemy. In short, empathy precludes enmity.

George Orwell has probably given us the simplest, most cogent account of this principle. He was serving as an antifascist volunteer during the Spanish civil war when he experienced the transforming power of empathy:

> At this moment a man, presumably carrying a message to an officer, jumped out of the trench and ran along the top of the parapet

in full view. He was half-dressed and was holding up his trousers with both hands as he ran. I refrained from shooting at him. It is true that I am a poor shot and unlikely to hit a running man at a hundred yards . . . still, I did not shoot partly because of that detail about the trousers. I had come here to shoot at "Fascists"; but a man who is holding up his trousers isn't a "Fascist," he is visibly a fellow creature, similar to yourself, and you don't feel like shooting at him.[13]

Unfortunately, the course of true empathy—like that of true love—does not always run smoothly. We have, for example, the "pathetic fallacy," named not because it is somehow pitiable (the more common use of "pathetic") but rather from the original meaning of "shared identification." Thus, the pathetic fallacy is a case of inappropriate empathy, the endowment of nature or other inanimate phenomena with human traits and feelings. (A classic is John Ruskin's phrase about the "undaunted cliffs of Dover.") Such attempts may be poetically pleasing, but for the self-styled "hard-headed realists," they can give the whole endeavor a bad name. There are many other obstacles to empathy, and it is to these that we now turn.

Umwelts and Attribution Errors

As difficult as it is to empathize with other human beings, it is even harder to know other living things in the deep sense of "understand" rather than the superficial one of "be familiar with facts."[14] This is because animals possess what is known as an *umwelt*, which is theirs and theirs alone. *Umwelt* is a German word that can loosely be translated as "environment," but more meaningfully as "environment, as experienced by the individual." Thus, the visual *umwelt* of a frog is bounded by such specialized receptors as "moving edge detectors" (for warning about approaching predators), "bug detectors," and so forth, but with nothing like the same picture of a pond as would be perceived, say, by a human being. Similarly, we simply cannot imagine the world as perceived by a housefly or bumblebee, whose eyes consist of thousands of hexagonal facets, or even the *umwelt* of our purported best friend, the dog, redolent with the olfactory calling cards of the neighborhood canines, a universe of hopes, fears, and excitement from which we are altogether excluded.

Umwelts are not the sole possession of animals. Human beings, too, are limited to the envelopes of our lives, prisoners of our perceptions. Not surprisingly, therefore, we commit what psychologists call the "attribution error." It works as follows: Each of us is likely to know, all too painfully, the various forces impinging on us, limiting our degrees of freedom, and sometimes forcing us to do things we would rather not, things that are "not really us." At the same time, when considering someone else—notably, someone considered to be an enemy—we see that person or persons as being remarkably *un*constrained. Whereas we may chafe under our own restrictions and compulsions, we view our enemies as possessing nearly complete freedom of action. Hence, we readily attribute our enemy's unpleasant behavior to nastiness and cunning, comfortably unaware that in virtually all cases, our opponent is every bit as constrained as we know ourselves to be. When our opponents do something bad, we attribute it to their nastiness; when they do something good, it is because they have been forced into it by circumstances beyond their control.[15] The attribution error comes from the misperception that whereas our own behavior is often a regrettable compromise forced upon us by the press of events, our opponent behaves nastily because he or she is, well, nasty.

Hence, during the height of the Cold War, many Americans pointed to the USSR's armed forces as being greatly in excess of its legitimate defensive requirements, attributing the large Red Army and the Kremlin's many missiles to its overall military malevolence. At the same time, our own bloated military was seen as due to our many (defensive) overseas commitments, economic and political pressures, and also—of course—the need to keep up with the Soviets.

The attribution error and all that it implied helped create what has widely been recognized as the "enemy image," the mask of inhuman evil with which people traditionally obscure the otherwise all-too-human face of an opponent. Such images tend to be especially resistant to change and, thus, likely to convey a false impression of how things really are. To this must be added the uncertainty that almost inevitably accompanies our attempts to "get inside" someone else. After all, most of us really are limited to our own pitifully narrow and personal *umwelt*, locked up as we are within our private envelope of skin with our intensely personal histories, our unique and idiosyncratic allocation of sense organs, and the tunnel vision that they generate. Take the resulting ignorance born of isolation and separation and combine it with fear, and the outcome, not surprisingly, is none too pretty. When Churchill, for example, called the Soviet Union "a riddle wrapped in a mystery inside an enigma," he gave voice not only to a widespread—and regrettably accurate—perception of the USSR of his day, but also to the fundamental loneliness, isolation, and distrust that characterizes much of the human condition. As we have seen, this condition is, if anything, exaggerated when it involves heavily armed Neanderthals.

To go beyond the attribution error and see the Other (whether a government, group, or individual) as motivated by problems, limitations, and aspirations no less legitimate than our own is to enter into a new world of relationships in which enmity can be replaced by empathy. It is not an easy journey: empathy is demanding, even exhausting, especially of our emotional resources. We cling tenaciously to our various belief systems, living as best we can within our own self-referential *umwelts*. To discard our belief systems is to become dangerously exposed, like cultists deprived of a leader, like a deep-sea crab caught in nothing but its soft and vulnerable skin, shivering and helpless between molts. Maybe such an experience offers the possibility of the kind of ecstatic transcendence that Eastern mystics tell about, and that Western skeptics discount but would kill for. Nonetheless, losing an *umwelt* is scary and dangerous, not something that happens lightly.

To a large degree, the end of the Cold War gave Americans an opportunity to expand their *umwelt*s in just this way, to free us from a past that had deformed our economy, our politics, and our society. Yet, as noted by Sidney Blumenthal, senior editor for the *New Republic*, the result was that everyone froze:

> The Cold War had polarized the elements of politics for so long that there was no idiom with which to speak about the new conditions. Concepts of weakness and strength, good and evil, optimism and pessimism—all had been politically defined within the old common frame of reference. Both Cold War liberalism and Cold War conservatism were now at an end, but no one of political consequence stepped forward to suggest what was next. There was a vast silence. Political society as a whole was stricken with aphasia. The end of the Cold War was like a stroke.[16]

It became a truism to note that George Bush's new world order looked suspiciously like the old one, except with the United States standing alone as the world's sole superpower. A truly new world order, one that included a switch to the brave new *umwelt* of global citizenship, would also carry with it an important and generally unspoken recognition: We would have to function without the comforting assurance of easily identified enemies. As we have seen, one of the benefits of having enemies is that their traits can be exaggerated, in the course of which we become ever more confident of just who and what we are. Conversely, the receding of an enemy and establishment of a new *umwelt* carries with it the threat that one's distinctiveness is at risk, since identity is often tied to one's enemies. Thus far, we have resisted anything resembling a truly new world order, settling whenever possible for a mixture of reaction and inaction.

Fortunately, however, the end of enmity can evoke other postures than paralysis, other, more creative consequences than a simple hardening of the categories. This is because there are various way stations along the road to dropping our enemies altogether, compromises that simply require us to refocus our tactics about dealing with opponents. Overcoming our enemies will almost certainly involve, for example, overcoming our tendency to force such interactions into the straitjacket of rigid, limited, and distorted perceptions of the Other.

Changing Attitudes

Fortunately, such changes do happen. They are, in fact, happening right now, with regard to public attitudes toward the former USSR. And as this account shows, they have happened in the past:

> In 1942 and again in 1966 respondents were asked to choose from a list of adjectives that best described the people of Russia, Germany, and Japan. In 1942 the first five adjectives chosen to characterize both Germans and Japanese (enemies) included warlike, treacherous, and cruel, none of which appeared among the first five describing the Russians (allies); in 1966 all three had disappeared from American characterizations of the Germans and Japanese (allies) but now the Russians (no longer allies, although more rivals than enemies) were warlike and treacherous. Data were reported for the Mainland Chinese only in 1966, and predictably, they were seen as warlike, treacherous, and sly. It is interesting that "hardworking" rates high for all these countries, whether friends or enemies, for besides being

true, it reinforces the images of both enemy and friend: a hardworking enemy is more to be feared, a hardworking ally is a greater source of strength.[17]

Writing in 1967, the author of the above paragraph was able to aver that "in American eyes, the bloodthirsty, cruel, treacherous, slant-eyed, buck-toothed little Japs of the Second World War have become a highly cultivated, charming, industrious, and thoroughly attractive people." By the 1990s, with the Cold War over and economic competition and a huge Japanese trade surplus looming large in the American psyche, the Japanese have come once again to be seen as troublesome, although more money hungry than bloodthirsty, while their industriousness has itself become less admirable and more threatening.

Attitudes toward Japan and the Soviet Union are not alone in having shifted markedly:

> The American image of the Germans is remarkable for having swung to opposite extremes twice within scarcely half a century. Before World War I the Germans were widely admired for their industry, culture, and scientific ability; during it they became the hated "Huns"; between wars the Weimar Republic, as a democracy, was looked on with great favor; then came the loathed Nazis; and now the Germans are again admirable chaps.[18]

Nonetheless, images of the Other tend in most cases to have great psychological inertia, at least in part because even though they are images of someone else, in actuality we are the ones holding them. In an important sense, they are *our* images. Changing them typically requires an empathic leap that only occurs when we are kicked hard by irresistible external events. In this respect, Caucasian Americans have been a generally favored people. For all of our

difficulty in reframing our views of others and dealing with the end
of enemies, we may actually be unusually good at doing so, compared
with many other people, who, compared with the white citizenry
of the United States, have historically been more traumatized and
victimized. Israelis (and Jews generally); Russians; Poles; black Afri-
cans; eastern and Mediterranean Europeans; the poor and despised
of Latin America, India, and Asia—these and numerous others have
every justification for holding a grudge, and, presumably, little call
for a change of attitude. In the long run, however, that may be precisely
what is needed.

It is easier to continue with the old attitudes and perceptions,
and sometimes even dangerous to tinker with patterns of thought
that, for better or worse, "work." "If it ain't broke," we are told,
"don't fix it." Yet, the persistence of animosities and resentments is
a sure indication that something is in fact broken, that there are rips
in the fabric of healthy relationships, whether the cloth is societal
or personal. The tragedy of the former Yugoslavia, for example, took
place because ethnic and religious hatreds were suppressed rather
than resolved. They simmered under decades of artful manipulation
and cynical suppression by President Tito, only to erupt once Communist control was lifted. The attitude of Slovenians, Serbians,
Croatians, Montenegrins, Macedonians, and Muslims toward each
other was never honestly confronted and, hence, it remained inaccessible to resolution and susceptible to manipulation when Yugoslavia
finally flew violently apart.

As we have seen, societies can be held together by shared enmity,
even as they are threatened when that enmity gets out of hand.
Similarly, there are marriages that are held together by shared enmity
toward a third party, and sometimes even toward each other.[19] In
such cases, the goal of effective marriage counseling may involve
a reorientation of attitudes not unlike that which is needed in many
societies, after which some marriages go through a difficult and

paradoxical transition, passing from the stability born of encrusted animosity (Edward Albee's *Who's Afraid of Virginia Wolf* comes to mind) to a relatively unstable and unsettling period in which the couple comes to see each other more clearly, if possible en route to another form of stability—a genuine one, this time—based on realistic perceptions and real caring.

It is harder than you might think, especially because the requisite changes must take place not just at the level of thinking, but also feeling. Consider, for example, how much easier it is to change one's mind than to change one's attitudes or beliefs. But it can be done, especially if we recognize the degree to which we are not simply bystanders or victims, but also active participants.

From Empathy to Complicity

Westerners typically have a hard time with the kind of profound philosophical empathy that is so important to many Eastern philosophies, such as the various forms of Buddhism; most of us are no more at ease, for that matter, with the self-abnegating love demanded by Gandhian *satyagraha*. Such levels of empathy may be ultimately enlightening and, thus, deeply desirable, but they are also disorienting. Another route—more accessible perhaps for the average Westerner— is to connect with our fellows (the Others) in a different way by recognizing our own contribution to most situations, from the personal to the societal, and especially our complicity when things go wrong. Most relationships, after all, require at least two participants, and when they go sour, it is very rare that one side is solely to blame and the other is an utterly innocent victim.

It may well be significant that the most dramatic and resonant statement recognizing personal responsibility—even, of self-as-enemy—is also perhaps the most notable and far-reaching tragedy of Western civilization: the tale of Oedipus. The story is widely known, especially in its relationship to the so-called Oedipus complex, the psychoanalytic notion that deep inside, boys long to kill their fathers and have sex with their mothers (and girls, at least to some extent, vice versa). But in fact, the power of the Oedipus myth goes far beyond this simplistic and rather questionable bit of Freudian dogma. It is more likely that Oedipus's hold on the human imagination derives instead from its tragic recognition of personal responsibility, in the context of a desperate search for an enemy who turns out to be none other than the searcher himself.

The nightmare plays itself out as Oedipus, powerful king of Thebes, seeks the culprit responsible for bringing a terrible plague upon his people. Oedipus vows to have the villain—whoever he may be—brought to his stern and uncompromising justice, only to discover, slowly and painfully, what the audience knows all along: that the enemy is Oedipus himself. Thus, as a young man, Oedipus had unknowingly killed the previous ruler, King Laius, who was also Oedipus's father. Moreover, Jocasta, Laius's widow, whom Oedipus took as his wife, is also Oedipus's own mother. Oedipus, and no other, was thus the enemy that he sought. (Significantly, as the awful truth begins to dawn on Oedipus, he first turns his fury on Jocasta's brother, Creon, accusing him of plotting against the throne and threatening him with death; like so many others before him—and after—Oedipus seeks to pass his pain along, blaming someone else rather than accepting personal responsibility.) But the truth is undeniable and eventually the distraught king turns his rage upon himself, piercing his own eyes and going forth in anguish as a blind outcast beggar.

Powerful stuff, this, and not nearly so much because of the incest or the violence as because it speaks to some of our deepest fears. Despite the purported insights of Freudian psychoanalysis, these fears are *not* that we might unknowingly do wrong, or that we might—

either accidentally or on purpose—act on deeply repressed, forbidden, incestuous libido, but rather that our own *umwelt* may someday be revealed to be so insignificant, so transparent, so connected to the world of others, that in fact, our sense of enemies *out there* will be replaced not simply with empathy but with the terrifying fact that oftentimes there really is no enemy except for ourselves.

"This thing of Darknesse," says the learned Prospero in Shakespeare's *The Tempest*, "I acknowledge mine." It is an acknowledgment that is ultimately forced upon Oedipus as well, and, through him, upon the rest of us. To be sure, whereas it is quite possible that many of us are Oedipal, virtually no one shares the explicit story of Oedipus.[20] And Prospero is not alone in having created monsters: The beastly Caliban is also ours, a creature of our own, internal darkness. Nonetheless, Caliban is a monster: foreign, distant, and basically repulsive. Thus, he is easy to separate from ourselves, whereas Oedipus is Everyman (and Everywoman). What makes Oedipus especially painful as well as powerful is that his story forces us to acknowledge that deep inside, we are all things of darkness.

The special appeal of tragedy, according to wise observers from Aristotle to the present day, derives from its offer of catharsis, the purging of emotions based on a recognition of similarity between the audience and the characters in the story. Rudyard Kipling encapsulated the power of empathy in the magical phrase by which the boy Mowgli gained entrance into the life of animals in *The Jungle Book*, and which also explains the horror and fascination that Oedipus holds for human beings, today no less than in the time of ancient Greece: "We be of one blood, you and I."

Blood, we are told, is thicker than water. Being of one blood, and acknowledging it, our empathy is aroused and ultimately, our enmity diminished. The benefits that human beings would derive from such a recognition are almost beyond imagining. Deep, true empathy holds the promise of smoothing and humanizing bumpy relationships from the societal to the personal. But it could go even farther: There is no reason why Mowgli's jungle greeting should be limited to the relationship of human beings with other human beings. It could encompass our relationship with the rest of the world, living and even nonliving. After all, as Zen masters have known for thousands of years, the human skin does not separate us from the rest of our environment; it joins us to it. Consider the following message, sent via walkie-talkie by a back-country ranger in the Glacier Peak Wilderness of Washington state: "Dead elk by upper Agnes Creek decomposing nicely. Over."

Decomposing Nicely

The report was matter-of-fact, and yet, startling. Anyone who has ever been close to a large, decomposing animal—especially in the summer—will recognize that "nicely" is perhaps the last word one might use: "grossly," maybe, or "disgustingly," "nauseatingly," "horribly," or "loathsomely." But of course, there is a deep wisdom in that ranger's description, because "nicely" is precisely correct, and one advantage that we have over the average elk is that we are able to understand this wisdom and to gain peace from it.

The elk, just like the rest of us, is going back to its primal stuff, with the help of various maggots, bacteria, beetles, earthworms, and perhaps the occasional nibble from a raven or coyote. Deposited on a busy street, a shopping center, or a formal dining room, a large decomposing mammal would be inconvenient to say the least, not to mention a public health menace. But out there in the upper drainage of the North Cascades' Agnes Creek, a particular dead elk is no one's enemy and everybody's friend. Moreover, the process of decomposition is not even unfriendly to the elk, which is being returned to the ecosystem from which, once upon a time, it was formed.

It may seem a truism to point out that "we are all connected," but we are, even though we tend to forget it. Among the molecules of oxygen, nitrogen, and carbon dioxide that we exchange with the atmosphere every time we inhale and exhale, some are the exact same molecules that were inhaled and exhaled by the soldiers at Valley Forge, and even—with a certain statistical probability—by George Washington himself. Some of those molecules also passed through the bodies of a rhinocerous from Africa, an Australian termite, a long-extinct dodo bird from Mauritius, even a *Tyrannosaurus rex.* For hundreds of millions of years, these and other substances have passed through—and thus profoundly connected—the living bodies of this planet. "Just passing through," we might say, disparagingly, of a transient journey to a small town somewhere. But that is precisely what we and all other forms of life are composed of: materials that are just passing through. All of us are just passing through. How, then, can we be enemies of our own substance, temporarily housed within what we call—by verbal convention—other bodies?

We each have somewhat more than two hundred ancestors who were alive, for example, in the year 1700, and quite likely several million ancestors from the year 1066. "If we could go back and live again," wrote Henry Adams,

> in all our two hundred fifty million arithmetical ancestors of the eleventh century, we should find ourselves doing many surprising things, but among the rest we should certainly be ploughing most of the fields of the Contentin and Calvados; going to mass in every parish church in Normandy; rendering military service to every lord, spiritual or temporal, in all this region; and helping to build the Abbey Church at Mont-Saint-Michel.[21]

What we identify as "ourself" is only a temporary collection of genes drawn from a much vaster, commonly shared genetic pool, which will shortly dissolve into that gangantuan, universal melting pot, and whose physical substance is shared with all matter, nonliving as well as living.

Eventually, we stop passing through, and the stuff of which we are composed begins a more one-directional process. We decompose, eventually to become recomposed in other ways. It is a good enough goal for us all: to decompose nicely, starting right now, even, in a sense, while still alive. Another such goal is to view our fellow creatures—elk, redwood tree, or human being—as fitting in, as belonging, as being a good and acceptable and even an appreciated part of the world we all share, to which all are connected, and to which all will return. According to Edward Abbey, such an attitude is "an expression of loyalty to the earth, the earth which bore us and sustains us, the only home we shall ever know, the only paradise we ever need—if only we had the eyes to see."

It will be a challenge, this business of living happily with dead elk in our favorite alpine meadows, crabgrass in our lawns, inconvenient or even threatening ideologies in our body politic, enemies in our midst. But when we think of them as part of a bigger process, contributors to a larger system that includes but is not limited to us—a vast natural system that incorporates our tiny, tidy enemy systems but is far more expansive, indeed, that is wildly inclusive in the very broadest sense—we might start seeing those "enemies" as tolerable, acceptable, and even downright nice.

Positive Visions and Dazzling Crystal

Empathy may be crucial for overcoming enmity. Although it may be necessary, however, in most cases empathy is not sufficient. Thus, empathy involves a recognition of ultimate connectedness, coming close to a union of the Self with the world, including as part of that world, the Other. But short of *nirvana* or a transcendent state of Buddhistic enlightenment, most of us remain largely stuck within ourselves. We may yearn for empathy, and even achieve it in fits and starts, but we also need something more (or less) than to submerge our selfhood in the great melting pot of existence. Therefore, we turn now to the second leg of overcoming: positive visions.

If life sometimes feels narrow, pinched, and unsatisfying, if joys and challenges are few and accomplishments rare, then at least our enemies provide something to strain and measure ourselves against. In a quicksand of disappointments, enemies provide a kind of solidity and structure, something by which to pull ourselves out of the muck of emptiness and despair. If, therefore, we are to overcome our enemies, and even more so, to overcome our need for enemies, we may well have to replace them with other things, more clearly demarcated than our empathic share of the great cosmic stew, and more gratifying than the essentially negative self-definition that comes from harping on what we are "not," what we oppose, and what opposes us. There is need, in short, for positive visions.

For this, two things are necessary. First, we need an affirmative sense of ourselves. Not the narcissistic, self-centered, "taking care of number one" attitude that characterized much of the the Reagan era 1980s, and not the feel good, "I-am-the-cosmos" New Age psycho-babble that—under one guise or another—seems to have percolated through much of the twentieth century. Rather, our need is for a realistic, clear-eyed yet compassionate self-assessment that acknowledges our shortcomings, recognizes the sources of our personal pain, and yet refuses to succumb to the temptation to pass that pain along, to create enemies as a salve to our own wounds. This positive sense of ourselves is damaged if we are abused as children, or if, as adults, we are told that we must be nothing less than tall, thin, rich, brilliant, and beautiful. It is further injured if our lives and aspirations are stunted by social injustice and environmental degradation. But it is there, latent within each of us, waiting to stretch and grow and flower, just as surely as the tree exists within the acorn.

Moreover, positive self-esteem can be wonderfully resistant—although not altogether impervious—to the insults of this world. It requires only those natural factors (equivalent to sunlight, water, and soil for a plant) that are part of every human being's birthright, and it offers each of us the opportunity of rising above the limited, enemy-bound existence to which so many have so long been restricted. But in many cases, the development of positive self-esteem requires that our baggage of prior wounds be healed. In short, if we are eventually to overcome, we need first to overcome our own weaknesses and injuries, to be made whole—emotionally, physically, spiritually—and thereby set free to nurture that which is positive and life-affirming within each of us. (Of course, this is true on the larger, social scale no less than on the personal; it was Lincoln's recognition of this necessity that led him to urge his countrymen to choose reconciliation over revenge.)

Blaise Pascal, the French philosopher and scientist, once said that if he had a place to stand and a lever that was long enough, he could move the world. Achieving our own peace, healing, and positive self-esteem would provide us with the place to stand, a secure place found only within ourselves.

The next requirement in our quest for overcoming would be a lever that is long enough; in other words, satisfying goals. In "What I Expected," the poet Stephen Spender wrote of his disappointment, even despair, that the world seemed lacking in worthy endpoints, that it was defined more by whimpers than by bangs. (It may not be irrelevant that this poem appeared in 1934, when Hitler was a dark, rising star without serious opposition in the West, while the Great Depression continued to hold sway throughout the industrialized world.) In any event, there is a timeless, universal validity to Spender's frustration over

> . . . the gradual day
> Weakening the will
> Leaking the brightness away.
> The lack of good to touch
> The fading of body and soul
> Like smoke before wind
> Corrupt, unsubstantial.[22]

Like most of us, Spender had expected something different. He had looked forward to a life that was meaningful, satisfying, filled with purpose and accomplishment, maybe even glory. In his own words,

> What I expected was
> Thunder, fighting,
> Long struggles with men
> And climbing.
> After continual straining
> I should grow strong;
> Then the rocks would shake
> And I should rest long.[23]

It seems that Spender had hoped for worthwhile enemies, for opponents against whom to struggle and strain, and who would help him to "grow strong." He wanted to climb and to shake the rocks and then to enjoy a lengthy and deserved rest: the kind that comes to those who have fought the good fight.

But his hope is more complete than this. Spender's magnificent if sad poem concludes with a yearning vision, one that pulls at our hearts precisely because it sings of our need for positive, affirmative goals that supercede the defeat of others and that reach toward the fulfillment of ourselves:

> Some brightness to hold in trust,
> Some final innocence
> To save from dust;
> That, hanging solid,
> Would dangle through all
> Like the created poem
> Or the dazzling crystal.[24]

Not many of us, in all likelihood, will create a perfect poem, will hold and preserve pure brilliance and innocence, or turn the stuff of everyday life into dazzling crystal. But even though such transcendence will always lie beyond our reach, it nonetheless remains for us to attempt the grasp, to strive for positive goals, for images of brightness and perfection. As we do so, maybe, just maybe, we can at least and at last begin to overcome that old itch for enemies, just as we scratch the surface of our own potential to become ourselves. The goal here is not necessarily a new human being, devoid of enemies or all penchant for having them, some sort of sugary sweet, goody-two-shoes *Homo amicus* ("the friendly"). Neither, however, would it be the old *Homo inimicus* ("the enemy obsessed"), but rather a creature that is far more complex, more empathic and more balanced, one that is neither less nor more than what we really are—or at least, what we have fancied ourselves to be—namely, *Homo sapiens,* "the wise."

Notes

1. Abraham Lincoln, *Selected Writings of Abraham Lincoln* (New York: Bantam, 1992).

2. E. Easwaran, *Gandhi the Man* (Petaluma, Calif.: Nilgiri Press, 1978).

3. Ibid.

4. Quoted in Joan Bondurant, *Conflict: Violence and Nonviolence* (Chicago: Aldine Atherton, 1971).

5. Quoted in P. Regamey, *Nonviolence and the Christian Conscience* (London, England: Darton, Longmann, and Todd, 1966).

6. Bertolt Brecht, *Poems* (London, England: Methuen, 1976).

7. Once, when asked his opinion of Western civilization, Gandhi replied, "I think it would be a good idea."

8. Quoted in N. K. Bose (ed.), *Selections from Gandhi* (Ahmedabad, India: Navajivan, 1957).

9. Ibid.

10. Richard Gregg, *The Power of Nonviolence* (London, England: James Clarke, 1960).

11. Ibid.

12. It could be argued that Catholic communion represents the ultimate in empathy, in which the communicants are supposed to partake of the literal body and blood of Christ.

13. George Orwell, "Homage to Catalonia," in *The Collected Essays, Journalism and Letters of George Orwell* (New York: Harcourt, Brace, Jovanovich, 1938).

14. In French, the difference between *comprendre* and *savoir*.

15. See, for example, T. Pettigrew, "The Ultimate Attribution Error: Extending Allport's Cognitive Analysis of Prejudice," *Personality and Social Psychology Bulletin* 5 (1979): 461–76

16. Sidney Blumenthal, *Pledging Allegiance: The Last Campaign of the Cold War* (New York: HarperCollins, 1990).

17. Jerome D. Frank, *Sanity and Survival in the Nuclear Age* (New York: Random House, 1982).

18. Ibid.

19. Consider, for example, the "cold war marriage" of Walter and Ellen, in chapter 3.

20. Satirist Tom Lehrer, in his song "Oedipus Rex," proclaims, "You may wind up like Oedipus," and then responds, hastily, "I'd rather marry a duck-billed platypus."

21. Henry Adams, *Mont-Saint-Michel and Chartres* (Boston: Houghton Mifflin, 1936).

22. Stephen Spender, *Poems, 1934* (New York: The Modern Library, 1934).

23. Ibid.

24. Ibid.

Index

301